Dear Dad,

I hope you will enjoy reading this interesting book while you are convalescing. Hopefully it will help pass the time and interest you! I hope you know how much I love you!

Rest, relax, heal!

x o x o

Colleen
#1 daughter

January 2013

Fight All Day, March All Night

Fight All Day, March All Night

A Medal of Honor Recipient's Story

WAYNE MAHOOD

excelsior editions

State University of New York Press
Albany, New York

Published by
State University of New York Press, Albany

Copyright © 2012 State University of New York Press

For information, contact State University of New York Press, Albany, NY
www.sunypress.edu

Production by Kelli W. LeRoux
Marketing by Fran Keneston

Excelsior Editions is an imprint of State University of New York Press

Library of Congress Cataloging-in-Publication Data

Mahood, Wayne.
    Fight all day, march all night : a medal of honor recipient's story / Wayne Mahood.
        pages cm
    Includes bibliographical references and index.
    ISBN 978-1-4384-4507-6 (hardcover : alk. paper)
    1. Brown, Morris, 1842–1864. 2. Medal of Honor—Biography. 3. United
States. Army. New York Infantry Regiment, 126th (1862–1865) 4. United States—
History—Civil War, 1861–1865—Biography. 5. New York (State)—History—
Civil War, 1861–1865—Biography. 6. Soldiers—New York (State)—Penn Yan
Biography. 7. Penn Yan (N.Y.)—Biography. I. Title.

    E523.5126th .M33 2012
    973.7'8092—dc23
    [B]   2012004398

10 9 8 7 6 5 4 3 2 1

Contents

Illustrations

Maps

Photographs and Documents

Preface

I was drawn to Morris Brown, Jr.—Captain Morris Brown, Jr.—for a number of reasons. First and foremost, he was a Medal of Honor recipient. Second, he attended the same college as I. Third, fortuitously a cache of his letters was obtained by Frank Lorenz, then Editor of Publications and Archivist at Hamilton College, Clinton, New York, and made available to me. Fourth, Brown's letters reveal many of the trials and tribulations of a Civil War soldier, including describing the unseemly, but all too human, infighting between fellow officers vying for higher rank. Importantly, Brown bared the fears of one who, as the war progressed in Spring 1864, came to believe that "We are now living as it were in our own graves."

When he wrote that to his parents, he was, in fact, living in a hole trying to avoid an enemy sharpshooter's fatal bullet. But, he also was acknowledging the reality that every soldier in combat must recognize: the next bullet might be intended for him, however much he wanted to deny it. The relentless Overland Campaign in Spring 1864 was to Brown, "fighting all day and marching all night." Yet, he sorely wanted to survive and to establish himself as a businessman in postwar America.

From over fifty of his letters carefully preserved, we also learn that Morris Brown, Jr. was mature beyond his years, ambitious as Lucifer, and a born warrior. Even had he not followed in his older brother's footsteps or succumbed to his father's ardent patriotism, likely he would have enlisted in the Union army during the American Civil War. Yet, he had an instinct for business, as well, unlike most of his Hamilton College classmates who generally prepared for the ministry or law. When not fighting or angling for promotion, Brown was socking money away for a postwar career as a land speculator or developer. In fact, he vowed to return home as a conquering hero, or one day, a successful businessman.

If it meant going West, he was willing to do so, as he wrote his parents on April 13, 1864, ignoring for the moment the imminent threat of more fighting. Or he might imitate his father who had prospered as a lawyer and land speculator.

But that was down the road. For now, during this awful, fratricidal period in American history, he was a warrior. However, his military career had begun on a sour note, one that proved a goad. He and the brigade to which the 126th New York Volunteers belonged had been captured intact at Harpers Ferry, September 1862, less than a month into service. For almost ten months he and his comrades were taunted as the "Cowards of Harpers Ferry."

Then, their fates were joined with that of Brigadier General Alexander "Fighting Elleck" Hays, who trained the men in the dishonored brigade to believe in themselves. And it paid off at Gettysburg in the first days of July 1863, where they redeemed themselves. Hays could proudly proclaim that their history was now "written in blood." That Captain Brown's and his fellow soldiers' heroism was not a fluke was demonstrated again and again—at Auburn and Bristoe in October 1863, at the battles of the Wilderness, Spotsylvania, Cold Harbor, the siege of Petersburg, and finally on the road to Appomattox.

Throughout, Morris Brown showed leadership, first as a company commander, and later, at age twenty-two, as acting regimental commander. Importantly, he offers glimpses of war that reveal the highs and lows, the unnerving calm and the awful bloodletting and the unseemly infighting among officers. Yet, he claimed to want to spare his parents and sisters what he was experiencing, for he didn't want to worry them. Nonetheless, he couldn't help himself. He had a story to tell.

Fortunately, we have access to much of his correspondence, mostly after Gettysburg, by which we come to know Morris Brown and the sacrifices experienced by Civil War soldiers and their families.

Acknowledgments

First and foremost I must thank Frank K. Lorenz, former editor of publications and volunteer curator of archives at Hamilton College, who realized what a find the scrapbook containing Morris Brown's letters was and who found a way for the college to obtain it. Lorenz also located and copied for me photos of Brown and fellow alumni who enlisted in the 126th New York Volunteers. Subsequently, I received help from the Couper Library administration and staff, including Randall L. Ericson, director, who graciously gave me permission to quote from Brown's letters; Katherine Collett, curator, whose helpfulness and thoughtfulness over the years seemed to come natural to her; and alumnus Jeremy Schmidt, who photocopied Brown's letters for me.

Staff and volunteers at Yates County Historical and Genealogical Society's Oliver House, including the late Catharine Spencer, former director Idelle Dillon, her successor, John Potter, Judy Wilbert, Katherine Doan, Martha Gifford Harris, and assistant director, Lisa Harper. Also, I'm appreciative of curator Chuck Mitchell, who magically managed to copy a framed drawing of Morris Brown.

Frances Dumas, Yates County Historian, spent valuable time to help with background on the Brown family, while Terry Bretherton, Hammondsport Village Historian, Twila O'Dell, Steuben County Historian, and Richard ("Rick") Leisenring, Jr., Glenn Curtis Museum curator, offered further assistance in tracing the Brown family. Nor can I forget the late William Treichler, who introduced me to historians Bretherton and Leisenring.

Roger Hunt not only corrected me as to the legal name of Morris Brown's older brother, but graciously gave me a photo of John Smith Brown and a biographical piece Smith Brown completed for the New York State Bureau of Military Affairs. This is the second, or is it the third, time Hunt has come to my aid.

xiii

Thomas Jones, who owns Morris Brown's pistol, has graciously permitted me to reproduce a photo of it.

I'd be remiss if I failed to mention Harriet Scruggs, former SUNY Geneseo Interlibrary loan manager and others at the library, including former director Edwin Rivenburgh, who must have wanted to hide when they saw me coming with another request.

Certainly, I also owe thanks to Amanda Lanne, Assistant Acquisitions Editor, James Peltz, Co-Director, SUNY Press, Kelli Williams-LeRoux, Senior Production Editor, Rafael Chaiken, Acquisitions Editorial Assistant, and Thomas Goldberg, copyeditor.

Words are inadequate to express my thanks to colleague and friend Judith Bushnell, a SUNY Geneseo alumna and SUNY Geneseo reference librarian emeritus, for her meticulous reading of the copyedited version of this book.

Finally, I thank Bobbi, who once more bore with me through my trials and tribulations.

CHAPTER 1

"How I Would Like to Lead Such a Regiment as This to Battle"

On April 27, 1861, Morris Brown, Sr., "President for the Day," was fired up, and he wanted his Penn Yan, New York, audience of between three thousand and four thousand equally inspired when he finished talking. Fort Sumter, the Federal military post located in South Carolina's Charleston Harbor, had been shelled by secessionists. That was treason, pure and simple, and he was not going to have it. Brown, a partner in the law firm of Judd and Brown, wanted the attendees "to consider the perilous condition of our country." This Union Mass Meeting, sponsored by the chairmen of both the Republican and Democratic Central county committees, was a wake-up call. "War is upon us," Brown asserted as he stood in the court house square. "Our beloved country, our pride, our joy, the wonder of the world, the polar star of the world struggling to be free . . . is involved in all the horrors and convulsions of civil war."[1]

If the brass bands and parade had not stirred the proper patriotism, he would do so. "The Stars and Stripes . . . ," he exclaimed, "have been ruthlessly assailed and trampled in the dust. Treason stalks abroad, as yet unrebuked, and red-handed Rebellion . . . threatens the very existence of the Government."

Brown, whose middle son, Theodore, had helped warm up the audience by playing the melodeon, reminded his listeners that "The question is not merely whether 'The Union must and shall be preserved. . . .'" "No, the government ["to which the heroes of the Revolution pledged their lives, their fortunes and their sacred honor"] itself is in danger."

1

Fifty-two-year-old Morris Brown, a lawyer and Oneida County native, was a relative newcomer to Penn Yan. Barely five years earlier, he had moved from Hammondsport, Steuben County, at the foot of Keuka Lake. He had been active politically, beginning in 1834 in Steuben County as an inspector of schools in the town of Urbana. Apparently, around that time, he used his political influence to have roads on his property moved (twice) and had property redesignated from one school district to another. In 1843 and 1844, he served as New York state assembly-man, followed by an appointive position as district attorney (June 1846 to June 1847) and, in 1854, as the town of Urbana (Hammondsport) supervisor. But rapidly growing Penn Yan, the Yates County seat located on Keuka Lake Outlet, held more allure. So Brown moved his wife, Maria (Mariah)—whom he married in the First Presbyterian Church in Cherry Valley, Otsego County in 1834—three sons, and two daughters there. He promptly proved himself an entrepreneur and man of means. Within three years, he had purchased or mortgaged three houses and lots in the village, including a large house on a six-acre lot on Main Street. In fact, almost immediately on his arrival in 1856 he bought two houses and lots, for which he was assessed a total of $3200 and paid $12.24 in taxes. Additionally, in 1857, he bought a large 848-acre timber tract for $28,000 in the hamlet of Milo Center just outside Penn Yan. (However, he may have been quite overextended, for the house in which he and his family would live at 322 Main Street would be purchased by Maria in 1862 and put in trust to Maria's brother-in-law James M. Gillett. Later, it was sold to Nelson Thompson to pay off a debt.)[2]

Thus, by 1860, when Brown returned to the practice of law in Penn Yan, at least on paper, he was prosperous enough to support a household of nine. This included his wife, himself, his namesake, eighteen-year-old Morris, Jr. and two daughters—Jennie (alternately Mary Jane or Jean) and Emeline (also called Lina), ages sixteen and twelve. Additionally Brown was supporting his father-in-law, John Smith, an eighty-four-year-old Presbyterian clergyman, two domestics (Hannah Grant, Smith's sixty-nine-year-old African-American servant, and a twenty-year-old female Irish immigrant) plus a twenty-three-year-old German-born male servant. (Brown's two older sons, John Smith Brown and Theodore Brown, had left home by this time.)[3]

Though an avowed Democrat, Brown declared that "this day, and here on this spot, I abjure all party . . . until the honor of the nation is redeemed." Before he would submit to those who were dishonoring the American flag, his "children shall be called 'fatherless' and my wife shall be a 'widow!'" Then Brown called upon others to disavow partisanship and pledge themselves "to maintain the honor of our country's flag [which] is to protect our homes, our wives and our children." These were not idle words, for two of Brown's three sons were of age to answer President Abraham Lincoln's call for seventy-five thousand volunteers, and his youngest, Morris, Jr. soon would be.

Brown wisely called for bipartisanship. It was crucial in this county divided over issues facing the nation. The odd name of the county seat, Penn Yan, is a giveaway. It clearly reflected a compromise between its New England (Yankee) and Pennsylvania (Penn or southern) settlers. Passions ran high over slavery. An armed battle near Lakemont in the southeastern most township in the county was only narrowly averted after some locals informed slave catchers that four Virginia runaways were working nearby. A local justice's ruling that the slave catchers had the necessary papers resolved the issue temporarily. Even Penn Yan's three Protestant Churches had split over the issue of slavery. The same ardor would carry over into elections. While the nascent Republican party received a majority of votes in 1856, Democrats crowed that their party had won the White House. The resultant pealing of church bells by Democrats, who had attracted Irish Catholic immigrants to their party, led to fist fights. Not surprisingly, the two Penn Yan newspapers, the Whiggish *Yates County Chronicle* and the *Yates County Democrat*, also reflected the opposing views.[4]

"President for the Day" Brown needed all his persuasive powers to ignite the county's citizens. Politics was only one problem. Yates County was the state's fifth smallest in population, with approximately twenty thousand residents, a vast majority of whom were New York State natives. Moreover, it was heavily dependent on farm labor. Boosters liked to claim that it was the greatest grain producing county in the United States, with a harvest of 174,181 bushels of corn and 169,000 bushels of wheat in 1854. The 2,794 farmers would need all the healthy men they could get to plant, cultivate, and harvest these crops. Other laborers were needed in the grist mills, powered by the waterfalls on Keuka Lake (or as it was generally known, the Crooked Lake Outlet).[5]

Leaving no doubt of his commitment, Brown concluded his talk with a rousing: "Hesitation is cowardice——delay is treason. . . . Today

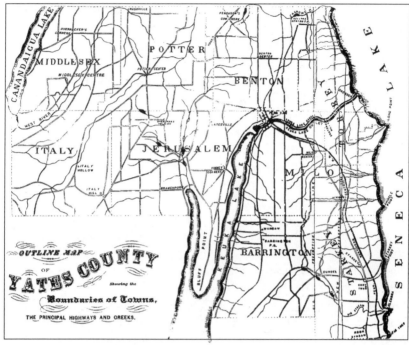

Yates County, New York, 1873 (*Source:* History and Directory of Yates County)

we talk——let us all talk——but tomorrow and henceforth it is our duty to fight." His words would come back to haunt him later.

The immediate upshot was the formation of a vigilance committee, which Attorney Brown was asked to chair. Three weeks later, the committee saw its first volunteers, the Keuka Rifles, off to Elmira, the newly created military depot. Nine days later, on May 27, Brown's first born, twenty-seven-year-old John Smith Brown, who went by his middle name (his mother's maiden name), took up the cause. Having abandoned the study of law and a teaching position in St. Louis, Missouri, he was then in New York City, where he enlisted as a private in what would become Company A of Colonel Hiram Berdan's First Regiment, U.S. Sharpshooters. It appears the younger Brown was visited by the same spirit that had led a great-grandfather to serve in the Revolutionary War and a grandfather in the War of 1812.[6]

Not content with his efforts, Chairman Brown presided over a meeting at Washington Hall in Penn Yan to organize a military company to serve as a home guard, followed immediately by initiating a subscription fund to provide "for actual necessity"—that is, board, clothing and a monthly allowance for the volunteers' families. In the same spirit, Brown spoke at meetings in various towns and villages in the county and moved that nine delegates be appointed to attend a "People's Convention" in Syracuse on September 10. Then in October Brown was appointed from the town of Milo (Penn Yan) to chair future meetings of delegates.[7]

John Smith Brown, U.S. Sharpshooters (*Source:* US Army Military History Institute)

But fostering the war effort was a frustratingly slow process. Not even a proposal by the state's adjutant general and governor to raise a regiment from the Twenty-sixth Senatorial District—which encompassed Yates and neighboring Ontario and Seneca counties—proved successful. Nor were the recruiting efforts by Brown's older son Smith more fruitful. Promoted sergeant major and then adjutant of the 1st U. S. Sharpshooters, Smith Brown had examined applicants in Albany and New York City. Shortly, he intended to focus on Yates County. In one of almost weekly letters to the *Yates County Chronicle*, he announced he would be in Penn Yan on August 29 to receive recruits for the Sharpshooters, which he had initially been authorized by Secretary of War Simon Cameron to recruit on June 15, 1861. As "Mr. J. Smith Brown, New York Agt" for the Sharpshooters, he appealed to those owning rifles with sights, who, at one hundred yards, could shoot ten consecutive shots averaging five inches from the center of the target for each shot. In a subsequent letter from Washington, in which he accused unnamed individuals back home of retarding recruiting, he tried another tack, advertising that a Sharpshooter, whose duty was likened to "the Indian practice of scouting," sported a distinctive uniform: dark green coats, green pants, and leather "leggins."[8]

Despite his, his father's and the military committee's efforts, recruitment up to the end of the year was disappointing. Yates County had no regiment of its own. Sharpshooter Brown continued to publish letters, often running three to four columns in the *Yates County Chronicle* well into 1862. However, by mid-June 1862, the tone of his letters took on an edge. The Peninsula Campaign, Major General George B. McClellan's attempt to take Richmond, had taken a toll on the eldest Brown son. He was utterly exhausted and railed about the soldier's hardships (though he acknowledged, "it is war") and about the inaccurate, even biased, newspaper reporting of the Union's battles. However, he saved his greatest wrath for his peers at home: "Have these young men [who think the war was nearly over] no aspirations, no patriotism?" By the end of July, he had another target for his wrath, Union officers. He absolved only McClellan and the enlisted men from blame for the failed campaign on the Virginia Peninsula, though he was willing to let wiser heads make the final judgment.[9]

By 1862, all hope for a short war had long since faded. More men were needed. Six months into the war barely five new state regiments claimed any Yates County men. So in early July a military committee, drawn from the Twenty-sixth Senatorial District, was formed, with Morris Brown and six others from Yates County appointed to it. The entire committee first met in Geneva, Ontario County, on July 11 to plan ways to raise a regiment. The Yates committeemen promptly called for a large war rally at the county courthouse on Saturday July 27, 1862. Speeches by the Hon. James C. Smith and the Rev. Mr. Frederick Starr "performed a glorious service," according to *Yates County Chronicle* editor and military committeeman, Stafford C. Cleveland, on July 31. The impetus was maintained by meetings throughout the county well into the next month. And the momentum paid off. By August 14, the *Chronicle* could report that Lieutenant Samuel Barras and Captains Truman Burrill were credited with recruiting ninety-two men, and William Coleman had signed up two full companies, which would be designated A and B respectively. (An infantry company had one hundred men, and a regiment had ten companies, or a thousand men.) Importantly, the county had met its quota of 220 enlistees, almost 10 percent of the county's population—proudly surpassing the efforts in Ontario County, though the latter would eventually supply the bulk of the enlistees. The *Yates County Chronicle* trumpeted that on Saturday, August 2, Captain Burrill's Company A steamed to Geneva and was "First in the Field." By the end of the war, the Town of Milo (Penn Yan) would claim 779, or 22 per cent of the draft eligible men, served in the Union Army.[10]

One of Captain Burrill's recruits was Morris Brown's youngest son, twenty-one-year-old Morris, Jr., who signed up on August 11. He would be joined by Smith Brown after the latter obtained a discharge from the U.S. Sharpshooters and mustered as a lieutenant and adjutant of the 126th later that year. But the middle brother, twenty-five-year-old Theodore, an accomplished chess and piano player, did not follow his brothers—electing instead to move from Newark, New Jersey to Germany to compete in international chess competitions. Theodore may have been a child prodigy, playing piano concerts at age eight, starting chess at age twelve, debuting at the New York Chess Club in 1855 at age eighteen and winning prizes barely three years later. Moreover, as the youngest Brown son would reveal in his letters, he and brother Smith were—at least felt—obligated to support Theodore's chess playing in Germany.[11]

Morris Brown's enlistment statement (*Source:* National Archives)

Likely, Morris, Jr. also was influenced by the martial air that prevailed at Clinton, New York's Hamilton College, a small men's school, just west of Utica. It was evident beginning in 1860, with a uniformed marching club—and even more so after the fall of Fort Sumter, when student activism included a drill company. President Samuel Ward Fischer fostered that spirit in a July 1862 address in which he declared that historic Hamilton would not shrink from defending the nation against "malignant traitors in our own land." That patriotic spirit led more than half of the 1861 graduates to enlist in the Union Army and ultimately something like 226 Hamiltonians to serve, mostly as officers, including 14 who became chaplains. That's a sizeable number for a small liberal arts college, the graduating classes of which averaged only about thirty. Twenty-five alumni gave their lives. Six from the class of 1863 died during the war, and six from Morris Brown's class of 1864.[12]

Six Hamiltonians enlisted in the 126th New York—including Brown; Corporal Myron Adams, a member of the class of 1863; his older brother, Edward P., from the class of 1858; Myron Adams's classmates George W. Sheldon and Henry Porter Cook; and Darius Sackett, Brown's 1864 classmate. Cook, Sackett and Sheldon were members of the Delta Upsilon fraternity and may well have been influenced by fraternity brother Myron Adams, the son of a Presbyterian minister and ardent abolitionist at age twenty-two. Brown, a Chi Psi, seems to have acted more independently, but was certainly prodded by his father's and brother Smith's enthusiasm for the cause.[13]

Cpl. Myron Adams (*Source:* Hamilton College Archives)

Cpl. Edward Adams (*Source:*
Hamilton College Archives)

Cpl. George Wright Sheldon
(*Source:* Hamilton
College Archives)

Cpl. Darius C. Sackett (*Source:* Hamilton College Archives)

On August 22, the 126th New York was officially mustered on the grounds of George N. Reed's White Springs Trotting Park in Geneva, the site chosen by the military committee. It was promptly dubbed Camp Swift, to honor retired Brigadier General Joseph G. Swift, the top graduate of West Point's class of 1800 and an Ontario County military district committeeman.

The 126th New York was a rather typical Union regiment, with twenty-three percent laborers, a fifth farmers, and the rest a mix of carpenters, clerks, shoemakers, blacksmiths, painters, mechanics, dentists, artists, marble cutters, and "boatmen." The average age was twenty-four. The selection of its colonel, forty-nine-year-old Eliakim E. Sherrill, was somewhat of a surprise. A former congressman, he not only had no military training; he had moved from Ulster County, New York, to Geneva only two years earlier. Moreover, he was the committee's third choice. State Senator Charles J. Folger and Darius Ogden, military district committeemen, had turned down the appointment. James M. Bull, thirty-six, a successful Canandaigua lawyer, was appointed lieutenant colonel, and

William H. Baird, a pre-war carriage maker who had served with the 38th New York in the Peninsula Campaign, was appointed major. Penn Yan's Dr. Fletcher M. Hammond, Morris Brown, Sr.'s brother-in-law (young Morris's uncle), became the regimental surgeon and would look after the young Brown throughout their service together.[14]

Mustering was delayed a week, until August 22, due to the lack of uniforms and blankets, allowing the men a weekend furlough. Meanwhile, a regimental flag was sewn of silk, which district committeeman "Colonel" or "General" Ephraim M. Whitaker from Penn Yan had purchased in New York City. But the flag presentation, with Penn Yan's Rev. Starr making the obligatory speech, did not come off as expected. Allegedly, carping by Genevans about "so much unexpected glory going to the ladies of Penn Yan" (who had sewn the 126th NY flag) necessitated an accommodation. Eventually on the twenty-second, the presentation came off in grand style, despite a blustery wind blowing dust in the faces of the recruits and eight thousand to ten thousand attendees.[15]

Morris, Jr. was mustered Orderly Sergeant (Adjutant) in Captain Truman Burrill's Company A, on August 22, 1862, and was advanced $21, a month's pay. (Typically he sent home his pay——a frequent topic of his letters——to be invested by his father.) Then, on Tuesday, August 26, sometime between 8:00 and 9:30 a.m. the recruits marched about a mile to Geneva's Steamboat Landing, where they boarded the three steamers that plied Seneca Lake, disembarking at the end of the lake at Jefferson (now Watkins Glen). There they boarded the Elmira, Jefferson and Canandaigua Railroad cars bound for the Elmira Depot. Once there, they got their first discomforting taste of army food: two loaves of bread that one non-commissioned officer used for footballs, two slices of cold beef, which he and some others tossed into the road, and two pieces of cheese. The non-com and others substituted pies they purchased from local merchants in the city for the unpalatable rations.[16]

At sundown, the 26th, Sergeant Brown and the other new soldiers aboard the Northern Central Railroad train were bound for Baltimore, via Harrisburg, Pennsylvania. The soldiers' fare in Baltimore was considerably more satisfying, courtesy of the "Union Relief Association." It was topped off by fresh peaches purchased from strolling peddlers. Five hours later they were on their way to Harpers Ferry, Virginia (now West Virginia) to relieve militia there. At midnight, August 27, the weary men arrived at Sandy Hook Station, just upstream from Harpers Ferry, where they lay for nine hours in the cramped railroad cars. Accompanied by the regimental band playing Yankee Doodle, they were marched to what Company E 2nd Lt. John H. Brough pungently labeled "the romantic, God-forsaken, pillaged and ever-memorable Harper's Ferry."[17]

Harpers Ferry, site of the ill-fated raid by abolitionist John Brown and his small band of followers in 1859, lay at the confluence of the Potomac and Shenandoah Rivers. Torched by fleeing Federals over a year earlier, with windows broken out of vacant houses and fences burned, the town seemed hardly worth defending. In fact, it was defenseless and would change hands four times during the war. The only justifications were its proximity to the vital Baltimore & Ohio Railroad and canal and its resting in the path of northward-bound Confederates. The new soldiers did not remain there long, moving uphill to Bolivar Heights the last day of the month. There, they began the inevitable adjustment to the military routine: 5:00 a.m. reveille, drills until dress parade twelve hours later, and "lights out" at 9:30 p.m.

Sergeant Brown's first letter home graphically describes what the newly-minted 126th New York Infantry encountered:[18]

Two miles below Harpers Ferry
Sunday
Aug 31st/62

Well my dear parents, here we are away down here about on the very outskirts of civilization.

How they came to place such a green regiment as ours, literly on the very outposts, I dont know. It is much pleasanter here than in Geneva for several reasons, one is, that we are not bothered with so many persons in our camp, & another which is a very important one is, that being so far South we are liable to have a fight almost any day. at least we see & hear enough to keep us considerably excited during most of the time.

Oh if we were only drilled a little slower how I would like to lead such a regiment as this to battle. If we have a chance we'll show you how to fight.

We are encamped on Bolivar Heights a lovely place on a high hill below Harpers Ferry, & the ground is where the battle was fought between [Lieutenant General Thomas "Stonewall"] Jackson & Col. Segoine when Col. S took all of Jackson's guns. The batteries are here now that stopped Jackson when he was after [Major General Nathaniel] Banks. About here one can find everything that a soldier came with & also pieces of shells, old guns &c &c & once in a while a skeleton & rebel soldier half buried & everything one would find on a field where there had been a hard fought battle. We get all sorts of reports here in regard to [Union Major General John] Pope & Jackson. The report to day is that Jackson is taken prisoner. How true it is I can't tell as I have only seen one newspaper since I left Geneva.[19]

Whether Smith [Brown] will ever get here or not I cant tell. Adjt [Albert S.] Wheeler resigned & the Adjt Gen. sent to Washington for Smith but we have not heard from him & the Col. is begining to fear that he wont be able to get him. If he dont come, then [Lieutenant Samuel] Barras will probably be appointed & in that case I will be promoted to a lieutenancy which would be nice now for me of course; but if we can get Smith here as adjt I will like it so much better for I have a very good place now. Capt Burrill is very kind to me & Lieut Barras will do anything for me, & [Second Lieutenant George] Carpenter cant do enough. Let 'em talk about Barras as much as they are a mind to, but dont you believe 'em. I say he knows more than all the rest of the regiment put together. I have watched him very closely & as yet I have not found anything but what was just right. He is far superior to those that talk about him.

So far, we have got along very nicely & everything has passed off very pleasantly; but Oh dear! what food. the first two days we only had raw bacon & such crackers as Smith sent home. Now we have some beans, pork; rice & sugar. I went two days without anything but about two inches of Bologna sausage. What do you think of that eh? Leave our table & go two days here without anything to eat.

If I had not dated my letter Sunday I would not know any difference between this & any others. We have just returned from inspection drill & in a few minutes we go out on dress parade.

The drum is beating now & I must go, so good bye.

Your aff. son
Morris
Address
Morris Brown, Jr.
Orderly Co A 126th N.Y.
Harpers Ferry
Va.

Be sure & send county paper & let all write. Send letters.

This is a characteristic Brown letter before 1864. He was full of bravado, uttering the usual complaints about food and conditions generally. But he was unusually laudatory of other officers. Criticism, ever more strident, would become the pattern for this ambitious young man. However, three items to which he alludes are significant. The first was the resignation of Adjutant Albert Wheeler, Hobart College Professor of Greek, who had agreed to serve as adjutant during the regiment's organization. This resulted in a vacancy that Brown very much wanted for his brother Smith and which may well have been discussed previously. Smith's resignation as adjutant of the 1st U.S. Sharpshooters had already been submitted, and his request for a commission in the 126th was in the works.[20]

The second item was the recurring rumor of the approach of then Major General Thomas ("Stonewall") Jackson's men. Fellow Hamiltonian Myron Adams, observing the concentration of troops there at the Ferry, was led to believe there was a "prospect of smelling powder very soon." Soldiers lived on rumors, and frequently they proved accurate, like this one. General Robert E. Lee, Army of Northern Virginia commander, planned an invasion of Maryland and had advanced the wings (later corps) of Jackson and of the soon-to-be Lieutenant General James Longstreet. However, Major General Henry Halleck, Lincoln's general-in-chief, inconveniently ordered the troops at Harpers Ferry, which stood in the way, to remain there, rather than to withdraw toward Washington. Necessarily, these Federals would have to be routed.[21]

The third item to which Brown alluded was how green the 126th troops were here on "the very outskirts of civilization." Barely a week in service, they were not only still learning drills and maneuvers, they had not fired their weapons. (Nonetheless, more than a few had experimented with their newly issued .58 caliber Springfield rifles and with revolvers they had obtained by various means, forcing Colonel Sherrill to order all enlisted men to turn in their pistols and revolvers and to permit no firing except immediately after guard mounting.) Shortly, they were brigaded with the 60th Ohio, the 9th Vermont and the First Independent Indiana Battery, which constituted the left wing on Bolivar Heights and was commanded by Colonel William F. Trimble, the 60th Ohio's commander. Unfortunately, these units were almost as raw as the 126th, though the 60th Ohio had met Jackson in the Valley Campaign in June. The 9th Vermont, evacuated with the Buckeyes from Winchester on September 2, had yet to see any fighting. The right wing, consisting of the 115th, 111th, and 39th New York and an artillery battery from the 15th Indiana Volunteers, was commanded by one of the more notorious officers in the war, the 39th New York's Colonel ("Count") Frederick G. D'Utassy. These units too were inexperienced, with the exception of the 39th New York (which acted as if it were, according to many who served with them). The two wings were designated the Second Brigade, Middle Department, Eighth Army Corps.[22]

More problematic was Colonel Dixon S. Miles of the 2nd U. S. Infantry, a forty-eight-year-old Maryland native, a 1824 West Point graduate, and a Mexican War veteran, who commanded greater than thirteen thousand troops at Harpers Ferry. Miles was an unlikely candidate, given reports of secessionist leanings, alleged drinking, and ineptness at First Bull Run. Though the charges may have been unfairly lodged, they tarnished Miles's reputation and caused General Wool to claim he gave the command to Dixon because "he was the only one [regular officer] I could place there."[23]

Finally, as noted, Harpers Ferry was virtually defenseless. Consider Shelby Foote's memorable prose:

> Low-lying Harpers Ferry, more trap than fortress, was dominated
> by heights that frowned down from three directions: Bolivar
> Heights to the west, Maryland Heights across the Potomac,
> and Loudoun Heights across the Shenandoah. Seizure of

Harpers Ferry, W. VA, Looking down from Maryland Heights (*Source:* Wayne Mahood)

these heights with guns bearing down on the compact mass of Union soldiers in the town below would be "something like shooting fish in a rain barrel."

More tersely, General Longstreet called Harpers Ferry a "man trap."[24]

Despite the arrival of the Union troops from Winchester on September 2, the defenders of Harpers Ferry sweated almost as profusely from tension as from the heat—and with reason. General Lee's Special Orders No. 191, the notorious "lost orders," issued on September 9, called for dividing his army, with Jackson leading the attack. (The "lost" refers to the fact that a copy fell into the hands of Army of the Potomac commander, Major General George B. McClellan.) Longstreet took part of his wing and headed for Boonsboro, Maryland. Jackson split his force into three columns—sending the divisions of Major General Lafayette McLaws's and General Richard H. Anderson, under the command of Longstreet, to capture Maryland Heights—and Brigadier General John G. Walker's division toward Loudoun Heights. Jackson led the third, fourteen thousand strong, to Winchester to capture the Federals, if still there, before sweeping down on Bolivar Heights. General Daniel H. Hill's division acted as rear guard, while General J. E. B. Stuart covered the route to Boonsboro.[25]

Capture of any of the heights, especially the eleven hundred foot-high Maryland Heights, would doom Morris Brown, Jr. and the other Union troops there, which is what happened. By early Saturday morning, the thirteenth, McLaws's division had clawed its way up the unfortified east side of Maryland Heights and bore down on the Federals who had laboriously climbed up the west side the previous night. Sergeant Brown's October 3, 1862 letter to his parents, countering newspaper accounts "evidently written by some malicious person or persons for the purpose of degrading our gallant 126th," offers a "brief account of our fight [with] and surrender" to the "unregenerate greybacks."[26]

Camp Douglas, Friday Evening
Oct. 3, 1862

My Dear Parents:.

When we reached the summit the different companies of the 126th were sent out on picket, Co. "B" holding the extreme left, which we all envied, as the enemy were encamped in that direction. The night passed away quietly, excepting a little skirmish which Co. B had with the rebels; but with the dawn of day [Saturday, September 13] came the rattle of musketry. But mark you no cannon were heard. Soon Co. A was ordered to march up the hill, to share her part in the hard and well contested fight in progress about a mile on our left. Joyfully the boys started, and as we took our course up the hill in single file [on a narrow bridle path], we first saw and began to realize in a slight degree the horrors of war. As the wounded and dying were carried by us it seemed only to hasten our steps as we wished to help our gallant regiment to drive the enemy from the mountain.

[Fellow Hamiltonian, Corporal George W. Sheldon of Company B, in a letter to a classmate back in school, placed the 79th New York (75 men) on the far left in the first line of defense, three companies of the 32nd Ohio to the 79th's left, the 126th except for Brown's Company A to their right, and Companies K and B of the 1st Maryland Cavalry on the far right. They faced General Joseph Kershaw's Brigade, while General William Barksdale's Brigade flanked the Union right.]

But this was not to be our good fortune: for as we reached the "Block House" the firing ceased, and soon the report came that our forces had been ordered to retreat.

Soon our gallant Col. SHERRILL ordered Co. A to go back to a narrow opening, to prevent a flank movement that was evidently intended by a regiment of rebel infantry.

As we reached our position the firing was resumed at the breastworks [just below a hundred-foot-long abatis and the second line of defense] which continued for about an hour, when the order was given to leave the works, and retreat down the hill. At once, every one in the regiment, from the highest officer to the lowest private in the ranks, saw that to give up Maryland Hights was to lose all; but we must obey, and down the hill we started.

When we had nearly reached the road, which is nearly half-way down the mountain, we received orders to reform the regiment and march back to the "Block House." Soon we were back within a quarter of a mile of our former battle ground, and ready in line of battle, for whatever might appear. In a few minutes the rebels appeared, and after having fired one or two rounds, we were ordered to retreat and fall back across the Potomac to our camp. The rebels quickly took possession of the hights, and from their signals, we knew that before another eve the hights would be bristling with cannon, ready at any moment to belch forth their thundering fire on our weakness in the valley below.

That night as we wrapped our blankets around us and tried to get a little rest (for we were nearly exhausted from the hard task we had performed that day) we knew that the following morning (Sunday) would reveal to us our weakness, comparatively, surrounded as we were on all sides with the forces of Jackson, Longstreet, and the celebrated A. P. Hill. About two o'clock the next day our batteries, at a given signal, commenced to play upon all the points where the rebel could be seen. Immediately the firing on both sides began in terrible earnest. While the rebels had seven batteries posted advantageously on the surrounding hights, we had but three to answer them. The firing was kept up until sundown, when, as if by mutual consent, it ceased.

About 9 p.m. the rebels undertook to capture one of our batteries on the left of the 126th, but were gallantly repulsed with great slaughter.

In a short time we were ordered out of our intrenchments toward the right, to give place for the 22d Ohio. This placed Co. A, F, and a portion of Co. D [of the 126th New York], in much more exposed position.

We had no sooner laid down on our arms than a large force of cavalry appeared on our right nearly in front of Co. A, and attempted to drive in our pickets, which were posted about twenty rods in advance. In less than two minutes we were again in line prepared to give them a warm reception. Here was seen the first instance of shirking on the part of Co. A. As two men were seen creeping away through the darkness, Capt. Burrill ordered them to halt, but they paid no attention to the command, when he drew his revolver and ordered them to return to the ranks, or he would shoot them. To this forcible argument they readily succumbed, for they well knew the Captain always did just what he said. In a short time the rebels were repelled with very little loss on our side and we laid down to rest.

As the moon arose, or about twelve o'clock, Capt. Burrill aroused the men and ordered them to dig some new trenches. To work we went, and in about three hours were ready to lie down and catch a few more minutes rest in our intrenchments.

At daylight the rebels again opened fire on us from forty or fifty guns, and having placed them during the night in much more favorable positions, were able to do with us about as they pleased. Soon our ammunition gave out, and as they were engaging [?] their fire, and getting a much better range of our intrenchments, we were ordered to leave them

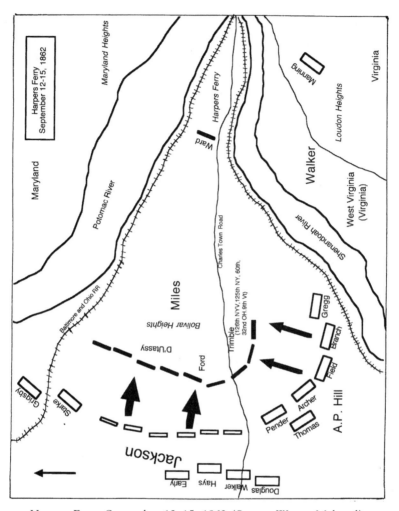

Harpers Ferry, September 12–15, 1862 (*Source:* Wayne Mahood)

and retreat down the hill to the Potomac. A few minutes before we received the order Col. Miles ordered the white flag to be raised, which every one refused to do.

As we left our intrenchments and started down the hill, the rebels seemed to increase their fire rather than slacken it although the white flag had been raised for some time. In about three-quarters of an hour the firing ceased, and the 126th who so manfully had borne their part in this contest, were prisoners of war. Soon we were formed in line, and with the other regiments marched up on Bolivar Hights, where having formed in line of battle, we stacked the guns we had received in Elmira less than three weeks before.

The next day the rebels gave us three hard crackers and a small piece of maggoty bacon, to the man, and started us off for Frederick, which we reached about ten o'clock the next morning. The next day we started for Annapolis and arrived there Saturday evening. The next Wednesday we left Annapolis for Chicago, and arrived here Saturday evening, having been nearly two weeks on the way from Harper's Ferry.

Until Col. Sherrill was wounded, everything seemed to go on prosperously; and if he had not been injured, we all think Maryland Hights would not have been evacuated.

A braver man never received a commission; and it is the wish of each one here, that his recovery may be speedy, and that he may soon be in command of the regiment, by whom he is much beloved and esteemed.

Too much praise cannot be bestowed on Capt Burrill. He had been sick in the hospital three days previous to the battle; but when he heard the firing and knew his company needed him, he filled his haversack and started for the Hights, but was ordered back by Dr. Hammond, who knew he was not able to climb that terrible mountain. But as soon as the company left the mountain he joined them, and did not leave them again until after the surrender. He has shared alike with the men in their toils and hardships, and by his coolness and bravery has now the confidence of his men; and if we are again called into action, with him as our leader, you can rest assured every man will stand by him, even though it be to die.

As regards the bravery and military capacity of Lieut. Barras (now acting adjutant) no comments are necessary. His bravery is unquestionable.

When the men were almost ready to give up from hunger and exhaustion, from his efforts the men were again rallied and formed in the line of battle.

Soon we hope to be again in active service, for paroled life in such a place as this, is anything but pleasant;—nothing to do—not even fight.

We are hoping that we will soon be ordered to Camp Swift, but that would be too good for prisoners, so I suppose we must remain here until exchanged.

Hoping to hear from you soon, I remain your affectionate Son,

Morris Brown, Jr.

As a prisoner of war, Brown not only had time to write this long letter, but, like his fellows, to rant. Accused of skedaddling, he and his comrades were being labeled the "Cowards of Harpers Ferry." In fact, fault finding and scapegoating occupied over 250 pages of testimony in Volume 19 of the *Official Records*.

A prior letter to his parents, written on September 23, reveals the intensity of his feeling and whom to blame:

The 126th N.Y. has received a very great injustice from some of those [unnamed] correspondents. All the fighting that was done on Maryland Hights was done principally by our regiment. The troops that had been in the service for six months retreated before ours.

Co A was not in the hottest of the fight. We were deployed to look out for the flank movements.

If proper precautionary measures had been taken we would never had to have surrendered.

There is no doubt but that we were sold to the Rebels by Col. Miles . . . the meanest & dirtiest traitor that ever drew breath. Oh, he was one of the blackest kind. . . . How happy we felt when we heard of this death. the old traitor.

Morris deeply resented reports getting back to Penn Yan and took it out on Colonel Miles, who was killed almost simultaneous with the raising of the white flag. Before long, it became a chorus of condemnation. One writer devotes an entire book to try to prove Miles's treason, and more than a few soldiers at Harpers Ferry suggested that Miles was intentionally killed by friendly fire. Yet, Brown is probably loath to admit that he was fortunate to escape without injury, for the 126th New York lost seventeen killed and thirty-eight wounded, the most of any Union regiment on Maryland Heights. (Only two privates from Brown's Company A were wounded.) His Hamilton College classmate Darius Sackett would be discharged because of his wounds. The most serious casualty may have been Colonel Sherrill, whose leadership the men had come to admire

Col. Eliakim Sherrill (*Source:* Roger D. Hunt)

in only a few short weeks. Sherrill was struck by a bullet that "passed through his left cheek and out the right, taking a portion of his front teeth of the lower jaw." The result was that he continued bleeding and had difficulty breathing or swallowing. Eventually a tooth was discovered buried in his tongue and an artery severed. The tooth was extracted, and the artery repaired in an operation that took close to an hour. However, Sherrill's recovery would take longer than anticipated by the attending doctor.[27]

Sergeant Brown had plenty of time to fret now. He lay idle, a Union prisoner of war at Camp Douglas in Chicago, Illinois, where he and his fellow parolees were guarded by Union soldiers. The camp, named for Illinois senator and 1860 presidential candidate, Stephen A. Douglas, sat near the windy shores of Lake Michigan some thirty blocks south of the heart of the city. The sixty-acre camp, built in late summer 1861, originally was to serve as a military depot and training site for the northern district of Illinois. Only later did it house Confederate prisoners. And Chicago's mayor was totally unprepared for the arrival of more than ten thousand parolees from Harpers Ferry, which he unsuccessfully protested as a menace to the city.

The whole bizarre episode began with the surrender at Harpers Ferry, on Monday, September 15. Actual arrangements the following day were in accord with the Dix-Hill Cartel, named for the signatories, Major Generals John A. Dix, U.S.A., and Daniel Harvey Hill, C.S.A. Prisoners were paroled, that is, they gave their word not to take up arms until properly exchanged for an equivalent number of captured enemy soldiers. Meanwhile, they were to be transported to "points mutually agreed upon at the expense of the capturing party." Major General A. P. Hill, who accepted the surrender and was in a hurry to join the Confederate army bound for Maryland, simply dumped the problem of where to send the prisoners into the laps of the U.S. military authorities. Unfortunately for the parolees, the Union Adjutant General had no place for them. Annapolis was already awash with prisoners, so the Harpers Ferry parolees were sent to Chicago to relieve Western troops which would be sent against Native Americans attacking frontier settlements.[28]

So, according to Company B's 1st Lt. Richard Bassett, it was "in quick & out quick."[29] Not exactly, given Morris Brown, Jr.'s description of prisoner-of-war life in a letter home written shortly before the October 3 letter describing the battle of Harpers Ferry and Camp Douglas:

Camp Douglas
Monday afternoon
29th Sept. 1862

Well, my dear parents, here we are after a long & very tedious
journey of two weeks, quartered in this lousy hole

We left Harpers Ferry two weeks ago tomorrow, &
marched to Anapolis which is about one hundred & twenty
miles from Harpers Ferry. I tell you that march tired us. We
even found out that war was no foolish matter.

You can bet I did'nt carry any knapsack. In our retreat
from the intrenchments at the Ferry I lost everything I had.
I stole a blanket of[f] some one else; & besides that, I have
nothing only what I have on. All those pocket silks, towels,
&c. &c. are gone. I bought a cheap shirt & a pair of socks at
Anapolis so as to have a change until I could send for more.

I wish you would make me two or more flannel shirts; &
send them to me, along with some hand kerchiefs & a couple
of towels. & some woolen stockings; & have John Brown
make me a pair of hip boots & send them along; & I would
really like to have one palatable meal. Since we started from
Harpers Ferry we have had only pork & crackers. I mean those
hard things Smith sent home. From Anapolis to Chicago we
only received our rations; & all the rest we had we bought
ourselves. There has not been a single day since I left Geneva
that I have had enough to eat. I dont know as I ought to say
that; but I have went to sleep many a night without anything
to eat—unless it was one of those hard crackers.

The commissioned officers get along well enough for
they can go & do as they please; but us poor ensigns have
to get along as best we can.

I like Capt Burrill & Barras very much but I think
Carpenter is a poor coward. He has not got the spunk of a
louse.

The day we had the battle on Maryland Heights Capt.
Burrill was in the hospital sick & Barras was acting adjutant
& so Carpenter was left in command of the company. When
the battle commenced we were off about a mile on picket

duty. We soon had orders to go & support the rest of the regiment & started up the hill. Well when we got where the bullets whistled pretty lively Carpenter was taken very ill & remained so until we had orders to retreat when he fell in & went back to camp all right. All that day I had the whole command of the company & I must say that since we left Geneva I have had command of the company more than all the rest put together, Capt. Lieuts & all.

Its too bad the papers accuse us of cowardice on Md Heights for if men ever fought anywhere they did there. It discourages the men & renders them unfit for future work; because they say if that is all the credit they are going to recieve they wont fight any way. I think this regiment will never recover from this defeat. It will never again be what it was when we went to Harpers Ferry. In my opinion it is becoming very much demoralized. They are going to have trouble here in this camp. This worries [me] the sixtieth Ohio regiment had an awful row. Our officers undertook to help stop it & they got used pretty roughly. Two brick bats struck Capt Burrill & Major [William] Baird's sword was taken from him by a private after he had knocked two or three down. Maj. Baird [the 126th New York's ranking officer at Camp Douglas] can be compared to the lowest scoundrel in Penn Yan He is a regular black leg. Everyone in the regiment came down on him. I hope Smith will be here before long If he dont come soon I hardly know what I am going to do. I had just as soon be in prison as here, for I think this is the worst place a person ever got in.

Until about three weeks ago, all the rebels that were taken at Fort Donalson [Confederates captured at Fort Donelson, February 6, 1862] have been quartered here; & if you never saw filth & lice you ought to come here. If I was in Penn Yan, all the money there could'nt get me in this scrape again. As long as we were in the field in action service I liked it very much; but since we have been prisoners we have been treated like dogs. We cant get out side of this dirty camp, & cant do anything—Just lie around here from morning till night.

I believe we ought to be sent home. Everyone of the soldiers think so, & I think if a person should desert they would not touch him.

If I could get a furlough & go up to Fonddulac [Fon du Lac, Wisconsin] I'd do it, or home either but that's impossible I suppose until Smith comes. I want you to send me ten dollars by return mail, for I must get something to eat once in a while. I have only spent $10 since I left home. Pinch _____ for me & say its all right. Remember me to all my friends in Penn Yan.

Good by
Your Aff. son
Morris

Why Brown showed interest in going to Fon du Lac, Wisconsin is a mystery. Was he intrigued by the name? Was this simply a place not far off to which to escape? Whatever the attraction, like other parolees, Brown was disgusted with the conditions since their sendoff from Annapolis on September 24. They had been crowded to suffocating aboard an insufficient number of steamers bound for Baltimore. Then, the "mortified, impoverished, disorganized" prisoners were escorted directly from the steamers into "plain" box cars (forty to a car), with newly mounted seats of "rough, unplaned plank" and were provided "neither water nor toilet facilities." Some cars lacked springs or seats, forcing men to sleep on the floor. A member of the 111th New York claimed that the former cattle cars were simply "swept out [with] a coarse broom."[30]

Not surprisingly, the 126th New York and the other paroled regiments arrived at Chicago with considerably fewer men than with which they had started. Some of the losses were outright desertions, others were "French leaves (short, unauthorized absences)." Sixty-three-year-old Brigadier General Daniel Tyler expected some desertions, but he was shocked at the "enormous loss of men" between Annapolis and Camp Douglas. Eighty-four members of the 126th deserted between Harpers Ferry and their ultimate exchange, November 24, 1862. It was virtually a daily occurrence, with twenty-three leaving en route to Chicago, seven from Brown's Company A.[31]

Once at Camp Douglas, if they had not thought of it before, many strongly considered deserting. Though the barracks were comfortable enough, they abounded in lice, aka "varmints." The low, flat land lacked drainage, and this resulted in standing water. More troubling, Sergeant Brown and the other parolees were destitute of clothing and food. (Their fare consisted of "Sour bread, wormy rice, old beans" washed down with "poor whiskey," a member of the 111th New York contended.) After visiting the camp, the future head of the Sanitary Commission, Henry W. Bellows, pronounced it "deplorable." Their condition was exacerbated by taunts from enthusiastic Illinois recruits who drilled nearby and called the parolees "cowards." But idleness would prove the greatest enemy—not only for the enlisted men, but also of the officers responsible for their conduct. The parolees could write only so many letters, read so many newspapers, pitch so many quoits—or play so many games of dominos, cribbage, checkers, rummy, and baseball. Earlier, their captors had led them to believe that they were forbidden to perform military duty and soon would be sent home. On the other hand, the Union officers seemed willing to carry out orders. This was a combustible mix.[32]

Signs of mischief increased as time wore on, leading to a series of explosions. Orderly Sergeant Brown alludes to an explosion when frustrated members of the 60th Ohio Infantry began what he called simply a "row." General Tyler regarded their actions as borderline mutiny. When Captain Burrill and Major Baird tried to intervene, it resulted in the melee Brown described. This may have been retaliation by the 60th Ohio after General Tyler's acting assistant adjutant general threatened to have the 126th New York replace the 60th and guard the Ohioians. Meanwhile, members of the 111th, serving as guards, protested unwanted duty by tearing down sections of outside fence and starting a fire, which spread to the 65th Illinois Infantry's barracks. (This too may have been a case of retaliation, for the Illini had not only relieved the 111th New York, but, similar to the 126th New York's experience, were ordered to guard the 111th.) The 9th Vermont "fired their barracks" and attacked the fire engine and crew with stones and clubs. Survival became the main concern for more than a few members of the 126th New York.[33]

In time, physical suffering was mitigated somewhat by better sanitary conditions, improved rations, and an issue of clothing, but relieving the psychological suffering proved more difficult. Trips to downtown Chicago helped some. Four members of a company at a time were issued passes to ride the street cars at five cents a ride to obtain a saloon dinner for twenty cents. This was not an unmitigated blessing. "Straggling" in saloons, theaters, and elsewhere became too common a practice, necessitating "patrols" by company officers. In fact, between 11:00 p.m. and 2:00 a.m. October 20–21, Company B Lieutenant Richard Bassett and five noncommissioned officers arrested twenty-seven "stragglers."[34]

Even with the improved rations and opportunity to get out of the camp, desertions increased as the time wore on. Finally, on November 17, 1862, Commissary General of Prisoners William Hoffman cut orders to have General Tyler notify the Harpers Ferry parolees to report to Washington for assignment. Two days later, all but the 9th Vermont and 65th Illinois were formally notified of their exchange and issued clothing, knapsacks, haversacks, and canteens—but they waited another five frustrating days, until around 3:30 p.m. on the twenty-fourth, to depart. This time they boarded passenger trains. By November 28, most of the "Cowards of Harpers Ferry" were at Camp Chase on Arlington Heights, just across the Potomac from Washington, desperately wanting to erase the stigma.[35]

CHAPTER 2

"Oh, That We Could Fight"

O n November 29, the parolees marched ten miles to Alexandria, Virginia, where they boarded flat cars of the Orange & Alexandria Railroad, bound for Union Mills, Virginia. Awaiting new Springfields and equipment, members of the 126th New York were starting the war all over again. In two months, they would become part of Major General Silas Casey's Division of Major General Samuel P. Heintzelman's XX Corps, Defenses of Washington. That is, they were to be garrisoned and commanded by superannuated or supernumerary generals, and they were responsible for the defense of the capital and surroundings. It seemed fitting for the men who bore the disgrace of Harpers Ferry.

Meanwhile, the carping that had begun in earnest at Camp Douglas continued, exacerbated in part by the absence of the wounded Colonel Sherrill. For example, on December 1, Company B's Lt. Richard Bassett, Officer of the Guard, and Lt. Philo Phillips, Company D and Officer of the Day, were accosted by Lt. Samuel Barras. Barras accused Bassett of saying that Barras "jumped his horse & run at Maryland Heights" and called Bassett "a God Damd liar." Phillips jumped up and called Barras a "Damd liar and & damd coward." Acting Adjutant Barras was the loser in this exchange and twelve days later when he was dismissed. Phillips had formally charged Barras with drunkenness, cowardice, and conduct unbecoming of an officer at Maryland Heights. The charge that stuck was absence from his post. Major William Baird, who had risked his life to stem a riot at Camp Douglas, too was dismissed (unfairly it would be shown later) for "bad conduct," based on a Court of Inquiry's finding. This was only the beginning of head-spinning organizational changes.[1]

31

Morris Brown, Jr. and his brother Smith Brown were beneficiaries of these changes. Smith had already been commissioned adjutant of the 126th and had joined his brother at Camp Douglas just prior to the trip to Washington. Better yet, on December 13, 1862, his ambitious younger brother enjoyed the fruits of his promotion efforts. He was now Company A's first, not second, lieutenant—a two-step jump—replacing the dismissed Samuel Barras. While still at Camp Douglas, apparently Morris had sought endorsements from two Hamilton College professors, Anson J. Upson, a Hamilton alumnus and adjunct professor of belles lettres, and "Old Greek," Professor Edward North. Upson had written that it gave "pleasure to express my good opinion of the character of Mr. Morris Brown." North was more effusive, writing that Brown possessed the "qualities that belong to a successful officer—physical courage and self possession, intellectual strength and sagacity with fine social gifts and a character unsullied."[2]

Likely, Morris benefitted more from a petition addressed to acting regimental commander Lieutenant Colonel James Bull by twenty-three members of Brown's company asking that he be promoted and jumped to first lieutenant. A photograph of the twenty-one-year-old in his officer's uniform, sent to Hamilton College for a class album, captures him well. Though light complexioned, his square face, full beard and piercing gray eyes show the determination, even aggressiveness, so evident in his letters home. Moreover, at 5 feet, 10 1/2 inches, he was over 2 inches taller than average. However, the high opinion of Brown was not unanimous at the time. Private Sidney D. Rice, for one, initially doubted Brown's fitness, but a change of heart after the Battle of Gettysburg induced him to praise Brown's "skill[,] daring and discipline. . . ."[3]

The 126th's Sergeant Harrison Ferguson could well have been describing young Brown when he wrote that "after a person has been in the service awhile, he becomes quite an aspirant, and goes in for 'number one' every time." Brown's letters clearly reveal he was such an aspirant, though his subsequent conduct would offer some justification. But his was only one of many promotions after Harpers Ferry due to a large number of officer resignations. Reasons varied. Quaker Captain Orin J. Herendeen claimed that "Some resign for want of pay. Some are sick, some are mad, some are discouraged, some are afraid." In fact, though he did not resign, he added, "most of us have all of these put together." Second Lieutenant George D. Carpenter's resignation may

Capt. Morris Brown, Jr. (*Source:* Hamilton College Archives)

have been brought on by Brown's promotion over him and an ongoing battle between the two.[4]

The 126th was now brigaded with other Harpers Ferry and Camp Douglas survivors—the 39th, 111th, and 125th New York—at Union Mills, Virginia. Nestled in the hills south of Centreville, barely twenty miles from the nation's capital, their camp lay on a flat plain crossed by Bull Run, the stream made famous by two ignominious Union defeats. Described by one unnamed member of the 126th as "no place at all," virtually nothing remained of what was once a flourishing town or the headier days when Confederates occupied it. Its thick woods had been denuded by soldiers to make camp fires and log huts. Worse, were the skeletal reminders of the earlier battles.

However, newly-minted 1st Lt. Brown was happily united with his older brother, which may have been as satisfying as the coveted promotion. He not only tented with Smith, but listened avidly to Smith's descriptions of combat experiences. For example, two days after Christmas the two rode to Bull Run with newly-mustered Lieutenant Dewitt Farrington of Company K and Captain Samuel Armstrong of the 125th New York. Smith described the Second Battle of Bull Run for his companions while they surveyed what was left of the fifteen-by-thirty-feet log huts, which extended some twelve miles on the plains of Manassas. And, for the most part, the younger Brown comfortably played second fiddle to Smith, including letting Smith correspond with their parents and with the *Yates County Chronicle*, which published many of his long letters. Only later, with the confidence gained from his own experience, would Morris seem Smith's peer.[5]

The only real downside was that they were basically noncombatants. In fact, many, if not most, of the troops in the Eastern theater were noncombatants, which frustrated President Lincoln. His commanding general, Major General George B. McClellan, "Little Mac" to his troops, had been ill that January, but when healthy had shown little desire to take the war to the Confederates. Contemptuous of Republican politicians, including Lincoln, he was not about to allow others to dictate to him. Even if inclined to attack, he always believed his troops were outnumbered. So, the Eastern front remained quiet. Nonetheless, Lieutenant Brown and others of the 126th New York had resumed their army routines—which, of course, included the dreaded, but inevitable, picket duty. For twenty-four to forty-eight hours, they were posted varying distances from the base camp and from each other, always on the alert for the enemy. It was tedious and tiring, and it took on an edge near where the Confederates had been spotted.

But as it had at Camp Douglas, time hung heavy. With time to gripe, the men did. Much of the griping was focused on the brigade commander, the 39th New York's Colonel ("Count") Frederick D'Utassy. The dress of the polyglot regiment out of New York City was as flamboyant as its unpredictable commander, who wore a green-feathered Italian black hat, a dark blue Hungarian hussar coat with scarlet and gold trimmings, and French trousers. A 126th sergeant contemptuously dismissed

D'Utassy as that "little Dutchman" who liked to show his authority. A lieutenant referred to the erstwhile count as "sour-crout D'Utassy." Lt. Richard Bassett was even more ethnocentric, reciting a ditty critical of him and the Germans in the 39th:

> I gets pretty drunk on lager beer,
> And fall in love mit de eagle.
> I leaves my vife in a lager beer shop,
> And goes to fight mit Siegle [General Franz Sigel].

The antipathy toward D'Utassy and his men seemed universal (and would continue through the war)—reinforced by various oddball exploits spawned by D'Utassy's fertile imagination.[6]

This changed dramatically upon the arrival of Brigadier General Alexander Hays, the newly appointed brigade commander. Hays's reputation had preceded him and had taken on a life of its own. According to Lieutenant Bassett's hyperbolic description, Hays "lost his leg in the battle of Shiloh: but he has a cork leg and you would hardly know that his leg was artificial: He is a large fine looking man about 38 years old, in every respect a gentleman and emphatically one of the best fighting gen'ls in the Army." Though wide of the mark, Bassett was correct that Hays had been wounded (three times), was a fighting general, and had a pronounced limp (the result of a minie ball at Second Bull Run). Before long, Bassett and others would come to highly admire Hays the person, not the reputation. (His cashiering of poseur D'Utassy shortly after he assumed command demonstrated his style of leadership, if any were needed.)[7]

The forty-three-year-old Hays, a Pennsylvania native, had graduated from West Point in the class of 1844, had served with upperclassmen Ulysses Grant and James Longstreet, and was cited for bravery in the Mexican War. More recent experience was acting brigade commander during the failed Peninsula Campaign. Six feet tall and weighing close to two hundred pounds, the bearded Hays even looked like a fighter. In fact, he had gotten into a bloody fight at West Point defending his cadet classmate, now Major General Winfield Scott Hancock, who was nearly five years younger and much smaller then. However, despite Hays's reputation, he protested that the insinuation "that I am too fond of fighting" is "ridiculously absurd." Most importantly, he would prove

Brevet Major Gen. Alexander Hays (*Source:* US Army Military History Institute)

inspirational, instilling in Morris Brown's brigade a merited pride. Within three months, Hays proclaimed that "Each day gives me more confidence in my command, and now that I have gained theirs, I think I can whip the Rebels here, in Centreville, five to one, and on any ground, even." That praise would be merited in their first battle under his command.[8]

Hays probably underestimated the admiration with which he came to be held. Company C's Captain Winfield Scott, a University of Rochester graduate and Baptist minister, labeled Hays "a princely soldier; brave as a lion. . . ." Hays's dash, recklessness, and enthusiasm reminded Scott of "one of the old cavaliers . . . we would have followed him to the death." Such praise of Hays would prevail throughout the brigade, with each regiment feeling it was Hays's favorite, despite the competition between them that he fostered. The 125th New York's chaplain virtually echoed Scott: "He [Hays] was among the bravest of the brave. Blunt of speech, and kind of heart. . . . His name was an inspiration to valor."[9]

For efficiency, Casey's Division, three regular brigades and one provisional, was posted at Union Mills, Fairfax Court House, Centreville, Fort Albany, Wolf Run Shoals and the capital itself. The division was a strange mix of veterans, untried soldiers, dismounted cavalry, and provost and post guards. Before long the 126th's camp assumed a martial bearing, with battalion and skirmish drills (the latter lasting up to six hours) occupying most of the men's time when they were not on picket or guard duty. Discipline also took on a harder edge. Most important for 1st Lt. Morris Brown, Jr. was attending the officers' school, created by General Hays and directed by newly promoted Major Philo Phillips. Consisting of drills and recitation based on Casey's Tactics, the Union standard, the officers met daily from 9:00 to 10:00 a.m. on stormy days, otherwise at night. The officers daily drilled five privates at a time to demonstrate their understanding of the various commands. Noncommissioned officers were drilled by Adjutant Smith Brown.

Being in a classroom again, this time as a soldier, served Smith's younger brother well—for in the unexplained absence of Captain Burrill, he drew extra pay for commanding Company A between January 17 and April 24, 1863. But he complained at length about "playing" company commander (filling in for Burrill), as the following letter demonstrates.[10] However, as was his wont, first he chatted about personal matters, including humorously chiding his older brother about his lack of musical talent and referring vaguely to his father 's obtaining a military commission.

Camp near Union Mills Va
Friday March 13th 1863

My dear Parents & Lina [sister Emeline]:

When I was a little boy if you remember correctly I used to get sundry "lickings"—yet quite often—If you remember well you will at once know that when I was young I was quite an adept at lying.

Well whenever I told a lie I would surely be found out in some way & get a thrashing. Perhaps you thought I was cured—well I was to such an extent that I cannot lie about that flute just to please pa because he took so much interest in buying it. While I was pleased with his motives & I also with the flute at first, yet I must confess I am sick of it for it is good for nothing. It is so much inferior to mine that I cannot bear to touch it. yet Smith keeps bothering me all the whole time to try some duet from "Martha"[?] or "Il Traviata" & he cant play ten notes correctly, that I am real sick of it. Perhaps though its because Smith keeps at me so with that old cornet of his. The idea of his spending thirty or forty dollars for a cornet when he never will learn ten cents worth.

He's a queer fellow—never will save a cent. You speak pa about writing to Capt Coleman & Col. Sherrill &c. Now I would'nt do any such thing; & hereafter I would believe just about one third Smith wrote you.

That matter between Smith & one or two Capts never amounted to a "row of pins." I hav'nt heard anything about it for two weeks.

Col. Bull went to Washington yesterday. He is personally acquainted with Gen. [John Henry] Martindale & will do all any one could towards getting you appointed Provost Martial.

Col. Sherrill would have gone, but Gen [Alexander Hays] Hayes is absent & Col. Sherrill is in command of the Brigade.

No appointment has been made yet & I am in hopes that you will get the place yet. Col. Sherrill & Bull are willing to do all they can for you & wont apoint anyone else. Get your influential letters & send them on immediately. I dont know what better you can do unless you have some one of those big men come to Washington & work personally. We will do all we can here anyway. I learn Capt Burrill is worse. What's the matter now? Can he ever come back? I wish he would either come back or resign. This playing Capt. is played out completely.

Barras ravings there in P.Y. I guess wont amount to much. Let him rip! Such a scoundrel cant infuse anyone. Perhaps I had better publish the charges which were preferred against him—They would set him kiting.

I have not seen the Dr. since we received the news of Mrs. Hammond death. I suppose it will make him feel terribly.

He has applied for a furlough to go home but now she is dead I guess he wont go. How are the rest of his family?

[Given later references to his wife, this must have been the Dr.'s mother.]

I have almost entirely recovered am on duty & feel about as well as ever. Why dont you send us some dried fruit sausages lots of butter &c. which you promised to send us when you were here.

You had it right to wait for us to send for these things but send em along. We will pay all expenses. We will probably be paid this month & then I will settle all of those little bills. You never sent in your bill for your trip down here yet. Send it along quick.

The rebels are reported moving on us from the South. How true it is I dont know, but let 'em come.

Will write again soon. You dont write often enough.

Your aff. son
Morris

Father

If Col. Sherrill gets a "leave of absence" he perhaps will try & recruit some men for the regiment. If he does I want you to get them all started on the right track & let Coleman slide. He has worked against us both ever since we "have had any authority."

Get Odgen & Starr & Morris &c., &c., &c. Capt. Coleman is like a little boy with a new pair of boots—now he is so far above his position when in civil life that he dont know how to act. He cant restrain himself.[11]

Now do your best & work hard.

Your aff. Son
Morris Brown, Jr.

I guess we will be paid again before long.

I guess the allotment system will be done away with.

It's a perfect nuisance.

Will write to the girls [his sisters Emeline and Jennie] in a
day or two.

Unfortunately, some of his references are vague. The disagreement to which
he refers (not amounting to a "row of pins") seems to have been between
his brother Smith and Captains Burrill and Coleman. (Smith Brown's
penchant for writing to one of the Penn Yan papers would eventually get
him in trouble.) Nor is the reference to provost "martial" any clearer. It
appears that Lieutenant Brown's father, the military committeeman, had
visited the 126th's camp at Union Mills and may have sought a place
in the army. How serious he was, and how seriously young Brown took
the matter also is unclear.

    Clearer are Brown's references to camp politics. Recriminations and
counter-recriminations would prevail much of the war despite serious
efforts to rid the army of incompetents who had been popularly elected,
the practice earlier in the war. Morris would continue to harp about
leadership or lack thereof in his company and later in the regiment. His
change of heart toward the dismissed Barras is amply demonstrated. He
also resented Captain Burrill's absences, even though they afforded him
the chance to command the company, because Burrill wore the captain's
bars and drew more pay. Why he felt such animosity toward Company
B's Captain Coleman, nine years his senior, is never revealed, though it
appears he considered Coleman, like Burrill, a shirker, an overly officious
one at that. (Apparently, later Coleman would get his feelings hurt and
extend his leaves of absence beyond the allotted time, as Burrill was doing.)
Brown's ardor both for promotion and a chance to lead his company into
battle magnified over time, as did his complaints about fellow officers.

    Brown was not alone, for backbiting and politicking were particularly
intense in March, when this letter was written. In part, the men, including
Brown, had too much time on their hands. The acrimony also stemmed
from the number of regimental vacancies and the martial spirit aroused
by new brigade commander Hays. As early as January, Hays had written

his father-in-law, "Although the brigade has been identified with one of the most disgraceful surrenders of the war and suffers a corresponding sense of humiliation, I have full confidence that in time 'the War Cry of Harper's Ferry' will incite them to rival the deeds of older and more fortunate soldiers." In fact, brigade commander Hays was convincing the men in each of his regiments that they were his favorite soldiers.[12]

Possibly affected by the martial spirit in camp and still smarting over the Harpers Ferry debacle, two months later Lieutenant Brown vented his spleen about fellow officers:

Centreville Va.
4th May 1863

My Dear Mother

Rcd your letter last evening, but have no time to answer regularly as it will be drill hours shortly & then I must go.

Now what Capt. Burrill said Col. Sherrill told him (that he did not know how he came to be discharged) is a confounded unmitigated falsehood & what he told about the companys wanting him to come back, or voting unanimously for him to be Capt. is another blackleg lie. No vote whatever was taken & [2d. Lt. Samuel] Wilson told me last night that some of the boys told him they did'nt want Burrill to come back—that he took no interest in their welfare, & everything that he ever had done for the men could be traced to my efforts.

The way Capt Burrill came to be discharged is this. Gen. Order No. 100/61 says in substance that all officers absent from their commands over sixty days on account of sickness, must be reported to the Adjt. Genl. at Washington for his consideration. Until Burrill had been absent over seventy days nothing was said about it; but when he went to Dr. Clymer & got the last twenty days absence Col. Sherrill himself made out a report of his case, or at least signed the report which was made out & sent it to the Adjt. Genl. himself. On this report I suppose he was discharged, for Genl. Order No. 100. 1861 distinctly says that an officer who is absent over sixty days must be reported & mustered out of service.

Capt. dont think I figured against him I guess, but he thinks Smith did it; & that is just the same. For him to go to Penn Yan & tell such abominable lies is outrageous. Oh! if he is mustered & comes back here there will be a grand old row. I used to have a good deal of respect for Capt. but I am fast loosing it. Such cussed works cant be winked at. The way he worked while he was here, & that during my absence has made me disgusted with him.

Day before yesterday Col. Sherrill came out to see the co's [companys] drill & as near as I could learn every one of them got a perfect drumming but me, because they [company commanders] brought out their companys looking so slovenly.

I could see him point to my company for an example & I could hear him tell them that "it was a darned shame for them to let so young an officer as me have the best company in the regiment."

When he got around to see me he says Brown you have got the best company in the regiment, & I consider Co. "A" with its officers to be a grand credit to any regiment—you always look the best & are the best drilled & your men seem to take an interest in what they are doing.

One day before this Col. Sherrill was out looking at us drill in the same way, & when he came along by me I was drilling the company in the loadings & firing & he was so well pleased with our way of drill that he went & made others do it as I did. He has consistently told me that my men always looked the best of any in the regiment. Now such notice as this is rarely taken by a Col. & to me it is exceedingly gratifying for I have taken a great deal of pains with my company & I am ready to brag a little on its efficiency of drill & discipline.

Capt Burrill never drilled the company but very little simply because he did'nt [sic.] know how. I have always drilled them, & now their excellence can be attributed to my efforts & no one else's.

If Capt says anything around there write me for there needs to be a settlement if he comes back.

Write often
Your aff. son Morris

Brown's obvious irritation with Captain Burrill is understandable, as apparently was Burrill's toward Adjutant Smith Brown. Smith's monthly reports may well have resulted in Burrill's dismissal (officially a disability discharge). Burrill's absence meant Lieutenant Brown continued to assume all the responsibilities for commanding the company. Still, Brown crowed—bragged, as he admitted—over the compliments he had received from Colonel Sherrill, who had recuperated sufficiently to resume regimental command. This is the consummate Morris Brown, Jr., showing a confidence bordering on arrogance. Yet, as he reveals in a letter two days later, he might have been satisfied to continue as a lieutenant rather than be subject to "frequent damnings which accompanies every military order" as a company commander.

Centreville Va.
Wednesday afternoon
6th May 1863

I received your letters this afternoon, my dear father & mother & hasten to answer them, for fear I wont get at it again in a week if I do not do it now. I feel very tired this afternoon. Just came off from picket—out in another terrible storm again for twenty four hours.

It is almost a proverb among the men that no matter how beautiful the day—if I go on picket, it will surely storm.

It would seem as though this was true for I have never been on picket but once, & that was the first time I ever went out, unless it rained or snowed. I dont think I ever suffered so much in my life as I did last night. No fires allowed, & only a rubber blanket [a poncho] to cover me & oh! how it did rain & blow.

$40 is enough for ___ in Utica. He dont deserve as much as that even. I will send you $150.00 the first chance I get. I lent Smith $50.00 & I keep $50.00 it makes about $60.00 which I have spent since I left Chicago. Pretty good, eh! I count my sword & belt in too.

I will send home about $200.00 more before the month is out, providing I can get a regular "leave of absence" for two or three days & go to Washington.

Mother, what Capt. Burrill told father in regard to Smith, & my swearing is nothing more nor less than an unmitigated lie. I can say & that with truth, that I have not violated the third commandment in eight years but once & that was when we lived in McAllasters house, when the old cow jumped over the low gate & made it clear up to the depot & then when I got her back in front of the house, she ran up on the Head[?] St.[?] & so alternatively for about two hours. That was justifiable. Capt. B. swears so much himself that the oath was as natural as the idea he advanced.

You dont answer the question which I gave you, father, in my last very satisfactorily, but rather evade a direct answer. It is the only possible[?] subject I have to deal with. Suggest something for my future. I dont know what Sam Hammond [the regimental surgeon's son] has been doing by what you have written us. Give us the details. Dr. feels very much worried about it, I guess, but then I dont believe Sam is any worse than we were when we were small. Just think of Thed's maple sugar arrangement, & also how he and I used to go to Adsits[?] store & buying six or eight dozen eggs would take them to Seneca Goodwins grocery & trade them off for oranges & candy. We have done it many a time; but we played the thing smart & didn't get caught at it. Sam will come out all right one of these days.

But then I believe if he were my boy I would offer up a burnt offering; or make a shooting match.

Capt. Burrill is trying hard to get re-instated. I dont care much whether he succeeds or not. I had as soon be 1st Lt. as Capt. if the Capt. will only tend to his business & he has got to do it, if he is restored, or it will go undone. A 1st Lt's position is ten times as easy as that of Capt. when the Capt. is present. You have no responsibility whatever, & none of the frequent damnings which accompanies every military order. You say you sent me three pounds of chewing tobacco. Now I recd about one pound. How can this discrepancy be accounted for? I saw Capt. Burrill about a minute to day for the first time since last Jan. He's gone to Washington. I will send the first $150.00 for that land at the first opportunity &

let those other chaps wait for _____ until I go to Washington. Then I can get $25 more, all of which I will send home.

What a terrible battle Hooker has been fighting near Fredericksburg [the Battle of Chancellorsville, May 3 and 4]. As yet the news we have received here is very meager, but from the booming of the many cannon which we have heard, even at this distance, we know a terrible battle has been fought.

How the poor soldiers who were wounded must have suffered last night, lying out in the rain. Night before last (Monday) we could hear the cannon nearly all night. How I wish our regiment was there! This guarding a lot of sand hills & stumps is getting pretty much played out.

I would run the risks incident to such a fight to be there. I want to get in one old whopper & then I will be contented to remain here, but not before. There is no glory to be gained about Centreville. The more I think of it, the more I hope Capt. Burrill will be restored. I expect every day that my commission as Capt. will come along, but I will willingly throw it aside if he is restored. Now I want you all to write oftener.

Your aff. son Morris Brown, Jr.

Another side of Morris Brown, Jr. emerges here, one rarely revealed: the moralist. First is his protestation about swearing, though it is hard to believe that he had not adopted a vocabulary common to army life, that is, if he hadn't exercised that vocabulary even earlier. (Later he does condemn another's alcohol-induced swearing, but the miscreant's drunken bravado may have troubled him more than the swearing.) Second, he lays out his child-rearing philosophy. And somewhat surprisingly, young Brown also shows a tenderness not often evident in his letters—a concern for Surgeon Hammond and his son's undisclosed misbehavior.

However, there are three other nagging matters for Morris: planning his future, investing his money, and testing his newly acquired leadership skills in battle. (A recurring concern is what to do after the war, and while he never spoke directly to the matter in his letters, it is unlikely he intended to return to Hamilton College.) More immediately, with time on his hands and flusher than he had ever been, he wanted advice about investing his money. Impatience, another characteristic, shows up in prodding his father to respond. Finally, his desire to see combat has been whetted by the drills and the study of military tactics. It was galling to sit on the sidelines there at Centreville, Virginia, listening to the cannon roar from Chancellorsville and learning that the Union army had been defeated again.

He picks up on these themes in a letter that appears to have been written just three days after the last one.

Centreville Va.
Sunday Afternoon
[probably May 9, 1863]

My Dear Father:

The Quarter Master goes to Washington to day & by him I send $150.00 to Stark for you to pay Jones if you think it best. This leaves me with only $30.00 & I owe about one half of that.

 I received from Pay Master $306.00
 I sent mother 20.00
 [ditto] Stark 130.00
 [ditto] Lieut Smith 50.00
 Paid Smith what I owed 30.00
 [ditto] 18.55 &c. &c.

Now if you think it more important to pay this money to Jones, rather than pay those little bills which have accumulated against me there in Penn Yan, do it.[13]

Do you suppose that Mr. Jones would take any advantage of me if I was behind hand in some of my future payments? I have'nt much confidence in him I must confess. Did you ever pay anything on the land? What are his terms if I buy the land?

How much will the next payment be & when will it have to be made? I wish you would give me a full explanation of all their different questions for I hardly understand what the bargain is & what its conditions are.

I am in hopes I can go to Washington in the course of a week or two & get the remainder of the pay now due me which amounts to about $250.00. If I can get that then I am all right & I can square up all my debts with every one & ___ too.

Frank Smith can wait for his pay until I get ready to pay him. He cheated me terribly on that coat & now he can shove it if he dont like it, because I dont send on the money to square up. I wish I were where I could tell him a "thing or two." No news from Capt. Burrill. I dont care whether he gets retired or not. He amounts to but little as regards military matters.

If you hear of any stories which he writes home or if he even hints at anything as though Smith or I figured against him I want you to write & tell me about it immediately. It will give me a starting point. "No news." Everything is all quiet about here. We have received orders to hold ourselves in readiness to "move at a moments notice" about a dozen times during the past week & now I have about come to the conclusion that we are booked for this place for all summer.

It is almost unendurable to think that we cannot go down to the support of Hooker; but I suppose we might as well make up our minds to make the best of it.

What a terrible fight Hooker has had down there & that with so little gain. Why could'nt we have been there? We could if we did'nt have such an old "granny" a[s] Genl [64-year-old John Joseph] Abercrombie for our leader.[14]

What a pity it is, that [Major General George] Stoneman did'nt capture Richmond, when he could have done it so easily, & brought Jeff Davis, Cabinet, Congress & all to Washington; but then we should be satisfied with what he really did, for it was enough for one "cavalry raid" to accomplish.

From all accounts I guess he could have taken Richmond & burnt the whole concern & retired in safety. Well let us try again & if we dont succeed we will try again & keep trying until the Union is restored, as it was or as fortune will make it different. Only keep those lousy Copper-heads down

& we will fight this thing out as it should be. Does Jennie correspond with Morris Sheppard yet?

Now I want you to write me all about this land speculation—everything, so I can understand better its objects.

This is a beautiful day—warm & sunny but I fear we are going to have another storm. It has rained enough during the past week for a month at least.

Your aff Son
Morris Brown, Jr.

P.S. I will send an order on Stark for the money as soon as I find what the express charges were. You need not charge one half of that money which Smith sent to Thede [brother Theodore] the other [day?]. At least if you do you must charge one half of that $100.00 which I sent to Thede last winter, to Smith for I did propose to pay a hundred dollars more than Smith.

Clearly Brown, settling his debts, intended to speculate in land like his father. (Except for his support of Theodore, then in Germany competing in chess tournaments, it's unclear why he, a former college student and a soldier for almost eight months, had run up so many bills at home.) He was flush due to the extra pay for commanding the company, one benefit of Burrill's absence. Though wrong about General Stoneman's raid, which was to draw Confederate troops away from Chancellorsville, he was correct that the Union defeat at Chancellorsville and the Army of the Potomac's withdrawal behind the Rappahannock was painful and disappointing. While it was an old story, it was especially irksome to the inactive Brown. He was simply drilling while a crucial battle was being fought close by. Also troubling, Loudoun Heights, overlooking Harpers Ferry, could be seen distinctly—a silent reminder of the brigade's ignominious surrender the past September.

While Brown blamed "granny" Abercrombie for the brigade's inaction, better explanations for withholding the troops there at Centreville were the need to defend the perimeter around the capital and the brigade's stained reputation. Brown's reaction seems to have been typical of those at Centreville, to which the brigade had moved. The days were beginning to drag. Still, in the words of Company H's Captain Orin J. Herendeen, it was a "dangerous calm." Enemy troop movements around Centreville demanded greater vigilance by pickets and induced a tension, one manifestation of which was an increase in desertions. Other manifestations were the construction of rifle pits and earthworks along with target practice.[15]

What is surprising about this and the two prior letters is what Morris Brown, Jr. did not say. On April 24, he was mustered captain of Company A, though he was not commissioned until May 9. Why he didn't brag—at least mention the promotion—is not easily explained. He alludes to it in the May 6 letter, but quietly drops the matter. Brown's reticence is uncharacteristic, given the fact that he would no longer be "playing" company commander. Now he would have the chance to lead his company if it ever saw combat, which seemed farther away each day. The monotony of camp life was eating at him, which is particularly evident in his May 25th letter.[16]

Centreville Va.
May 25th 1863.

My Dear Mother

It's time for me to write you, but I have not a word of news to write. Smith sent such a monstrous letter this morning that you ought not to expect anything further from us in a month at least.

Here we lay in this camp, which although very beautiful (Gen. Abercrombie says the finest he ever saw) is becoming so monotonous as to be almost insufferable. We ought to move. We want to go some wheres where we can fight & do some good. This laying here & guarding these same banks & old stumps is getting about "played out." Oh that we could fight & gain the name which some of those two year regiments take home with them; because we can lie here through eternity & nobody would know anything more about us than that which happened at Harpers Ferry. I wish I had went with Capt. Munger in the 44th N.Y. We will never gain the name which they have.[17]

Its terrible hot here now, & such steady heat too, but the nights are cool and comfortable.

I came across some "tulip trees" to day; & if ever I have a chance I will send two or three home. Such beautiful flowers I never saw. Just the shape of a tulip, but their color is green & red with a little projection in the center very similar to a cucumber. There are a few of these trees up around Canandaigua but I guess they were imported. Anyway this is the first time I ever saw one of them. They are magnificent.

You ought to see one of these great large trees covered with these flowers to form an idea of what they are. I cant describe them. My pen is inadequate to the task.

I guess Capt. Burrills blow will be stopped when that letter of Col. Sherrill comes out in the Chronicle. What a fool he has made of himself & that too when any man of common sense ought to know he would be overwhelmed by telling such outrageous lies.

Well let him rip & tear. I got my commission now & all his blowing wont avail him, only the disgust of a people of sense, & that is all I care for. He can blow about me as much as he wishes, for I defy anyone to bring a single thing that I have done since I enlisted that was not right, & just as near correct as a person of my years could accomplish. By my promotion I am placed the tenth in rank, but that makes no particular difference. In two more months I'll show you the model company of this regiment.

Only last night some of the boys of my company told me that if I had only been their Capt. in the start, they would not be compelled to go on the left of the regiment now [the place occupied by the second best company in a regiment]; & added that now they would follow me to hell if necessary.

I have had so many different officers & men tell me the excellence of my company lately that I am really getting to be quite proud of myself. Even the enlisted men in other companies are talking of the improvement that has been made in my company since I took command of it.

You may think I am "bragging," but I have a right to, I am the youngest officer in the regiment & when I have the Col., Lt. Col., Major, Capts & all tell me that my company has grown from the poorest, to be the best, its enough to make anyone vain. Its my nature to brag & I am going to keep it up as long as I have so many compliments thrust upon me from almost every direction. I presume some of my company hate me (one or two) but they are those whom I have punished. I have'nt punished but two or three yet since I enlisted—never had a man refuse to obey me. I punished one or two pretty severely & they know what will surely come; if they dont tread up to the scratch. I dont have any trouble & never did. Every man is perfectly obedient without a word of grumbling. Let Burrill slide he cant hurt anyone. Col. Sherrill started for home today—"if he can get a furlough." Smith has just tried but couldnt

I hope the glorious news we recd to day from Grant [the capture of Vicksburg, Mississippi] will be confirmed to morrow. What a glorious victory. Bully for Grant Hip hip!! Hurrah. He will take us home soon.[18]

Your aff son Morris Brown, Jr.

Though frustrated by the inaction and suffering the Centreville heat, Captain Brown was quite self-satisfied, with some reason. He was eight years younger than the regimental average, although Company G's newly promoted captain Sanford Platt was just two years older. Brown's company was on the left of the regiment, the second highest place of honor. And he was, as claimed, tenth in line to command the regiment. (The three line officers and six company captains still outranked him.) Whether he was as respected as he would have his parents believe, of course, is unknown. Clearly he was feeling his oats and chafing from inaction. He wanted to prove his worth as a company commander in name and fact. Only combat could do so.

And he had his infantry captain's $60 a month to invest his in postwar future, leading to a letter to Oliver Stark, the money exchanger, and a confirmation letter to his father.

duplicate Centreville Va
May 26th [1863]

Oliver Stark

Pay to Morris Brown Sr. $150 & place the same to my account.

Morris Brown, Jr.

Father

Being a little fearful that something may delay the order I sent the other day I write another to make it sure.

We will be paid again before long I guess. Aint the news from the west "bully"?

No news!

Your aff. son
Morris Brown, Jr.

Monday Morning [May 1863]

Mr. Stark

Dr Sir

Being more fortunate Saturday than I had anticipated I will leave $25 of the $50 I recd. from you asking that you will let father have the same upon application

I am Sir
Very Respt
Capt 126 NY

Brown's attention was drawn back to the war one June night when pickets observed "a great lot of small fires" and an unexpected commotion.

Daylight revealed soldiers wearing the I Corps insignia, and on Monday, June 15, the dusty, hungry, and hard looking men of the III and XI corps appeared. The next day another corps arrived, cramping another forty thousand troops into the Centreville camp. The unexpected arrival of Hooker's Army of the Potomac (and the equally abrupt departure of two corps on the seventeenth) led to all kinds of speculation. Company H's Captain Orin J. Herendeen probably spoke for most as he watched the "steady tramp, tramp, tramp, tramp, rattle and rumble all day and far into the night." He estimated that the XI Corps's five hundred wagons stretched over six miles and that the wagon train of the six army corps extended over thirty miles.[19]

Likely, the event that left the most lasting impression was the arrival of the II Corps and the reaction of brigade commander Hays. The hungry II Corps soldiers planted their guns and promptly raided the sutlers' tents, foraging "cheeses, cakes and tobacco." General Hays "rode his big grey horse into their midst, sword in one hand and revolver in the other and ordered them to disperse and threatened to shoot some of the most violent who just said 'shoot and be damned.'" These veterans may have viewed Hays as another bandbox soldier softened by garrison duty, but they were brusquely disabused of that notion. He promptly ordered three pieces of artillery aimed at them, and they dispersed just as promptly. Then the fearless Hays "sent word to General Hancock, whom Hays had defended at West Point, to take care of his troops," which then were sent to outposts. If Hays's men harbored any doubts about his fighting spirit, they were now dispelled.[20]

Though the camp at Centreville seemed strangely empty on Tuesday, June 23, the tension was turned up a notch. The issuance of eight pounds of rations, orders to be ready to march, an unusual stirring at headquarters, and the packing of surplus materials confirmed that Hays's brigade was being readied for a movement. But where were they going and would they finally have the chance to redeem themselves?

At approximately 2:00 p.m. on June 25, "all style both in dress and living," Hays's brigade marched out of Centreville, their home for the past three months. Unaccustomed to long marches, especially on gummy, rain-soaked roads, before long they began ridding themselves of what they considered expendables, including their knapsacks. Ten hours and ten miles later, they dropped to the ground at Gum Springs. The next day they caught up with the II Corps at Edwards Ferry on the

Potomac, the significance of which is captured by the corps's historian, Brevet Brigadier General Francis Walker.[21]

"Here joined, for the first time, a body of troops destined to bear a conspicuous share in all the future labors and dangers of the Second Corps, from the fast-approaching conflict on the bloody slopes of Gettysburg to the final triumph of April 1865. This was the brigade of the dashing Alexander Hays—General Hays, who had greatly distinguished himself on the peninsula."

Joining the II Corps was memorable for Captain Brown and other brigade members (effective June 26, the Third Brigade, Third Division), but for a different reason. Hancock's veterans taunted them as the "White Glove Brigade," stemming from the veterans' impression of Hays's men "on duty at Centreville, with white gloves, blacked boots, etc." The veterans badgered the untried soldiers with a reminder that they "would yet have a chance to smell powder." The newcomers were doubly condemned: "The Cowards of Harpers Ferry" and the "White Glove Brigade."[22]

Unknown to them, they were hell-bent to catch up with the Confederates who were taking the war north. There would be no letup for the Union soldiers, of which they were made painfully aware after stopping for barely an hour and a half in the bleak early hours of the twenty-seventh. They did not enjoy another rest until late afternoon near Barnesville, Maryland. After a quick breakfast on the twenty-eighth, they stepped out as briskly as their tired bodies would allow, prodded by constant reminders to "close up," and made another twenty-five miles. They rested briefly again at Monocacy Junction, consoled, if any, by the beautiful countryside and hospitable inhabitants along the way. The longest and severest march was on June 29, somewhere between thirty and thirty-five miles on dusty roads, with occasional rests totaling three hours at most. Straggling peaked before the marchers reached Uniontown around 10:00 p.m. But, as Sergeant Ferguson wrote home, "it does no good to fall out, for the first thing we meet is the point of the [file closer's] bayonet."[23]

Perhaps it is not surprising, given the forced march and responsibility for making sure his company kept up, there are no letters from Morris Brown, Jr. Also, it is likely that he continued to let his brother Smith, the adjutant, conduct their correspondence. Captain Brown would have to let his actions speak for him, and they would—loudly. Shortly, he would have the chance he sought so ardently to prove his leadership and thereby to help erase the stigma that gnawed at him.

CHAPTER 3

"Morris is a Hero"
The Battle of Gettysburg

On the march, Captain Brown could only have been dimly aware that ahead was General Robert E. Lee's Army of Northern Virginia, which had boldly struck out for the north again. The first time, which culminated in the Battle of Antietam, near Sharpsburg, Maryland, had been a disaster for Brown and his comrades who simply had been in the way at Harpers Ferry. This time General Lee had additional reasons to make the bold move. He needed to find better foraging for his men than available in Virginia, where so much of the fighting in the East had occurred. He also believed the Confederacy might be recognized by Great Britain, and bolstered by the success of his army in defeating Hooker at Chancellorsville, he confidently expected a reprise, if the opportunity presented itself.

The opportunity would come at the little southeastern Pennsylvania crossroads town of Gettysburg, toward which Lee's three corps were concentrating. In the lead was Lieutenant General Richard Ewell, now commanding the late General Jackson's II Corps, headed for Harrisburg. He was followed by another newly appointed corps commander, Lieutenant General Ambrose Powell Hill, who had arranged the surrender at Harpers Ferry ten months earlier, while Lieutenant General James Longstreet, Lee's "warhorse," was pushing his I Corps to catch up with Hill's near the town of Chambersburg.

Though apprised of the Confederate movement, Army of the Potomac commander Hooker was unaware of its destination. Worse, his support from the Lincoln administration had eroded, and when he argued for more troops—those at defenseless Harpers Ferry—he was not only spurned, his precipitous resignation was accepted. So, effective early morning, June 28, Lee's army, which had been Hooker's quarry, was now Major General George G. Meade's. The forty-seven-year-old Meade, who was jumped over his seniors in rank, was as surprised by his appointment as anyone. And he faced an awesome challenge: finding Lee's army and confronting it with close to 113,000 men (seven corps, nineteen divisions, fifty-one brigades) and 372 guns widely scattered.

Meade promptly assigned Major General John Reynolds, whom Meade felt should be commanding instead of himself, to lead the left wing, the I, III, and XI corps—while Meade directed the others, the II, V, VI, and XII.

Forced marches were ordered. On June 29, Major General Winfield S. Hancock, the II Corps commander, pushed his men thirty-two miles in eighteen hours. Wet from rain, faces streaked from dust earlier, feet blistered, the men were thoroughly exhausted. But there was no letup. The next day, they were issued three days' rations and sixty rounds of ammunition, the awful telltale signs of combat.[1]

That night, Morris Brown's 126th New York and others in the II Corps reached Uniontown, where, after mustering for pay, they fell to the ground like dead men. They lay there until around 11:00, July 1, when they were pushed against their wills to Taneytown, Maryland, on the Pennsylvania-Maryland border. Many straggled, some simply gave out despite constant exhortations to move on and bayonet pokes in the back. Company A's Private Sid Rice, who initially had been critical of Brown, his commander, was eternally grateful to him when the Captain shared his canteen with his men en route. "When they got done he [Brown] wet his own parched lips."[2]

So, more than two hundred thousand soldiers, though only seventy thousand Confederates and ninety thousand Federals would be engaged, converged on Gettysburg, bordered by two north-south streams and approached by ten roads. Gettysburg was also marked by parallel ridges, three of which would play important parts in the upcoming battle: Seminary to the west, with the Lutheran Seminary atop it; Cemetery, beginning just north of Little Round Top and culminating at Cemetery

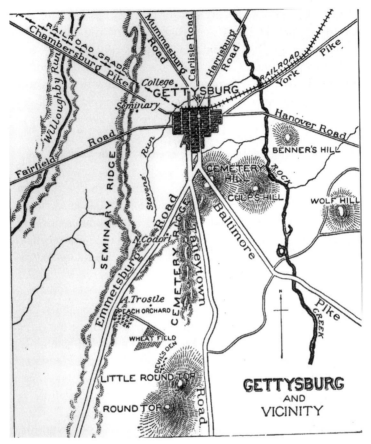

Gettysburg, 1863 (*Source:* History of the Second Army Corps)

Hill, south of town; and a low, broad ridge running along Emmitsburg Road and obliquely traversing the field between the two other ridges, of particular concern to the Union II Corps.

Before the Harpers Ferry debacle, Brown had written home how much he "would like to lead such a regiment as this to battle." Now he was part way to his goal, commanding a company, and it would be a frightful experience.

If there had been any doubt about what beckoned the weary marchers, the booming of cannon they heard on their way to Taneytown dispelled it. A battle was raging ahead: a battle begun unexpectedly when

Major General Henry Heth's division of Hill's Corps ran into Brigadier General John Buford's cavalry division west of the village. Buford's men held off the surprised Confederates long enough for Reynolds's I Corps and Major General Oliver O. Howard's XI Corps to stem the tide momentarily. But by late afternoon on July 1, after heavy fighting and large losses, the Union's two corps were driven back through the village by the combined attack of Hill's and Ewell's larger corps. Another Confederate success loomed.

With 14,347 men (the second largest of Meade's forces) the Union II Corps would play a large role. It had been commanded by General Hancock less than a month. Hancock seemed born to command, but with three large divisions he had his hands full. Brigadier Generals John C. Caldwell, John Gibbon, and Alexander Hays commanded the First, Second, and Third respectively. Hays represented the most recent change in command—having on June 28 replaced Brigadier General William French, who was directed to reoccupy Harpers Ferry. Hays's subordinates were Colonels Samuel S. Carroll, Thomas A. Smyth, and George L. Willard—commanding the First, Second, and Third brigades.

Late on July 1, Hancock's corps dropped to the ground near the southeastern base of what would come to be called Big Round Top and tried to rest. Sleep was virtually impossible, for the eerie silence was broken by intermittent musketry fire. Even had there been no firing, one Third Brigade member readily admitted that he slept little because the soldiers' "minds were too much on the coming battle." The groggy men were aroused at 3:00 on that sultry, misty July 2 morning and stumbled to their feet. Five hours later, Captain Brown and the footsore soldiers halted near the Cemetery, then moved to their left at the crest of Cemetery Ridge. A few managed to find sticks to build fires to boil coffee and nibble on hardtack, but most went hungry.[3]

To their right was the village of Gettysburg, to their left woods, and straight ahead a valley that rose gradually to Seminary Ridge on the west. Their vision was unobstructed for miles. Directly in front was a low stone wall and an old rail fence. The first order of business was for Brown's brigade to build breastworks while ducking the cannon shelling, which rocked the ground and belched shrapnel. Shortly the brigade extended its right flank past the abandoned Brian Farm to the cluster of trees near the elevated crescent-shaped area known as Zeigler's Grove.[4]

During the day, Captain Brown's Company A was spared the inconclusive skirmishing to take the Bliss Barn, which proved so attractive to both sides as a shelter for sharpshooters. Still the desultory firing and fear of an attack rendered it an anxious time for Brown. Then, around 4:00 p.m., General Longstreet's corps attacked the Union's III Corps, badly mauling it and opening a gaping hole in the Union line. Roughly three hours later General Hancock, commanding the III Corps after General Daniel Sickles's wounding, sent an aide to General Hays. Hays and Colonel George Willard, who were closely watching the unfolding contest, were told that Hancock wanted Hays to send "one of your best Brigades over there." Turning to Willard, an army regular replacing Hays as brigade commander, Hays said, "Take your Brigade over there and knock the H—— out of the rebs." By calling on Morris Brown and fellow members of the "Cowards of Harpers Ferry," Hays was demonstrating his faith in them.[5]

The brigade, screaming "Remember Harpers Ferry," ducked "grape, canister, and shell" raining in on them and charged through the brush toward the swale known as Plum Run. Their formations were broken up when they crossed the rocky, slippery bottom of the swale, necessitating a realignment that usually only veterans performed successfully. Reformed, they ran uphill some eight hundred yards in an open field and into a canister from Confederate guns, which slashed through their ranks. Then they ran smack into members of General William Barksdale's brigade of Major General Lafayette McLaws's Division, which delivered a withering fire. Given the chance to redeem themselves and with their fighting spirit aroused, Company B's Lt. Richard Bassett claimed that they met the advancing Confederates "at the muzzles of their muskets and the points of their bayonets." Their inspired charge resulted not only in their overrunning the Confederates, but it caused them to become dangerously exposed to a flanking fire from two brigades of Major General Richard Anderson's Division. Men continued to fall in alarming numbers, so they were ordered to withdraw across Plum Run.[6]

What followed, even who gave the order, depends upon the narrator. One version has it that having accomplished its purpose and not wanting to risk greater casualties unnecessarily, Colonel Willard reformed the brigade to withdraw, but he was killed before he could issue the order. Another version is that the order to pull back was given by the

126th New York's Colonel Eliakim Sherrill, the senior officer, on his own account after Willard's death. Whatever the explanation, when Hancock saw the brigade withdraw, he loosened a stream of profanity, as only he could, and ordered Colonel Sherrill arrested. He then directed Colonel Clinton MacDougall of the 111th New York to command the brigade. To top off a rather bizarre conclusion to what otherwise was restoration of the maligned brigade's reputation, Captain Morris Brown, Jr. assumed he too might be under arrest. As soon as he could, he penciled the following note to General Hays's adjutant general, Captain George Corts:[7]

July 3 1863

Capt Corts

Supposing it to be possible that I may have been put under arrest last evening by the commanding General through a misapprehension of the facts I desire it my privilege briefly to state that while executing the order of Col Willard who was in command of the Brigade which was to have the Regt fall back he fell[.] Upon observing in __that I was then the ranking officer I made the announcement and halted the Brigade[.] about this time Lt Col Crandle [Levin Crandell] in command of the 125th N Y Vols said to me, they are flanking us on the left [F]or Gods Sake move us to the Right[.] as I could discern no enemy in front it seemed to be that this might be the reason for retiring the Brigade[.] I at once Right faced the Brigade.

Why Colonel Crandell might have requested Captain Brown to relocate the brigade and why Brown figured he was the ranking officer are unknowns. Nothing has been discovered to explain Brown's note, but the arrest of Colonel Sherrill is documented. (The next morning, acting brigade commander Colonel MacDougall asked General Hays to intervene on Colonel Sherrill's behalf. The much-admired Sherrill was duly restored to command by General Hancock—only to be killed later that day.)[8]

That night the thoroughly exhausted, hungry, but vindicated brigade marched back to Zeigler's Grove, where they rejoined Colonel Smyth's

Second Brigade, the 14th Connecticut, 1st Delaware, the 12th New Jersey, the 108th New York and a battalion of the 10th New York. With only two brigades—Carroll's brigade had been detached to help defend Cemetery Hill—General Hays was forced to stretch his force to cover the ground that three had been expected to defend. Moreover, these two brigades were understrength. For example, the 126th reported only 455 men present for duty (less than half of its authorized strength) before they became engaged on July 2. It was imperative that Hays properly deploy his men, given Meade's late night council of war and anticipation of an attack on the Union center in the morning, the 3rd. If it materialized, General Hays's demi-division would be a target.

Captain Brown spent a fitful night, while his brother, Smith, the regimental adjutant, suffered a sleepless one. Apparently, the latter assisted the surgeons in the hunt for the dead and wounded. It was, as a witness reported, "dismal and appalling . . . to turn up one dead cold face after another." Lieutenant Benjamin Thompson of the 111th New York recalled that the "most doleful sounds that broke the night stillness were the cries for water and help that came from the poor sufferers on the field." By the best estimate, Captain Brown's Company A had lost one man mortally wounded, First Sergeant David Goff, and five enlisted men wounded.[9]

General Ewell's predawn artillery attack on Culp's Hill ushered in the fighting on Friday, July 3. While Ewell failed to smash the Union right, Hays and his division were no less anxious. Most of the men "quivered with instinctive readiness," Lieutenant Thomas F. Galwey of the 8th Ohio recalled, and peered ahead. However, skirmishers were already at work, resulting in the usual exchange of musketry. The bulk of the exchange occurred as the two sides contended for the Bliss Barn, which sheltered occupiers in disputed land between the competing armies. Finally a member of the 111th New York was ordered to torch the house and barn and did so, leading to another pause in the fighting.[10]

Fortunately, Captain Brown was spared the savage and unrelenting skirmishing that morning, which proved fatal to three fellow company commanders—Captains Isaac Shimer (Co. F), Orin Herendeen (Co. H), and Charles Wheeler (Co. K)—and resulted in the severe wounding of Captain Winfield Scott (Co. C). Instead, Brown's detached company, in reserve to the skirmish line, was positioned near the Trostle House in front of and on the brigade's right, along with Captain Samuel Armstrong of the 125th New York. Also Brown did not have to accompany Armstrong, who shortly was ordered to attack the enemy skirmish line, "a bad blunder" resulting in the casualties of five of his officers before he ordered a retreat.[11]

Shortly thereafter—some time between 10:00 and 11:00 a.m.—an "ominous deathlike silence . . . fell athwart both armies." Hays's men clutched their weapons. Many had two, a few had four, having been instructed by Hays to "hunt up all abandoned small arms, clean and load them, ready for use." They had reason to be fearful. "I could not help wishing all morning that this line of the two Divisions of the 2nd Corps [General Hays's and Major General John Gibbon's] were stronger," noted Lieutenant Frank Haskell, Gibbon's aide. "It was, so far as numbers constitute strength, the weakest part of the whole line of battle." Yet, as historian Stephen Sears has observed, Gibbon's and Hays's divisions "were as good as the best in the Army of the Potomac."[12]

Then around 1:00 p.m., an ear-splitting and earth-shaking cannonade began. "The heavens looked like a continuous ball of fire. Shells striking the ground, dirt, gravel, stones and pieces of shell" splattered the Federals. Something like 150 Confederate cannons were aimed at the Union forces. A cross fire struck the II Corps's right flank, where the Third Brigade huddled. Shortly Brigadier General Henry Hunt's artillery answered the Confederates with between 100 and 120 guns. Confederate artillery Colonel E. Porter Alexander described the cannonading as a "volcano in eruption." Hunt, his Union counterpart, called it a sight never "witnessed on the continent, and rarely, if ever, abroad."[13]

"Large limbs were torn from the trunks of the oak trees under which we lay and precipitated down upon our heads," recalled one combatant. In Zeigler's Grove, Lt. George Woodruff's battery suffered as much or more than the infantry. Wheels were knocked off the guns, horses fell in heaps, and the guns collapsed under their own weight. General Hays, the restless division commander, rode the lines in front of his fearful men, pressing his "'boys' to stand fast and fight like men. Shell, shot, nor bullets . . . seemed to intimidate him in the least."[14]

After greater than an hour of the unprecedented cannonading (estimates run from an hour and a quarter to two hours), again there was silence—signaling the fateful Confederate infantry attack, thereafter known as "Pickett's Charge." Burly General Hays, standing by his old brigade and waving his sword, called out, "Now boys, look out; you will see some fun!" Immediately afterward, he shifted them up to the crest of the ridge to close the two hundred-yard gap on the right between him and portions of the I and XI corps to the northeast.[15]

Despite his bravado, General Hays had some concerns. Rocks, bushes, and stunted trees on the rough ground immediately in front of his division offered cover for the attackers. More worrisome was the lack of reserves to stop a breakthrough that, like the previous day, threatened the whole Union front. So, Hays took the unorthodox step of mixing his two brigades to double the strength of his line and thereby double his fire power. In places, his division was four deep.[16]

Hays's division, now only two brigades, extended close to three hundred yards. The 8th Ohio was on the extreme right and west of the

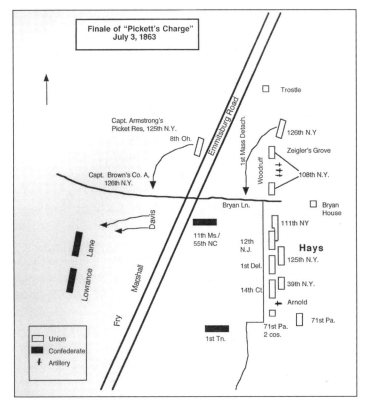

Finale of "Pickett's Charge," July 3, 1863 (*Source:* Wayne Mahood)

Emmitsburg Road. The 126th New York held the right behind the road in Zeigler's Grove, with the 108th New York to its immediate left. The 111th New York's line, to the 108th's left, jogged backwards; thus the 12th New Jersey overlapped the 111th's left. The 1st Delaware rested to the 12th New Jersey's left and the 14th Connecticut to its left, touched the right of Webb's 71st Pennsylvania. The Third Brigade's 125th and 39th New York were immediately behind the 1st Delaware and 14th Connecticut respectively. Supporting the infantry were two artillery companies. Lieutenant Woodruff's I Company, 1st U.S., which had taken a beating from the enemy cannonading, immediately fronted the 108th New York. Battery A of the 1st Rhode Island Light, Capt. William A. Arnold commanding, was left and slightly rearward of the 14th Connecticut.

At 3:00 p.m. Seminary Ridge came alive. "All at once, over their works and through the bushes that skirted them, came a heavy skirmish line," the 126th New York's Captain Winfield Scott recalled. "The skirmishers were about two paces apart, covering about three quarters of a mile on our front. Behind them about twenty rods came another heavy skirmish line. Behind them, about the same distance, came out the first line of battle." The much anticipated Confederate attack had begun. The mile-wide line of battle moved forward like "a stream or river of silver." Despite the apprehension, the Federals gaped at the bayonetted rifles at right shoulder and the plainly visible guidons marking the advancing troops. Captain Scott marveled that the Confederate movement was "grand beyond expression."[17]

Kneeling behind what there was of the stone wall, Hays's men awaited their commander's order to "Fire." Approaching them were three Confederate divisions, approximately thirteen thousand men. Toward the Union left, came Major General George Pickett's Division of Longstreet's Corps, which consisted of the brigades of Brigadier Generals Richard B. Garnett, James L. Kemper, and Lewis Armistead—the latter's, in support. About three quarters of a mile back of the Emmitsburg Road and left of Pickett was Major General Henry Heth's Division of A. P. Hill's Corps, commanded by Brigadier General James J. Pettigrew, replacing the wounded Heth. His four brigades, from right to left were: Brigadier General James Archer's (Colonel Birkett D. Fry commanding); Pettigrew's own (commanded by Colonel James K. Marshall); Brigadier General Joseph R. Davis's Fourth Brigade; and Colonel John Brockenbrough's

Second Brigade. Davis's brigade was left of center in Pettigrew's front line, while Brockenbrough's was to Davis's left—both appeared to be aimed at Hays's division. Finally, behind Pettigrew's, roughly a mile and a quarter from the Emmitsburg Road, was Major General William D. Pender's Division (Major General Isaac Trimble substituting). Trimble commanded two Tarheel brigades, Brigadier General Alfred M. Scales's (Colonel W. Lee J. Lowrance commanding) and Brigadier James H. Lane's, a member of which correctly prophesied that "blood must flow and gallant spirits must take their final flight."[18]

A similar feeling prevailed among the Federals. Even after the passage of more than twenty years, Lieutenant John L. Brady of the 1st Delaware remembered feeling that "the odds against us was [sic.] indeed appalling." He saw the Confederates, flushed with pride at previous success against the Union, looking for an easy conquest against his "thinly scattered line," ducking behind its "hastily constructed works of defense."[19]

Pickett's Division had barely begun its advance when it was met by severe Union artillery fire. Shortly, the other two divisions suffered from similar shelling. The shelling was followed by small arms fire, which became "a ceaseless storm." The closer Pickett's men got to the Union line the harder the fire storm rained on them. General Henry Hunt's guns, concentrated to produce a wicked cross fire, poured solid shot and shell, then canister, even double canister, creating a tempest that blew away the advancing army "like the chaff before the whirlwind."[20]

But somehow the Confederates kept reforming and coming and became entangled due to the murderous artillery and small arms fire, causing them to veer toward Hays's division. "The shock of the assault fell upon the 2d and 3d divisions [Gibbon's and Hays's] of the 2d corps," General Hancock later testified. Finally, when the attackers were within two hundred and three hundred yards of them, division commander Hays shouted "Fire," though some of his anxious men had already anticipated his command. They rose up and fired away, with something like seventeen hundred muskets and Woodruff's battery to answer the Confederate charge.[21]

When the full force of the attack on his right did not materialize, Hays pivoted the 126th New York and the 125th New York reserves forward to connect with the 8th Ohio. An excerpt from Adjutant Smith Brown's letter to his parents, written on July 4, summarizes the results:[22]

Morris is a hero. Captured a rebel flag. He charged the rebel line with 10 men & captured it. . . . Morris's flag had inscribed on it "Shepardstown," "Malvern Hill," "Manassas Junction," "Sharpsburgh," "Harpers Ferry," "Mechanicsville," "Hanover," "Ox Hill," "Cold Harbor," "Frazers Farm," "Manassas," "Cedar Run. . . ."

Captain Morris Brown, along with Captain Samuel Armstrong of the 125th New York, had been ordered to strike the Confederate left with his small company. (Brown estimated he had barely eighteen men). After advancing about a quarter mile, Brown deployed them so as to strike the left flank of Davis's broken and retreating brigade. After the firing died down, the youthful Brown, at the head of his column, proudly returned with an estimated fifty Confederate prisoners and, especially symbolic, a Confederate flag. It was, the 28th North Carolina's, which proclaimed the regiment's capture of Brown and the Third Brigade at Harpers Ferry.[23]

"It was a terrible fight & I don't wish to get in another unless necessary," Morris confessed in a letter written twelve days later, but he still gushed over his role:

When I captured that flag (I was about a quarter of a mile away from the rest of the brigade) I formed my company with about fifty prisoners which I also took & marched up to the Brigade carrying the flag myself at the head of my column. Oh!!! you ought to have heard the whole brigade cheer me. I bet you too would have yelled "bully" for another of those "miserable Browns." It was a proud day for me I can tell you.

I cant see nor can I ever tell why I was not taken prisoner for I was on the left flank, & almost in the rear of the whole rebel army. I captured three times as many prisoners as I had men. Bully for me.[24]

The capture of the enemy's flags was a particular point of pride. A regiment's flag was its embodiment, its identity. Its capture by the enemy was an acute embarrassment. Necessarily, captors of flags were heroes. Imagine the feeling when the II Corps's Lieutenant Colonel Morgan reported the corps took thirty-four flags, of which officially Hays would claim his division took fifteen. Five were attributed to Hays's redeemed Third Brigade—for which three captors, Captain Morris Brown, Jr., Sergeant George Dore, and Private Jerry Wall of the 126th New York, subsequently were awarded Medals of Honor. From all the evidence, they had clearly captured the flags—not simply plucked stray flags off the ground—an important distinction. It remains that the number of flags obtained by Hays's division reflects how intensely it was engaged.[25]

After the fighting died down, the tragic proportions of the Battle of Gettysburg began to sink in. As General Hays lamented, "The angel of death alone can produce such a field as was presented." Despite discrepancies in reports, the number of casualties through July 4 is

Sgt. Maj. Henry Porter Cook (*Source:* Hamilton College Archives)

"Morris is a Hero"—The Battle of Gettysburg / 67

revealing. The II Corps lost 4369 men, almost 40 percent of those engaged. General Hays's division had suffered 1291 casualties (killed, wounded, and missing), or greater than 35 percent of those engaged. Two of Hays's regiments lost greater than half of those engaged. The 111th New York and the 126th New York—representing the "Cowards of Harpers Ferry"—sustained 63.8 percent casualties (fifty-eight killed) and 50.8 percent (forty killed) respectively. Brown's Company A was eleven men fewer, with one noncom killed, another wounded, and nine enlisted men wounded in their two days of fighting. Brown must have felt the loss of Sergeant Major Henry Porter Cook—the 126th New York's top noncommissioned officer and a year ahead of Brown at Hamilton, who was mortally wounded on the third day of fighting at Gettysburg. General Hays could rightfully report that "The history of this [the Third] brigade's operations is written in blood."[26]

Smith Brown's letter in its entirety reveals the awful ordeal that he, his brother, and the brigade had undergone, but also the Brown ambition:

Gettysburgh [sic]
July 4th 1863
9 a.m

My Dear Parents.

Had a terrible battle 126th annihilated Little over 100 left. (76?) Sixteen officers shot Col Sherrill killed. Capt [Isaac] Shimer do [ditto] Capt [Charles] Wheeler do Capt Herndorn [Orin J. Herendeen] wounded & prisoner. Lt [Meletiah] Lawrence shot in leg. Not dangerously Capt [John] Brough shot " " [ditto] Lt's [Jacob] Sherman, S[ydney]. E. Brown. G[eorge] Sherman. &c shot None dead Morris [Brown, Jr.] & [Samuel] Wilson all right Forshay [Sgt. Charles Forshey] ran away. Col Willard killed Col McDougall shot. [Col James] Bull commands brigade Brigade reduced from 2000 to 500. Col. Sherrill shot in grand charge of rebels. Morris is a hero. Captured a rebel flag. He charged the rebel line with 10 men & captured it. Our regiment captured 5 flags. We went in with 375 men & 27 officers. We have been fighting now continuously for 60 hours. are losing rest of our men very fast. I just came out to carry Co Sh[errill's] body to the rear. Morris flag had inscribed on it "Shepardstown," "Malvern Hill" "Manassas Junction" "Sharpsburgh" "Harpers Ferry" "Mechanicsville" "Hanover" "Ox Hill" "Cold Harbor" "Frazers Farm" "Manassas" "Cedar Run" It belonged to 14th N.C

Rebels laid down their arms & came in and no one to make them. This is 4th day of battle. Send me New York papers from June 25th every day. Have not seen a paper since June 25. *We had no food for 50 hours* No mail. We are beating the Enemy I will write [*Yates County Chronicle* editor] Cleveland a detailed acct. Am writing on a pint cup do not know how I can send this. no battle going on now. It will be renewed soon. Wonder if you have sent my horse? If so, where he is Some stragglers may come in. In haste

Smith

[On the edge of the paper, Smith added] Can you not Pa get me a Colonelcy now.[27]

Had Adjutant Brown left it at that—just the letter to his parents—he would have escaped his arrest by General Hays on August 6, 1863, for violating Section 220 of the Revised Army Regulations. Hays charged the adjutant with making "false and perverted statements regarding battles of Gettysburg, Penn, previous to official announcements of the same." As he had done since his initial enlistment in the 1st U.S. Sharpshooters, Adjutant Brown had written a long, five-column report on Gettysburg to the *Yates County Chronicle*. He singled out his younger brother twice, though it is only a very small part of the report. However, apparently relatives of other soldiers at Gettysburg were offended by what they regarded as too much credit given Captain Morris Brown, Jr. and his Company A. When Hays released the adjutant from arrest nine days later, Hays made it clear that he was not excusing him. The adjutant had shown a disregard for the reputation of others. "If each and every scribler [sic.] gives accounts which should deviate from official sources which are responsible, it cannot be expected that truth will always be

```
Adjutant General's Office,
2128 A.C.O.1888,

                                        Washington, May 21,1888,


C.A.Richardson,Esq.,
        No.17 Atwater Block,
                Canandaigua,New York.
Sir:-
        In compliance with your request of the 14th instant,I have the
honor to transmit herewith a copy of letter from Lt.Col.James M.
Bull,126th N.Y.Vols.,commanding 3d.Brig.3d.Div.2d.Corps,dated July
17,1863,receipting to Capt.Morris Brown,Jr.,Co."A" of said regiment
for one regimental banner,captured at Gettysburg,Pa.,July 3,1863;
and an extract copy of Statement from Headquarters Army of the
Potomac,dated October 17,1864,showing capture of flags at Gettysburg
Pa.,July 3,1863,by Sergt.Geo."H" Dare,of Co."D." and Pvt.Jerry Wall
of Co."B" 126th N.Y.Vols.
        The flags captured by Captain Brown and Sergt.Dore are now in
custody of the War Department,and the one captured by Pvt.Wall may
be also,but,if so,it can not now be identified.
        No additional information,pertaining to capture of flags by
members of the above named organization,appears to be of record.
                        Very respectfully,
                            Your obedient servant,
                                J.C.Kelton,
                                    Assistant Adjutant General.
```

Brown's record of flag capture (*Source:* Official Records)

told." Let this be a lesson to others, he was saying in effect. Individuals did not win battles; the army did. Hays's reprimand of Smith Brown did not go unnoticed by others in the 126th New York.[28]

In fairness to Smith Brown, his report reflected the content as well as the context of the battle. Not long after submitting that piece, but before his arrest, he also submitted the regiment's monthly reports to the paper, including what could have been regarded as much more disturbing to sensibilities, the listing of deserters from the 126th. But nothing seems to have come from that posting.[29]

Apparently Morris himself had no time to write anything for another nine days. He and others in the Army of the Potomac were racing to catch up with Lee's retreating army. As General Meade had written, his men were "making forced marches, short of rations, and barefooted" because General Halleck—safely in Washington—criticized him after Lee's army had safely retreated from Gettysburg.[30]

By Monday, July 6, Hays's division, wet to the skin, had made twenty miles before halting. The next day was a repeat, with the men dropping to the ground outside Taneytown. Nothing—not illness, exhaustion, or painful blisters—excused the marchers. On the 8th, they reached Frederick, Maryland, a twenty-four-mile hike. Their quarry, General Lee's army, was racing just as rapidly to reach the pontoon bridge left earlier near Falling Waters, Maryland, just north of Williamsport. By the twelfth, the Army of the Potomac was within striking distance of the Army of Northern Virginia—which was stalled by the raging Potomac, making its return trip via pontoon bridges dangerous to impossible. Again, as he had done on July 4, General Meade held a council of war and again the vote was not to attack, for Lee still had an intact army. Trapped as it was, it could be even more dangerous to the tired Union pursuers.

Pumped up over his heroism at Gettysburg and intent on routing the Confederates after the forced marches to catch up, Captain Brown spoke for many when he protested Meade's decision not to attack on the thirteenth, as he made clear in his letter of July 16:

Camp near Harpers Ferry
July 16th 1863

My Dear Parents

Just think! I hav'nt written home but once since I left Centreville twenty days ago.

But Smith writes every few days & that is just the same. Cant sit down by the side of the road & pen a letter the way Smith can. it's impossible. I must have something to write on or I am afraid my correspondents will suffer.

Now, I have so much to write about, that I dont know where to commence. But the one thing which makes me feel the worst & which discourages us all is that Meade let Lee get across the river so nicely.

Every man almost in the Army of the Potomac was willing yea eager to attack Lee on the 13th of July; & every man would have fought like a tiger if the word "forward" had only been given. It is incomprehensible to every subordinate officer why Meade did not attack Lee when everything seemed—just as it turned out—to indicate that the rebel army would have been compelled to surrender, or have been utterly routed. Their rear guard which our cavalry captured told us that they all fairly trembled in their boots on the 13th inst for fear of an attack. I believe if the attack had been made it would have been the ending up of the war. Perhaps though there is some good reason for not advancing which we know not of.

Ere this, of course you have heard all about the battle of Gettysburg. It was a terrible fight & I dont wish to get in another unless necessary. When I captured that flag (I was about a quarter of a mile away from the rest of the brigade) I formed my company with about fifty prisoners which I also took & marched up to the Brigade carrying the flag myself at the head of my column. Oh!!! you ought to have heard the whole brigade cheer me. I bet you too would have yelled bully for another of those "miserable Browns." It was a proud day for me I can tell you.

I cant see nor can I ever tell why I was not taken prisoner for I was on the left flank, & almost in the rear of the whole rebel army. I captured three times as many prisoners as I had men. Bully for me.

I have'nt had anything to eat to day save a small piece of ham without any bread. Pretty rough but I can go it yet a while. Never was better in my life. None of those old head-aches which used to bother me so much, trouble me now.

I am ragged & dirty & look as bad as any little rag-muffin you can pick upon in the streets of Penn Yan.

Will write again in a day or two.

Whether he kept that promise to write cannot be determined. The next available letter was almost six weeks later. Strangely, in the immediate letter, he did not mention a very unsettling incident for some of the marchers. An executed spy's body hung from a tree to remind would-be spies and passing troops the punishment for breaches of discipline.[31]

Weariness might explain Brown's later lack of correspondence, for day after day the Army of the Potomac forged its way south. By July 25, the marchers had reached White Plains, Virginia, back in the "enemies country." Marching daily, sleeping infrequently, eating poor food, and suffering wet clothing took a toll. Men were falling out in greater numbers, and those who endured were griping.[32]

Command changes explained some of the complaints. James Bull, replacing the deceased Sherrill in command of the 126th New York, had requested promotion to colonel. But some officers preferred Major Philo Phillips. Lt. George Yost (Company I) wanted Captain Coleman, "our Senior Capt, to be made Major" and grumbled "that Adjutant [Smith Brown] is working his bigest [sic] licks for it and [I] should not wonder a whit but that he got it." Company B's Captain William Coleman was even more acerbic, protesting that he "could never serve under that fellow Brown, for I know him to be a rascal and coward who owed his continuance in the service to my forbearance." Unnamed officers had submitted a petition supporting Phillips for colonel and Coleman for major to forestall the return of Lt. Col. William Baird, who had been reinstated just prior to Gettysburg. Lt. Richard Bassett may have been one of those officers, for he protested Baird's appointment on the grounds that promotions belonged to those who had "passed through what they did at Gettysburg." But he said nothing about promoting Smith Brown.[33]

Though there is no direct evidence, likely the Browns were actively seeking the majority for Smith. The key was getting to the Democrat governor, Horatio Seymour, who had authority to grant promotions. Though the senior Brown had argued for bipartisanship, he and his sons intended to use their ties to the Democratic party and the elder Brown's role as military committeeman to secure promotions. The losses at Gettysburg and the expiration of nine-month enlistments portended a thorough reorganization. At the beginning of the year, the corps's aggregate strength was 32,529—while at the end of July, it was 20,104, with only 7,681 (38.21 percent) present for duty. The 126th New York's

Surgeon Hoyt reported fewer than two hundred in his regiment at dress parade by mid August.[34]

Smith Brown, the target of more than a few barbed letters by fellow officers, was one of the absentees. Apparently, he had returned home due to ill health, and his absence may have induced more worries among his fellow officers. That is, he was better situated to further his cause for promotion. His enemies' worries were not groundless, for he would be commissioned regimental major on November 13, 1863—while, ironically, he was on detached service as U.S. Inspector General of Wisconsin in Madison. His promotion while on detached service could not have sat well with his fellow officers, for he held the rank but was not actively performing the requisite duties.[35]

The end of August found his brother, Morris, at Elk Run, Virginia, eight miles from Warrenton Junction. The old camp routine was accompanied by tightened discipline, induced by an influx of "bounty jumpers" and "professional deserters," and court-martials and military executions. This was somewhat offset by the issuance of equipment, necessitated by the fact that the men seemed bereft of everything, including clothing and arms. Health was another concern, leading to an order from the medical department reminding the soldiers to boil and bake, rather than fry meats, exercise regularly, and move camps to higher ground. Rations were supplemented by fresh vegetables, pickles, rice, and pepper. The combination of measures led to generally improved health.[36]

For now, Captain Morris Brown's and his comrades' immediate enemies were rain and heat that ranged from "one to one thousand," according to division commander Hays.[37]

CHAPTER 4

" 'I Rallied on the Right'— Charged 'Bayonets' "

In early September, Morris missed Smith, who was home on leave, and was beginning to sound more like the older, rather than younger brother. In what appears to be his first letter home in almost two months, he is miffed with his brother. He doesn't like having to pick up after him and risk a fight with 2nd Lt. Samuel Wilson.

Sunday Evening
Sept. 6/63,

[Smith]

Pretty lonesome here to day. Your being absent with the thought that I must remain in this benighted region indefinitely. I trust the receipt of Carries letter will satisfy you regards her future intentions. You left your traps—horse, bed, blankets &c. in a pretty fix. Whoever you wanted to have them you should have left them with & not with each one separately. I expect to have a regular quarrell with Wilson about your horse for I am bound to have him to ride while you are absent hit or miss. We went over to Div. Hd. Qrs to church to day. I sent one of my men after the horse not knowing when we are going. He (Wilson) went & took the horse away from him. So you see he expects from what you told him that he could have the horse, & even all your things. If you really want him to have the things—write me fairly & Ill not trouble him

Brown

Idleness and organizational changes would create greater problems for the young company commander and the others near Warrenton Junction, located on the Orange and Spotsylvania Railroad about forty miles southwest of Washington. Surprisingly, he did not comment on one major change—the August 12 appointment of Major General Gouverneur Warren as II Corps commander to replace Brigadier General William Hays, who had substituted for the wounded Hancock after the Battle of Gettysburg. The waspish Warren, West Point 1850, was only thirty-three, but he had proven himself as lieutenant colonel of the 5th New York in the May 1861 Battle of Bethel Church, as brigade commander at Gaines's Mill on the Peninsula, at Second Manassas, at Antietam, and on July 2, when he alertly directed troops to occupy Little Round Top.

Nor does Brown suggest any interest in the appointment of Brigadier General Joshua Owen to command the Third Brigade, to which his 126th New York was consigned. Owen, a Welsh native and graduate of Pennsylvania's Jefferson College, had commanded two different Keystone State regiments during the Peninsula Campaign, which led to his promotion. Except for an accusation of drunkenness later, Brown also ignores Lieutenant Colonel (soon to be Colonel) Bull's appointment to command the 126th New York and similar changes in the 126th's fellow brigade regiments.

The two opposing armies settled down until mid-September, when the Union camp routine was interrupted by orders to cross "the famous Rappahannock, making the third experiment of our army to invade this section of the sacred soil," Division Commander Hays wrote his wife on September 14. "May it be more successful than the two preceding," referring to the failed Fredericksburg and Chancellorsville campaigns. General Meade had learned that Longstreet's Corps had been sent west to support Major General Braxton Bragg in Tennessee. So, on September

11, Meade ordered his army to move out. But his intentions were not clear to others. In fact, he reminded General Warren that this was only a reconnaissance ("Don't bring on a general engagement."). The Army of the Potomac was now engaging in what *New York Times* reporter William Swinton dubbed "A Campaign of Maneuvers." Per orders, Maj. Gen. Alfred Pleasonton's Cavalry Corps had crossed the Rappahannock, driving the Confederates back behind the Rapidan. The infantry, including Morris Brown and others in the corps, followed. Pleasonton reported the capture of seventy-five prisoners and three guns, but the affair amounted to little and is only mentioned in passing by Morris Brown.[1]

Though a quiet prevailed, Brown and others encamped between the Rapidan River and Cedar Mountain were constantly reminded they were at war. First, with the enemy close, one whole brigade was on picket duty, while the other two brigades were in reserve. The occasional exchange of fire between pickets forced greater alertness. A more troubling reminder of war occurred on September 16, when two Connecticut conscripts charged with desertion were executed. It was an awful affair for all. "One was shot five times," but not killed, according to the 126th New York's Sgt. Harrison Ferguson, forcing a member of the firing squad to hold the muzzle of his weapon to the unfortunate's head and to blow "his scalp off." But, as Ferguson concluded, it was "the only way to stop desertion."[2]

The executions stemmed from an increased sense of urgency. Not only were the ranks reduced, they were not being filled fast enough. Worse, too many conscripts or bounty jumpers deserted soon after their arrival. General Warren reported that ten conscripts had deserted on August 17. Four from one Massachusetts company were still at large the next day. Desertions and absences without leave would continue well into the new year, though executions remained rare. But witnesses did not forget them easily or quickly.[3]

While Captain Morris Brown rather lightheartedly anticipated "a big fight," he enjoyed a much needed rest. He and his men had marched over five hundred miles since leaving Centreville at the end of June. They had bloodied themselves at Gettysburg, subsequently had endured oppressive heat and drenching rains, had eaten poorly, and were dead tired. Moreover, they were reduced to the barest of essentials: possibly a quart cup to boil whatever was available (with coffee generally a staple), a jacknife to cut meat, and a whittled stick as a fork to cook and serve what was called meat. And money was in short supply, proving especially exasperating now that there was time to spend it.

Morris Brown's letters home offer a glimpse of life there near the Rapidan River, which narrowly separated the armies.

Camp near Rapidan Station
Sept. 22d/63

[To Smith Brown]

Here we are yet. not moved since I last wrote you.

To day we recieved eight days rations—five in knapsacks & three in haversacks.

This looks wonderfuly like a big fight. for of course we are going to move forward.

If Lee has sent a portion of his troops to re-inforce Bragg of course we wont have much trouble to thrash 'em, but if he has not you can bet a big fight is in the future & that not far off.

We cannot move forward one hundred rods without exchanging shots with the rebs. Our line is very close to theirs—so close that we exchanged papers with them yesterday when we were on picket.

Our whole Brigade goes out on picket now every third day—General & all.

I would like it very much to see to day's paper to learn whether Rosecrans was really whipped or not. I dont believe it, unless as I said before Lee has sent a large number of troops to help Bragg.4

You have not yet sent me a complete list of my debts there in Penn Yan. Get Frank Smiths bill & all the others— get pa to help you. & send 'em along. Send for Theodore for he must come home.

Find out exactly what I owe Stark. Explain everything.

I guess we will be paid before a great while & when we do I want to get rid of my money as soon as possible.

In your next [letter] tell me when you are coming back to the regiment.

When you come, bring a hatchet. That's all!

Love to all
Your aff. brother
Morris

With time on his hands and anxiously awaiting muster for pay, Brown was toting up his mostly unexplained debts. Finances were never far from his thoughts.

His letter a week later offers a few clues about his debts:

Camp near the Rapidan
Sept. 29th/63

[To Smith Brown]

Received your letter enclosing Surgeons certificate all right. gave the certificate to [Col.] Bull.

Also received mothers letter & will answer it as soon as I have a single thing to write.

I sent Stark $500 yesterday, which I guess will sit him all right.

You dont seem to pay any attention whatever to my request asking you to send in the difference amounts I owe them in Penn Yan.

I wish you would make an effort to get me their bills for I want to settle up my accounts now while I have the money. Dont fail!!! Wilson paid me $23.85 [Capt. Benjamin] Lee $3.50 & I owe you $59.95 which makes total owed you $87.30 They deducted from my pay $51.60 for employing Baker as servant & I paid him $15.00 for you & Sam & I, as __ present. Your share of this is $22.20. I paid Bull $20.00 & Q.M. [John K.] Loring $33.33 which taken together makes $75.53 I have paid out for you. This leaves me in your debt

$11.77 Will write mother in a day or two—as soon as I can find anything worth writing.

The 1st, 12th & a part of the 5th Corps have left for Washington, or at least a large portion of them. Where they go of course we dont know.

Perhaps to Rosecrans & perhaps not.

You pay Millspaugh for my flute $4.50 & send me his receipt.

I will send you an order for $50.00 on Stark. As I owe you $11.77 & if you pay for flute $4.50 it will leave you $33.73 in debt to me.

Our picket line is only about five rods from the rebs. We are on picket two days out of six. I dont think now that we are going to have battle here. I think we will fall back to Culpepper or _____ in a few days. If the rebs find out how many of our troops have left us they will "get" us out of this pretty quick.

Your aff. brother
Morris
Recieve [sic.] lots of papers.

Having mustered for pay, Morris was flush. He wanted to settle accounts and bank the rest, which explains his sending $500 to Oliver Stark, the closest thing to a bank in Penn Yan at the time. While he sought to invest his pay, Morris had other money concerns. Officers were not issued clothing or rations as enlisted men were. Also apparently, though it is not on his military service record, he was taking advantage of his brother's and Lt. Samuel Wilson's servant. But army practice demanded that the servant's monthly pay be deducted from the officers' pay. Morris felt obligated to pay his brother his share. Further, he had to obtain food and other necessities from sutlers, whose prices typically were what the traffic would bear. With pay coming only bimonthly, officers often incurred some fairly sizable debts, as apparently he had.[5]

Although anticipating a battle (or a withdrawal to Culpeper), Morris Brown seemed preoccupied by concerns over money, and with recurring picket duty, he had time to try to reconcile accounts with his brother, Smith.

Oct. 1st 1863

Smith

Enclosed find $20.00 which give to mother. This makes $845.00 I have sent to Penn Yan since enlistment.

In my last letter I sent you an order on Stark for $50.00 which left you owing me $33.73. Yesterday I paid Q. M. Loring $9.25 which you owed him for clothes which leaves you in my debt to the amount of $42.98.

Now you say I owe you $162.60 on Thedes [Theodore's] account—subtracting—& I owe you $119.62 for which I enclose order.

Get all debts from father which I am to pay & I will enclose orders for the amounts. Sent Frank Smith an order for $34.50. Ask mother if it is correct. Be sure & pay Millspaugh for flute out of the fifty dollar check.

When you return bring a hatchet, two or three knives & forks & a brass kettle holding about six or eight quarts, & nothing more!!! for we cannot attend to anything else till we go into Winter Quarters.

No News. Theodore must come home! Send for him before I return. I will furnish the money.

Your aff. Brother
Morris
On picket

Oct. 2d/63

My dear all

Since I wrote you yesterday & told you Theodore must come home immediately I have received yours & mothers letters of Sept. 28th enclosing a part of Theodores last.

Now as regards Thedes coming home you can do as you at home can agree.

If it is going to make so much difference to Thedes if he comes home now as he represents, I think he had better remain there till the first of April next.

Hereafter we will have no trouble sending him his allowance, for I will get my pay regularly.

If I had my way & as my heart feels he should remain there thru years yet. & the only reason that Smith & I came to the conclusion that he had better come home is that Smiths health is so poor, & my life is so uncertain. But we must incur [?] some risk & now do as you please & I will be satisfied.

Send for him, or let him remain—anything will be satisfactory to me.

It seems to be the impression here that the army will fall back within the defences of Washington ere long. I dont believe we can get out of this without a fight for there are no troops this side of Culpepper but a part of the 2d Corps.

Your aff. Morris

[Written upside down atop the first page of the two-page letter:]

sent Mother $20 dollars yesterday

Morris's and Smith's apparent support of their brother Theodore is the most intriguing aspect of the two previous letters. Why the two were (or felt they were) required to underwrite Theodore's chess playing in Germany, and why Theodore was not self supporting is never revealed in Morris's letters. However, nothing indicates that Morris or Smith begrudged him the support.

In this next letter, to his mother three days later, Morris offers an unusual experience with two Confederates also on picket duty.

Camp near the Rapidan
Oct. 5th 1863

I believe my dearest mother that I have received two letters from you since I last wrote but then as I have written Smith so frequently of late & knowing that the only thing which I can possibly write of any interest is that I am well. I perhaps have neglected writing longer than I ought.

Tell Smith I cannot send the letters he wants before the tenth [A]t present there is not a sheet of paper in camp fit to write them on & the train is back on the other side of Cedar [?] Run & they wont allow any but ration wagons to come here in the "front." The Head Quarter Wagon did come up for a short time the other day but I was on picket.

I dont think I would send them anyway for he must come here & then he can attend to them better than I.

The Dr. [Hammond] said last night he [Smith] must come here, for he didnt want him to think of going into the "Invalid Corps." I guess Col. Bull dont want him to go for he never can get another such an Adjut. I think Major Phillips can stand it as long as Smith, although there may be some doubts.

Picket duty is quite interesting here. We are so close to the rebs that we are talking & blackguarding each other continually. The other night I could hear one swearing away because he did'nt have any shoes, blankets, or overcoat said he was [of?] a good notion to desert. Another one told him not to talk so loudly or the Yanks would hear him. he said he did'nt care a damn for he would go over to there the next day anyhow.

The next morning he saw me eating my breakfast & yelled out & asked me what I had to eat. I told him & asked him to come over & eat breakfast with me. he said he would do it if I would let him go back, which I agreed to. Down on the ground went his gun & over he came, & oh! you ought to have seen him eat & drink coffee. Well we talked & chatted quite a while when he concluded he would go back & away he went. The next day another fellow after making the same bargain came over & after seeing how much we had to eat in comparison with theirs concluded not to go back & went out on the "outpost" & told his comrads to go to hell with their confederacy he was'nt going to fight for 'em any longer.

Him I sent to Head Quarters. We frequently exchange papers. You can bet there was a great hub-bub in the rebel camps the other day when they heard of Braggs victory.

Write often Morris

[Atop the page and upside down, the following:]

A rumor is current that we are to be relieved by an other Corps, & we go back to Culpepper Court House. I hope it is true.

Interaction between pickets was not uncommon during the war, but Brown's story is unusual in that a Confederate was induced to desert by what seemed to him better fare with the Union. Moreover, Brown's narration is surprisingly matter of fact.

Camp about one mile north of Culpepper Court House
[Oct. 9, 1863]

Smith.

Here we are, having been relieved from picket duty on the Rapidan by the sixth Corps. We were ordered out but the order was countermanded.

Received two letters from you to night both of Oct. 5th. Enclosed find order on Stark for $50.00 If I knew you wanted any more money than what I have given orders for you could have it. We are square now. You must be mistaken about paying [lst Lt. John] Stainton, or rather that you did not receive any clothes from [Quarter Master] Loring. You can settle that when you return. When you return bring me a sole leather valise. thick—square & of fair size. You can tell best what I need to carry my books & papers. It will cost from six to ten dollars.

Bring a hatchet or small axe, an eight-quart brass pail or kettle, three knives & forks, with whatever provisions you wish. Fill my valise full.

Dont bring anything only what you can take care of yourself. Express boxes are played out. Fill a trunk & bring that. If you can find me a nice cap or hat in Washington buy me one. I have an abundance of money to last me till next pay day.

Received mothers letter to night—Oct 9 will write her in a day or two.

I am pretty busy now with my monthly & Quarterly Returns &c. Sam [Wilson] wants a box of good cigars. Bring me three lbs. Emmons Best chewing tobacco. I will send order for 69.30 & then you pay Hamlin & Latimer & take receipts. Tell mother not to buy anything more of Latimer. I would rather go without than buy of him. No news. Bull has been dead drunk two or three times since we left Elk Run the day after you left for home.

Came a good ways to see you.

Dean of Albany, my old chum in college is drafted & wants [to] join my company. His father wishes to pay the $300 [for a substitute?] I am going to write him not to join the army short of a Brigadier. Do not allow that young Stark to enlist. You know very well, it will be the ruin of him. Tell him, as you told me, to cut his throat & be done with it.

Your aff. brother
Morris

Camp near Bealton
Sunday evening
Oct. 11th /63

[To Smith Brown]

Here we are [,] having left Culpepper at 3 a.m. to day. Terrible march. The whole army is moving. Five different & distinct columns were on the road at once. We hear all sorts of rumors. One is Lee is again on his way into Pennsylvania. Another that he is making for Washington via Falmouth &c.

Of course we dont know yet what is up & cant tell for several days.

Enclosed find notice of letter in P.O. at Washington. Hope you received all my orders on Stark all right. Pay those debts at Hawkins & Latimers. Take receipt.

No prospect of killing the grey man. Be sure & bring me that sole leather square valise. Fill it full of cake & Chestnuts. Bring me three pds of Emmons best chewing tobacco. I will write again soon.

Morris

[Clearly, Captain Brown wanted to go first class: an "eight-quart brass pail," knives and forks, a leather valise (small suitcase) filled with cake and chestnuts and the best tobacco from Emmon's store in Penn Yan. Apparently the valise and tobacco were essentials, given his repeated requests for them.

Surprisingly he passes over Col. Bull's drunkenness rather lightly. A regimental commander's drunkenness should have been cause for greater concern unless drunkenness was more common than reported.

The five different troop columns he saw on the road, to which he seems to pay little attention, were a portent of some significant changes occurring in the front. The events ahead would critically involve him and his regiment and would prove fatal to more than a few.

The Army of the Potomac's repose had been forced on General Meade when he had to send the XI and XII corps to reinforce the Army of the Cumberland the third week of September after its defeat at Chickamauga. This offered General Lee an opportunity to "seriously cripple Meade" and to bring an end to the Army of the Potomac's campaigns long enough for Lee to reinforce his hard-pressed Western army under Maj. Gen. Braxton Bragg in Tennessee, to whom Morris Brown had alluded. Lee intended to flank Meade, forcing the latter to attack on ground favorable to the Confederates. One of the first indications of Lee's intentions was reported by Brigadier General Joshua T. Owen, who had replaced the late Colonel Willard as commander of Hays's Third Brigade. Owen's pickets had detected "unusual activity" in the enemy's camp on the first of October. Railroad cars had run all night, which indicated to Owen "either the arrival or departure of troops." His superior, General Hays, more amused than alarmed, was reminded "of the old woman's opinion of the quality of indigo." If broken up and tossed into water, it "would 'sink or swim,' she did not know which." In fact, the Confederate activity presaged an advance which was confirmed later by spies and Federal signal men who had broken the Confederate code.[6]

In early October, with something like forty-six thousand men, Lee was on the move. By Friday, the ninth, Ewell's and A. P. Hill's corps had crossed the Rapidan. Hill was to make a wide sweep northwest and then swoop down upon the Union army at Warrenton, while Ewell took the direct route through Jefferson to unite with Hill. The next day Meade, now fully aware that Lee had slipped around his right flank, ordered his army across the Rappahannock and northward along the path of the Orange and Alexandria Railroad. Corps commanders were to remain at the rear of their commands to receive instructions. General Warren's II Corps, now 587 officers, 8,243 men, and thirty-two manned pieces of artillery, began its march along the familiar route to Bealeton on the eleventh. The October Virginia Campaign had begun.[7]

Though preparing to meet an attack, Meade and others believed that Lee's move was only a demonstration in advance of the upcoming elections in the North. That is, it might offer support to those disillusioned with the war who sought a rapprochement with the South. However, shortly circulars to the corps commanders demanded they move at "the utmost promptitude" and "celerity" while observing the "utmost vigilance." The II Corps was to support General Irvin Gregg's cavalry and cover Major General William French's III Corps. The corps marched all night of the twelfth, and by 1:00 a.m. of the thirteenth linked with Gregg at Fayetteville, a bone-weary, thirty-six mile trek. At Fayetteville, still fearful of being struck from the rear by Ewell's Corps, Meade prodded his army. But the II Corps, in battle line, anxiously awaited the arrival of the III Corps, which Warren regarded as inexcusably delayed. Finally, around 11:00 a.m., after discovering a parallel route, Warren's dead-tired corps moved on to Auburn, with Caldwell's division in the lead, followed by Hays's and Webb's (formerly Gibbon's) divisions. The other corps, I (Major General John Newton), V (Major General George Sykes), and VI (Major General John Sedgwick) were well on their way to the army's destination, Centreville.[8]

October 13 was an anxious night for Warren's isolated command, which stretched along the road three miles. It was without a crossing place and faced Ewell's Corps barely five miles away at Warrenton. At 2:00 a.m. on the fourteenth, Warren received orders to push his troops on to Catlett's Station, staying on the south side of the railroad. The "prescribed course" would take them to the right in the valley and then down to Cedar Run, "making a sharp angle in the route, the point toward the enemy." It was a difficult and dangerous move up the extreme incline and then down the narrow path leading to Cedar Run. Ewell's and Hill's corps too suffered from delays and confusion, but by 5:00 a.m. on October 14, Ewell had moved out, intending to cut off Meade's army. Both armies were in a race that to the opposing commanders was irritatingly delayed. Awakened between 3:00 and 4:00 a.m., Brigadier General Alexander S. Webb's Second Division and then Colonel Samuel S. Carroll's First Brigade of Hays's division were ordered to guard the 100-wagon train and 125 ambulances, while the rest of the corps advanced through a heavy fog from Three Mile Station to Auburn. But the train got mired in the mud, forcing Warren to send Caldwell's and Hays's divisions ahead through the fields.[9]

At 6:30 a.m., Brig. Gen. John S. Caldwell's First Division finished crossing Cedar Run, and Hays's division moved through the heavy fog onto St. Stephen's Road. Shells, likely from Major R. F. Beckham's seven guns of Stuart's Horse Artillery, landed among Hays's surprised troops, killing eleven and wounding twelve. One shell alone killed seven men. Though Caldwell ordered his men to move to high ground, II Corps commander Warren faced what appeared to him to be a terrible dilemma. Stuart's cavalry was blocking the way, while two divisions of Ewell's Corps were rapidly advancing. "Attacked thus on every side, with my command separated by a considerable stream, encumbered with a wagon train in the vicinity of the whole force of the enemy," Warren later reported, "to halt was to face annihilation, and to move as prescribed carried me along routes in the valley commanded by the heights on each side." At 10:00 a.m., too late to do any good, Major General Andrew A. Humphreys, Meade's chief of staff, wired Warren to scout routes to retire on if "repulsed and outflanked."[10]

Major General Robert E. Rodes's and Major General Edward ("Old Allegheny") Johnson's divisions of Ewell's Corps were rapidly advancing on Caldwell's and Hays's beleaguered divisions. Because of the difficulty of fighting there, Warren ordered Hays to "break through the enemy" with his division. Hays ordered out five companies of skirmishers from the 125th New York. However, they met some of Stuart's dismounted cavalry and a part of General John B. Gordon's Brigade, and in the words of the 126th's Sergeant Harrison Ferguson, the Union skirmishers "ran like sheep." Hays bluntly blamed the failure on "the chickenheartedness of a major commanding my skirmishers."[11]

In fairness, at Auburn the situation was confusing to the participants. Neither side recognized what it faced, particularly General Hays, whose men now seemed to bear the brunt of the attack. As historian William Henderson observed in his treatment of the affair, "Hays struggled to deal with an enemy of unknown size whose positions were inexactly known." But it seemed made for Hays. It was time for him to inspire his men, as he had done during the Peninsula Campaign and at Gettysburg. He was not about to let his "blue birds" fail.[12]

So, General Hays "selected" the 126th New York to "Find out who is in those woods." Bull's men and Ricketts's battery met the 1st North Carolina Cavalry's charge, Hays recalled in a letter home, "with a withering volley" that "instantly" covered the plain "with riderless horses." Officially, Hays tersely reported that the engagement "was short, but very decisive." In fact, the main attack by Ewell's troops had not materialized, which Warren soon realized.[13]

Main attack or not, it was a harrowing experience for Hays's division. "The moment was critical," the 126th New York's Captain Winfield Scott recalled.[14] There was no time for Colonel Bull to issue commands; rather, various company commanders individually tried to meet the attack. Morris Brown offers a vivid firsthand account in an excerpt from his letter home:

Centreville Va.
Oct. 15th/63

My dear Parents:

Here we are again at old Centreville after our long & fatiguing march from the Rapidan. The whole army [Army of the Potomac] is here with the exception of the 1st & 6th Corps which are at Thoroughfare Gap.

Our Division carried the retreat. Yesterday morning about day break, having marched about a mile we were attacked by the enemy in force. Our Regt. was sent out as skirmishers & you can bet we had a "right smart" of a fight, but we drove them out of the woods in front of us, from which the 125th N.Y.V. was driven like so many sheep.

A whole regiment of rebel cavalry charged on the right of our line where my company was but I "rallied on the right"—charged "bayonets" & broke their regiment in two parts—one part going to our rear when it was captured & the other repulsed. We (my Co. A) captured Col. Ruffian [Ruffin] (ex U.S. Senator from North Carolina) with his Adjt. & several enlisted men besides killing eight or ten enlisted men together with several horses.

You can bet my dear parents my company "did themselves up proud." Capt. Seabury, Gen. Owens Adjt Gen said that the right of the line was all that done anything. The other company did their duty, but as the rebels charged directly on the right of my company we had a better chance for "deeds of valor" than the rest. Gen. Hays remarked to Dr. Hammond, "The 126th have done nobly. They have remembered poor Col. Sherrill & have shown him up another round. This mornings work has covered them with glory." All the forenoon every time he rode by the regiment he would yell out "you did bully boys." Once he even halted the regiment & yelling out "You did bully this morning boys" & giving the order "forward" rode on.

What makes it so much better for us the 125th N.Y. Vols a rival regiment of ours in our Brigade, was driven away like so many sheep from the very spot where we deployed & drove the "rebs" out of the woods. Well this was'nt the end of our fighting yesterday by any means. The fight above mentioned happened at a little place called Auburn a little distance northeast from the railroad between Warrenton & Warrenton Junction.

Indeed, it was not the end of Brown's combat that day. Before 9:30 a.m., the road cleared, the II Corps struck out again, with Hays's and Webb's divisions in the lead. By noon, Meade, impatient with Warren, directed the II Corps commander to advance as fast as he could. The enemy was headed for Bristoe Station, not Centreville, and Sykes's V Corps was waiting for the head of Warren's column before moving on. At 2:00 p.m. General Humphreys, Meade's chief of staff, was still unaware that the II Corps had been engaged at Auburn and asked Warren if he were delayed. Hays's Third Division was instructed to take the southeast side of the railroad, while Webb's division with two artillery batteries was to take the northwest side. Caldwell's division would act as rear guard. Hays then ordered the 111th New York's Colonel Smyth to send out flankers on the right of the road, after which the rest of Hays's column moved out. Each commander was "acting on his own judgment," according to Warren, which demanded spontaneity.[15]

General Lee, acutely aware of the extended Union advance—and its vulnerability—advanced Major General A. P. Hill's Corps toward Bristoe. The goal was to destroy the Army of the Potomac piecemeal. The littered clothing ahead suggested to Hill that the Federals were exhausted from marching and countermarching—as they were. To the impetuous Hill, the time was ripe. A half hour's delay "and there would have been no enemy to attack," Hill claimed. Then he spotted his quarry, Sykes's V Corps, waiting to ford the swift-moving Broad Run. Mistakenly assuming that he had overtaken the rear of the long Army of the Potomac train, Hill ordered General Henry Heth's Division and Major W. T. Poague's artillery battalion to attack the unsuspecting Union troops. (Major General William French's III Corps had gone ahead, while Sykes awaited Warren's approach.) The initial shelling at approximately 3:00 p.m. forced Sykes's men to clamber wildly across Broad Run and around 4:00 p.m. encouraged Heth to direct Walker's, Kirkland's and Cooke's brigades to charge.[16]

Warren ordered Hays and Webb to halt, face left and double quick to Bristoe Station ahead. Now both Confederates and Federals were furiously racing toward the raised railroad embankment, which made for "an effectual breastwork for whichever side could first reach it." Skirmishers from Hays's Third Brigade, including Morris Brown's 126th New York, scrambled across Kettle Run, some on the railroad ties, others on the flat stones in the stream. Unfortunately, their straggling rendered them more vulnerable to the Confederate shelling. Warren reported that "A more inspiring scene could not be imagined. The enemy's line of battle moving forward, one part of our own steadily awaiting it and another moving against it at a double quick, while the artillery was taking up position at a gallop and going into action." However, to those in Hays's division, it was anything but inspiring; it meant another bloody charge.[17]

Every minute might determine the contest. Hill's advance on the Greenwich Road and Ewell's approach by a parallel route to the south created a pincer movement. Its success "would have meant little less than the complete destruction of the corps," according to Colonel, later General, Francis Walker, the II Corps' historian. The 126th New York's Captain Brown wrote home that even before Hays's old brigade, the Third, reached the embankment the "showers of bullets" were the worst he had encountered, including at Gettysburg. Walker believed that even the II Corps veterans were appalled.[18]

But Hays's "impetuosity which his presence always insured," would help them carry the day, wrote Charles W. Cowtan, the 10th New York's historian. Hays's and Webb's divisions finally reached and ducked behind the railroad cut. They formed with Caldwell's division on the extreme left, Smyth's brigade to Caldwell's right, Owen's to Smyth's right, next to which were Colonel James E. Mallon's and Colonel Francis E. Heath's brigades from Webb's division. They formed a continuous line on the right, resting at Broad Run. Lieutenant Fred Brown's 1st Rhode Island Battery B, occupying high ground in the rear, opened fire with spherical case, and Captain William Arnold's Battery A soon followed suit. They slowed, but did not stop, the charging Confederates. Once behind the embankment Hays's and Webb's divisions directed their fire toward the Confederates advancing down the slope toward them. The "deadly fusillade" by the Federal infantry and artillery "swept the field," according to the 11th North Carolina's Colonel W. J. Martin. General Cooke's unattached brigade was driven back, but General Kirkland's North Carolinians still came on, with the left of their line reaching the railroad and momentarily dislodging some of the defenders. Though "hardly a battle in all that implies," the 14th Connecticut's Sergeant E. B. Tyler recalled, "for a short, sharp and promptly decided little fight, it was a rare specimen."[19]

Here is how Morris Brown remembered it in his October 15 letter to his parents:

> After driving the rebels away from our front we marched out to Catletts Station, & thence took the road leading to Manassas Junction along the rail road track.

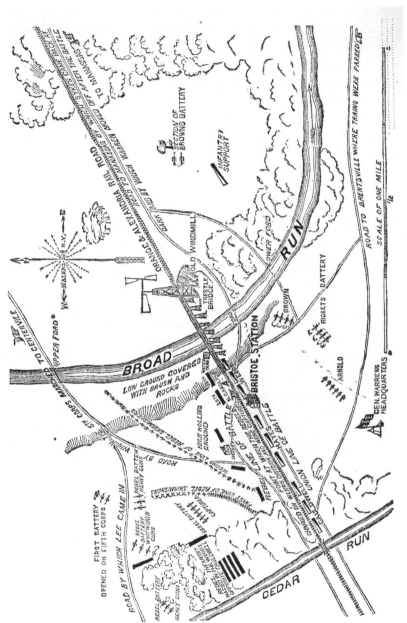

Bristoe Station, Va., October 14, 1863 (*Source*: G. K. Warren Papers, New York State Archives)

When within about a mile of Bristoe Station heavy firing commenced directly in our front. Well we hurried on & just as we came opposite the Station or a few rods south of it the rebs opened on our column, from the woods across the track.

Soon came the order "By the left flank, double quick, march" & away we went for the rail road which was directly toward the enemy & of all the showers of bullets that ever I passed through this was the worst. Gettysburg was not a circumstance for bullets. The distance from where we started, to the track, was about thirty rods [195 feet], across a plain with not a bush on it. Here we suffered severely.

But we reached the track & got into the cut before the rebs had formed their line sufficiently to charge on us from the woods about twenty rods off.

As soon as we reached the track the "rebs" advanced from the woods—a long line extending about a half mile. Now we opened with musketry & cannon. On came the rebels in the beautiful "line" which they always keep, until within about ten rods of us [about the width of a football field], when they reached a house which was on the left of their line. About this time a well directed shot swept away a large number of them about the length of a regiment from their left, which so broke their line & confused them, that those on their extreme left, broke for this house & huddled up around it like so many sheep. Bang! Bang went the canister & spherical case into this crowd,—when they scattered for the woods & their whole line with them. We sent out our skirmishers immediately after them & captured that whole house full of rebs together with a great many others who gave themselves up voluntarily.

We kept on into the woods and took five pieces of artillery which they abandoned in their precipitate retreat.

By & by they formed & came out again but we repulsed them again. this ended the infantry fighting but the artillery kept up an incessant firing till dark.

We took (I mean our division) some three or four hundred prisoners with five pieces of artillery & killed some two or three hundred more. "Big thing!"

About nine oclock we started for Centreville—everything being done without a word being spoken by anyone for the prisoners reported Lee close to us with his whole force, & it was necessary for us to get out of that before morning or we would be overwhelmed with numbers. We could see the "sky lit up" for a long distance with their camp fires & by this the prisoners reports were confirmed.

We encamped between Centreville & Bull Run creek about four oclock this morning, having accomplished one of the best, & hardest days work since I entered the service. When the rebels attacked us at Bristoe Station it was their intention undoubtedly to break our column & cut us off but the point—the railroad track which was necessary for that side to pass which would surely win, once gained, was reached by us about five minutes before the rebs.

If they had reached it before us I have no doubt we would all have been captured or badly cut up, for it was an admirable position—a deep cut with quite a bank thrown up on our side.

But time favored the Confederates. Another Confederate charge might decide the contest in their favor. "It would have been impossible to withdraw from my situation in daylight in the presence of such superior forces of General Lee," Warren later reported. He counted on Lee's uncertainty about the size of his force. Any movement by Warren would reveal how outnumbered he was, with only three thousand infantry and three batteries against two corps. General Sykes, responding to Warren's report of his situation, urged him to move toward Manassas at dark, if not before. Delay would only invite an attack. But Warren had no time to consider the advice, for the situation on his left was threatened.[20]

Near sunset, the fighting slowed to skirmishing and to a contest between the competing artillery. Heth, convinced that he faced "one, if not the greater portion of two entire corps," did not order another attack. But Warren still needed to extricate his corps. The opportunity came for most of the units around 9:00 p.m., but Hays's men lay in the cut until 11:00 p.m. when their commander "came around and ordered us in line as quickly as possible without saying a word," according to the 126th New York's Sergeant Ferguson. Once more, Morris Brown and others in the 126th were in the rear after a battle and in the van as they approached another. The corps did not complete its withdrawal in a dreadful rainstorm until around 4:00 a.m. on the fifteenth. Wet and starved, they remained along Bull Run that day, though skirmishing and a noon artillery shelling reminded them how close they were to the enemy.[21]

General Meade would praise the II Corps for repulsing the enemy "after a spirited contest," which resulted in the capture of 450 prisoners, five guns and two colors. Colonel Morgan, assistant inspector general and close observer of the action, was more effusive. He claimed that Warren had not only met the enemy, but had effected a change in formation "in the face of a powerful advance of the enemy." The corps commander was equally quick to praise his subordinates, whom he recommended for higher rank when openings occurred. Hays received the lion's share. While Warren noted that Webb's division had sustained the "larger portion of the enemy's attack," Hays had not only cleared the way for the advance from Auburn, but he had gone "into action at the critical moment [at Bristoe Station] with that inspiring courage which has made him so well known." But Hays's men had paid dearly. The Third Division lost one officer and nineteen men killed, eleven officers and 134 men wounded, and 37 men missing or captured, a total of 202, compared with Webb's loss of 133 and Caldwell's 184. Reminiscent of Gettysburg, the Third Brigade, in whom Hays had placed such faith, had suffered 125 casualties, over half of those sustained by his division. His "blue birds" were paying an awful price for his approval, but minor compared to the Confederate losses of 1900 men, almost four times the Union casualties during the hour-long contest.[22]

Morris Brown confirms how intense the fighting was in the remainder of his letter.

> I lost more really than at Gettysburg from my company. The following is a nominal list of killed & wounded in Co. "A" with description of wounded—which I wish you would have published in the Chronicle as emenating from a private letter of mine, with such remarks as you see fit, only be careful not to bestow any praise upon me or Co. A. Be sure though & get in what Gen Hays said in regard to the 126th Regt. to Dr. Hammond.

[In a letter written on the 17th, he added:]

Publish this list in [Penn Yan]Chronicle

I had forgotten to give you a list of killed & wounded in my company but here it is.

Killed Oct. 14th
  Thomas Tobin,
  Thaddeus [Thadeus] B. Twitchell
  Barnard F. Gilder [Gelder]

Wounded
  Sergt. Daniel W. Finch in leg, severely,
  Corpl Wm. Strobridge " " & Shoulder "[23]
  Corpl David E. Taylor " hand "
  Private Charles M. Nicholson " Breast "
  " A[rthur]. W. Middleton " leg "
  " O[rson]. R. Linkletter " Hip slightly

[The quotation marks mean ditto, or the same.]

These losses reduced Brown's Company A further. At the first muster in August 1862, his company had a full complement: a captain, two lieutenants, five sergeants, seven corporals, and eighty-three privates. After Gettysburg, thirty fewer privates mustered. At the end of October, his company was reduced to two officers, Brown and Samuel Wilson, five sergeants, six corporals, one musician, one wagoner, and forty-three privates. Morris also reported to the local newspaper that he had received a letter from Private Daniel J. Beyea, listed as missing after the battles at Auburn and Bristoe, that he was a prisoner in Richmond along with five others from Company A, including Finch and Middleton, who had been wounded, and a member of Company B.[24]

Brown offered an even bleaker picture on October 17, in a post-script to his October 15 letter home.

Forshay [Sergeant Charles Forshey] run again—the poor poltroon. This time he will catch fits. Not one from Co. B. was touched. I dont know the number killed & wounded in the regiment. I have only 14 guns [men] left in my company from the ninety eight original ones. It is rather discouraging to have so few men—only 14.

I guess I will reduce Forshay to the ranks, for it takes so long a time to get anything accomplished by these Courts Martials. It would go much worse with him though, if I should let the law take its course.

The company as a whole are perfect heroes & its rough to have one such coward among them.

This is a beautiful day—warm & sunshining after the hard rain of yesterday & last night.

I suppose Smith has started back before this time. If not tell him Lt. Coste one of Gen. Owens Aide de Camps was killed at Bristoe Station.

Morris Brown, Jr.

Brown's count of fourteen men likely refers only to those present for duty. Others were on detached or special duty, absent sick, or other excused duty. His disgust with Forshey needs no explanation.

Lee's decision not to pursue Meade was based on the latter's nearness to fortifications in Washington and Alexandria. Lee had done all he could to harass the Federals with only two thirds of his army, including tearing up the Orange and Alexandria Railroad back to the Rappahannock. However, the Confederates had paid quite a price to rid the area near the Rapidan of Union troops, which Hill ruefully admitted. He had "made the attack too hastily" against a force "of whose presence I was unaware." Lee was blunter; it had been a "disaster."[25]

"Fighting Elleck'" Hays's official report of the affairs on the fourteenth tersely described his division's part, as if it were an everyday affair. However, he offered a different account to his wife. Assuring her that despite the hard marching and fighting, he was safe after his men fought "one of the prettiest affairs I have ever seen." His men had "flogged [the Confederates] terribly" while experiencing "comparatively light" losses. Credit for the repulse of the Confederates was due Colonel Bull and the 126th New York of his old Third Brigade. Morris Brown, Jr. would have readily agreed.[26]

Five days later, Captain Brown and his heroic regiment were bivouacked back at Centreville, but there are no letters from him until December. Part of the reason is that he had been busy. General Meade, being pressed by Lincoln to take advantage of the weather, suggested moving his base to Fredericksburg, from which to attack Richmond. Lincoln brusquely disapproved; the object should be Lee's army. So, Meade changed plans. The opportunity (or pressure to do so) occurred when there were reports of a Confederate movement. If Meade were to succeed, he had to beat Lee to the punch—so on November 7, he began an advance with two columns. Major General French commanded the left, the I, II, and III corps, while Maj. Gen. Sedgwick led the right with his VI Corps and Sykes's V Corps. The cavalry was to clear the way. By 9:30 that night, Meade reported a successful crossing of the Rappahannock. Hays's Third Division was in support of the III Corps, which did most of the fighting with Lee's rear guard, but Lee's army had successfully withdrawn behind the Rapidan.[27]

The key to Meade's success in what would become known as the Mine Run Campaign would be crossing the uncovered fords along the Rapidan and striking Ewell's and Hill's separated corps before they could unite. Assaulting Lee's entrenchments along Mine Run, a tributary of the Rapidan, required a different approach from customary. Meade would have to cut loose from his base of supplies, advance and attack Lee's widely spread line running southerly along Mine Run across the two main roads between Orange Court House and Fredericksburg. First, however, Meade had to concentrate his forces and clear the path to the Rapidan. Clearing the path took longer than he intended. So, once more, Meade's army was stationary.[28]

Finally, on November 22, General Humphreys reported that the railroad had been reconstructed, and General Warren observed that the roads to Mountain Run were drying up. However, near Mine Run, where they planned to meet Lee's forces, the path was belly deep for horses. Meade intended to move out anyway, but bad weather forced him to suspend the movement on the twenty-third. His patience exhausted, Meade ordered the cavalry to cross the Rapidan at Ely's Ford and his infantry to move out at daylight the next day. The II Corps, in the lead, was to cross the Rapidan at Germanna Ford and proceed to Robertson's Tavern on the Orange Courthouse Turnpike. The III Corps would support the II Corps in its crossing and join with it, while the VI Corps was to cross and post in the rear of the III Corps, with Sykes's V Corps following. The I Corps, in support, was to head for the Orange Courthouse Plank Road.[29]

Before they embarked, Captain Morris Brown was ordered to appear as a witness in the court martial of Company A's thirty-nine-year-old Private William Hainer, the charges and the outcome of which are unknown. (Ironically, Private Hainer would play a rather critical role after Brown led a charge on June 22, 1864 during the siege of Petersburg.)[30]

On the 26th, Thanksgiving Day, Meade's Army of the Potomac successfully crossed the Rapidan, but from then on, Meade had nothing for which to be thankful. Nothing seemed to go right. First, it turned cold, leaving a heavy frost cover on the tentless men who were not allowed to build fires. Next, General French's corps took the wrong road, forcing the other corps to halt. When the army resumed its advance, a pontoon bridge had to be built. Then a short, but sharp, skirmish with forces from General Robert Rodes's Division slowed the advance again. Newly promoted, Major Smith Brown led one group of skirmishers on the twenty-seventh, including his brother, Morris, who was struck by a spent ball and only slightly wounded. Next, General French's corps collided with Major General Edward Johnson's Division of Ewell's Corps, and General Warren engaged other Confederates, whom General Hays claimed were "driven pellmell . . . with great loss." But Hays lost between fifty and a hundred men. On November 28, General Warren moved out again and reconnoitered for a favorable spot to launch an attack. Given Warren's report, Meade ordered an attack for the 30th.[31]

At 2:00 a.m. on the thirtieth, a bitter cold morning, General Hays's division was awakened and ordered to attack at 8:00. What the Federals saw was, in the words of a member of the 108th New York, "another Fredericksburg calamity trap," referring to the Union disaster at Fredericksburg a year earlier. Major Smith Brown recalled they "stood face to face with death." "Fighting Elleck" Hays labeled the attack a "death warrant." After another examination of the situation, General Warren was like minded and called it off, which left General Meade apoplectic, but resigned to accept Warren's decision.[32]

On the bitterly cold last day of the last month of the year, Meade ordered his army to withdraw behind the Rapidan; again, the Army of the Potomac had failed, and once more Morris Brown had time on his hands, time to settle accounts again and invest in his future.

Dec 1863

Father

I have been thinking about my buying that mortgage & the question arrises, what good is it going to do me, or how is it, that I will have anything more saved when I pay for that than now?

Now I'll tell you what I will do. You owe me $150 to begin with. I paid when home $61 & some cents to pay interest on property which you had bought & which you could have been compelled to pay before you received your full title to the land.

I will pay the balance due on the mortgage if you will have the land deeded to me, which will square the $150 & the back interest on the mortgage. Now I have a certain object in view which at present I do not wish to make known. If you can explain to me what better off I would be, by holding that mortgage, when you or mother holds the deed, than at present I would take it. If I should take the deed I would make a will so that mother would have it in case anything should happen to me.

I want to know also, the exact amount interest & all—you yet owe on the house & lot, which you now live in.

Now write me immediately in regard to these matters for by the first of March I will have four or five hundred dollars to invest up there somewhere.

Be very careful & leave no doubts about anything.

Your son
Morris

Apparently Morris and his father were engaged—entangled seems more accurate—in some real estate purchases, and the son now was as prone to give as to receive advice from his father. At any rate, he was clearly thinking ahead, even anxious about his future. It also may have been that his father's fortunes were dimming; in fact, it may have been that the older Brown was heading into or was already into bankruptcy. On December 27, Morris wrote Lt. Col. William Baird, replacing Colonel Bull, that "Important business long neglected demands my presence at home" and requested a ten-day leave of absence. But, however "important," it would have to wait.

CHAPTER 5

"You Can Bet We Are Going to Have a Terrible Battle"

Spring 1864

According to the editor of the local paper, Captain Morris Brown, who was "looking extremely well," had visited him in Penn Yan a few days before January 14, 1864. The editor also reported Morris was home again on February 25, along with Colonel Bull, Captains Richardson and Scott and ten enlisted men. Thus, it appears Brown had obtained a brief leave in January, had returned to duty and was furloughed again from mid-February to sometime in March. Likely, a particular incentive for coming home in January—beyond checking his investments—was to see his brother Theodore, who had returned to Penn Yan in late November after two years in Europe.[1]

Morris's second leave—to recruit—was critical, for the II Corps was badly decimated by this time. By the end of December 1863 only 11,092 officers and men out of 22,340 were present for duty. Moreover, it was a bitter cold winter with sub zero temperatures in parts of the north and below normal readings in Virginia. Those on duty huddled in their log huts, (tents built atop logs dug into the ground and finished off with stick and mud chimneys). It was not a good time to recruit. Nor was the Yates County Board of Supervisors' offer of commutations particularly helpful. Greater than two hundred draft eligible men in the county bought their way out of serving by paying $300, thirty-five in Penn Yan alone. Offsetting this, the supervisors voted a bounty of $300 for volunteers and $552 for veterans who reenlisted. Meanwhile, Morris's brother, now Major Smith Brown, was acting commander of the 39th New York, which was inundated by four hundred recruits, many enrolled by their colonel home in New York on recruiting duty.[2]

Apparently Morris was on recruiting duty on February 22, when the II Corps had its grand ball, which historian Bruce Catton labeled "the most brilliant event of the winter." It had all the glitz and glamor that a military camp could muster. Yates County Military committee-man Darius A. Ogden and his daughter, visiting the 126th, were duly impressed. They had entrained from Washington and took up quarters in the absent Brown's tent. Among the dignitaries were Army of the Potomac commander Meade, II Corps commander Warren, VI Corps commander Sedgwick, and cavalrymen Judson Kilpatrick and Alfred Pleasonton. Representing the 126th New York were Major Smith Brown, Lt. Col. William Baird, and Lt. Meletiah Lawrence. But the review the following day was somber, with rumors of increased fighting ahead, given warmer weather and drier roads.[3]

Moreover, changes were afoot, beginning at the top. In late February, Congress revived the rank of lieutenant general, previously held only by George Washington, and on March 2, the president duly promoted the man for whom the revived rank was intended—Ulysses S. Grant, the hero of the West. He would command the Union Army, but he chose to accompany the Army of the Potomac rather than to occupy a desk in Washington. And on March 5, coinciding with his first review of Meade's army, a reorganization was announced. Following General Meade's earlier recommendation, the Army of the Potomac was reduced to three corps, retaining the II, V, and VI Corps. The I Corps would be incorporated into the II, while the III Corps was split, with its First and Second divisions joining the II Corps, which was thus enlarged to four divisions.[4]

The biggest change for Morris Brown, Jr. and others in the Third Brigade was the appointment of boyish-looking Francis Channing Barlow to command the II Corps' First Division. The military career of the twenty-nine-year-old Harvard graduate and prewar lawyer had been meteoric. In scarcely sixteen months he had risen from private to brigadier general, was twice wounded and left for dead at Gettyburg, and now commanded a division. But this meant "Fighting Elleck" Hays, who had imbued the Third Brigade with his legendary bravery, would no longer lead them.[5]

Capt. William Coleman (*Source:* New York State Adjutant General's Office)

Changes at the regimental level followed. One of the first was the resignation of Company B's Captain William Coleman. Rumor was Coleman had protested that he could not serve under Smith Brown, whom he considered a "rascal and a coward." Officially he was resigning "on account of health." (He later regretted his decision.) Ironically, given Coleman's huffy resignation (and Morris's criticisms of Coleman), a testimonial to Coleman by the regimental and company officers was signed by both Browns and William Baird, whose promotion Coleman also had protested.[6]

Another change, greatly affecting Morris, was Smith Brown's absence, beginning March 24, when the latter returned home on recruiting duty. Five weeks later he was appointed by Secretary of War Stanton to serve as inspector general of Wisconsin in Madison. Additionally, Morris's Hamilton cohorts were all gone. Darius Sackett had been discharged after Harpers Ferry. Henry Porter Cook had been killed at Gettysburg. Edward and Myron Adams had been discharged and had enlisted as 1st and 2nd Lieutenants in the 2nd U.S. Colored Infantry and later the U.S. Volunteer Signal Corps. George Wright Sheldon, Class of '63, would be killed in September, while serving as Captain, 6th U.S. Colored Infantry.[7]

Morris's letters would reveal not only how much he missed his older brother, but his relief that his brother was not present for the bloody combat that was about to begin. Morris also was battling on another front. In the first week of April, his father and attorney D. B. Prosser were suing "agent Ebenezer B. Jones" on Morris's behalf, asking the court to compel specific performance of a contract by the defendant. While the details are unknown, it appears that the younger Brown had purchased a twenty-five acre plot in the Town of Milo and was suing Jones to compel compliance with his part of the bargain. Clearly the ambitious younger Brown was promoting his postwar future.[8]

Despite a flood of circulars and dispatches from headquarters and the lengthening of picket lines along the Rappahannock, which created an extra sense of urgency in camp, Morris was in a playful mood in early April. Not even the cancellation of furloughs and the April 8 instructions not to reveal to the press anything about the "near approach of . . . active operations" seemed to destroy that mood.[9]

[Partial letter n. d. to parents, but after April 5, 1864.]

commenced to think of the short time I had to remain & to dread the time for starting. I want Jennie, if Josie Eaton has not left Penn Yan yet to go & thank her, for her kindness to me while there. She did really exert herself for my benefit & I am just the one to feel grateful for it. I believe I would fall in love with her if it was not for the trouble I had with Frank _undage when we lived at Hammondsport for the sleepless nights which I then passed frightened ___ even when I think of such a thing as ____. And there's the widow too. La me.

Our boxes have not come yet. I dont know why. It seems to me it's high time they were here.

We are looking anxiously for those sausages &c. Perhaps I will get home again sometime in the spring. I guess I can if I choose too. Well I will see about it. I guess though ten days in a year is enough. I dont like to see an officer in the service of the United States who is drawing his regular pay lounging about home one half or more of his time. Twenty or thirty days ought to satisfy anyone. Tell Emma[?] Franklin I will send her one of my vignettes when I receive them but dont either of you now go & give her one for I may change my mind.

Smith seems to be very well—exceedingly so. Will write the girls a long letter in a day or two.

Love to Lizzie.
Your Aff. Son
Morris

P.S.

Hand this piece of paper to Mr. Jones & tell him as the fellow said who had his prayer pinned to the bed post in cold weather "them's my sentiments."

I guess you need'nt say anything to Ellis about the pictures. I will write him

I want Jennie to thank Mrs. Charley Hamlin for coming over to the depot to see me off. Now dont neglect this.

"Rogy"

I have given Mr. Ellis direction to let you have the large photographs, but none of the small ones.

Capt.

But he was not playful about his desire for promotion, as his letters increasingly reveal.

In Camp
April 7th 1864

Father

Smith tells me he forwarded a recommendation to Gov.
[Horatio] Seymour for [John] Randolph to be 2nd Lt. of
my company. If you have it, keep it until further orders. I
would rather have Sergt. [Ira Hart] Wilder if I can get him.
If [military committeeman Darius] Ogden has not gone to
Albany yet start him off immediately. If he succeeds, I will
pay him well. Be sure and have him prep those grounds I
wrote about yesterday.

Have him tell the Gov. [that] Baird recommended
Munson simply because he is from Geneva & not through
any military motives whatever.[10]

I wont be under Munson. No sir! If [Captain Winfield]
Scott or [Captain Charles] Richardson got it I would not
care so much; but I cannot & will not remain in this Regt.
if Munson is placed over me.

Seems to me that if Angel and Post should go to the
Gov. and tell him that they are republicans but recommended
a democrat because they know him to be meritorious, it would
have a good deal of influence with the Gov.

At any rate give Ogden and Sunderlin Genl [Joshua]
Owens letter and start them off to Albany, for I would rather
spend that much money & be satisfied, than always to be
thinking that perhaps I might have secured the commission
by a little more work than otherwise would be accomplished
or expended.

What do you think of my going into a darkey Regt?
Answer definitely.

Your Aff son
Morris

Put these pictures in my album Dont allow them to lie around
the house

Ever ambitious, Morris Brown was not about to let fate determine his future. Nor was he prone to cloak his feelings about his regimental comrades. So, he appealed to his father, the district military committeeman, to work behind the scenes. But it was too late to block Randolph's promotion, which had, in fact, already occurred. Moreover, Randolph was made first lieutenant, effective April 1, though Wilder would be promoted first lieutenant in August. Brown's dislike of Randolph and Munson becomes clearer in his April 21 letter. He desperately wanted the majority of the regiment, a post coming vacant with his brother's promotion, and he wanted his father to spare no effort.

Despite attempts by Grant, the new army commander, and others to eliminate this practice, many promotions were still political. Efforts to examine candidates for promotion had been underway for some time, but they had not—and would not—rid the army of incompetent officers. This would stick in Morris's craw as it would in others'. Wrangling would continue, but over time combat attrition would come to be a greater determinant of rank than political pull.

The next day, Morris was writing home again to retrieve critical papers he had left home when on recruiting duty.

In Camp
April 8/64

Father

You know I left a bundle of Ordinance Returns at home which I wished carefully forwarded. I brought them down stairs one morning when I came to breakfast. Well I want you to get that bundle and hunt up the part marked 4th Quarter 1863, down in left hand corner, and "pick out" the papers with this printed on the top "Triplicate to be retained by the officer signing this Return" and inside at the bottom you will find Column marked "On hand to be accounted for in regt Return" Copy this part very carefully and send it to me by return mail. For instance (So many) Springfield Rifled Muskets Cal. 58 " " [ditto] Bayonet Scabbards &c. &c. &c.

It is very necessary that you should be exact for all my future rations will depend upon it. Make the figures very plain

If you dont understand take the papers to Capt Root and tell him I want the amount (on my return for 4th Quarter 1863) I dont see why I did'nt copy it myself, but I did'nt.

Send it immediately for its high time my return for 1st Qr. 1864 was sent in.

Recd one months pay to day & will send $100 to Stark which if not spent in getting in a commission will go toward Sheppard mortgage. Guess I will be examined for colored regiment. Shall not remain here if Munson is made Maj.

Will resign and go so far West first that I cannot get home without making enough money to pay such expenses.

Your Aff Son
Morris

Brown's sense of urgency was real and seemingly justified. First, as company commander he was responsible for all equipment issued to his company. That is, he had to pay for losses. For example, if a member of his company deserted, he would be charged $30 for clothing per deserter. It was imperative that he make an accurate accounting. The second cause for urgency was the bustling around in camp, increased discipline, greater secrecy, and reorganizational changes which portended imminent resumption of the fighting. The next day, April 9, General Grant informed Army of the Potomac commander Meade of his plans to move "all the armies . . . toward one common center." Grant had already directed Major General Nathaniel Banks to prepare to take Mobile, though he realized that it would take almost a month for Banks to assemble his scattered forces. General William T. Sherman was to coordinate his move to oppose Confederate General Johnston and take Georgia along with Meade's move south. General Franz Sigel would move to control the Upper Shenandoah Valley, while General Burnside's IX Corps was directed to reinforce Meade, combined with naval operations on the James River. Then, to Meade the clincher: *"Lee's army will be your objective point. Wherever Lee goes, there you will be also."* [Italics added.][11]

Yet, four days later, when nothing had happened, Morris again wrote home about three apparently untended matters. First, he wanted action on his lawsuit against "Agent" Jones. Second, he was tired of supporting his older brother, Theodore. More important, he wanted to know what was happening back home for his promotion, which offered a command equal to his perceived leadership–and more money for his postwar plans.

In Camp
Wednesday
13th April 1864

Well my dear parents I have not heard from home yet since I arrived in camp except through a letter which Smith had from you last night & through Aunt Sarah's letters to the Dr. [Hammond]

Aunt Sarah writes that Jim Longwell and Mr. Jones had a great quarrell over our lawsuit—that Jones told Jim he swore falsely &c. &c.

Seems to me if I were in Jim Longwells place I would'nt allow a man to talk that way to me.

Well Jones undoubtedly will get in trouble on all sides. He ought to. he wont be any the less rascall, even though the law beats us. Perhaps if we beat him he will carry it higher—if he does—meet him. How long will it be before the present trial will be settled?

I want you to write me all the particulars.

You write that you sent Theodore $75 which you expect us to pay as soon as possible. Now that you have sent the money of course we will pay it; but he wrote us for it, and I woud'nt send it. He must support himself hereafter.

[Then he got to the meat of his letter—his promotion:]

If Munson is made Major I intend to go before the board in Washington to be examined for a Field Officers commission in a darkey Regiment & if I fail then I am bound to resign, &, if I should resign I will need every cent I can possibly save between now & that time. Dont draw on Stark for any more money for Thede. You see how I am situated. I have only six or eight men left in my command (the rest have been taken for a Provost Guard at Corps Head Qrs.) and I am unwilling to remain here & only command from five to ten men, or to expose my life leading that number of men into battle.

They have taken so many men out of our regiment for this Provost Guard that now there are only about six men left to each officer (average).

Write me just exactly what you think of the matter providing it comes to a resignation. I can gain no more honor by remaining here with these few men, than I already have, & as for staying just for the pay I cant do it. Any young man who has any snap whatever can get in some kind of business which will be permanent, and I might as well commence now, as to wait until our regiment is mustered out (Aug. 1865)

If I remain I dont believe I will ever save anything. I can go to Idaho, New Mexico, California or even to the East Indies and come back to Penn Yan all on the square in a few years. I never would settle down in Yates Co. unless I could have some capital to commence with, & to have a good beginning.

You see now how the matter stands, & I want your opinion & advice freely expressed

Now dont be bashful. Tell [me] just what you think, & that plainly. It all depends on whether I get a commission as Major or not. Exert yourselves and do what you can for me and if you fail then we will try something else. [Colonel] Bull is not out of the service yet, but will be the latter part of this week or the first of next. When Bulls papers are back there I will telegraph you "Charles [Richardson] is better" so that if Ogden should receive any encouragement from the Gov. this time him and Sunderlin can both go when the Gov. receives notice of Bulls resignation being accepted. It wont do any harm anyway to send the telegram.

Have a petition signed by the prominent democrats of Yates County if you think it will do any good. It will be safe to tell the Gov. that Munson bought Bairds recommendation, and that he is a bitter republican.

Seems to me you ought to be successful. Cant you tell the Gov. just what kind of a man Baird is and influence him in that way? [Quartermaster] Loring goes in strong for me & says when he gets to Albany (He is absent on sick leave) he will go to Miller (the Inspector General on [Governor]

Seymours staff) and tell him exactly how matters stand—that I ought to be made Maj. so as to give some character to the Regiment. It is all whiskey now. Do what you can.

Morris

And he was at it again, two weeks later. A new competitor for the majority of the 126th had emerged. Morris's tone was even more strident.

Camp of 126th Regt. N.Y.Vols.
3d Brig. 1st Div. 2d A. C.
April 21st 1864

Received your real good, long letter last night, my dear mother, and right glad was I too, for just think, here it is over three

Lt. Col. William Baird (*Source:* New York State Adjutant General's Office)

"You Can Bet We Are Going to Have a Terrible Battle" / 113

weeks since I left home, and this the first and only letter from you.

Seems to me it is very singular you hav'nt heard from me for I have written two or three times since I arrived at the regiment. It is only yesterday I was over to Dr. Hammonds tent and he [was] asking me if I had heard from home when I told him no, and added that I was'nt going to write another letter till I received one, said he should suppose they could or ought to write you oftener. Well I think so too.

I think is very singular pa does not write me about that lawsuit—how it passed off and what the prospects are—giving full particulars. Also what the Gov. said when he ^Ogden^ visited him &c, &c—who the prominent candidates are and all about it. Now I want to know all about these things. [Newly promoted Company B] Capt. [Richard] Bassett tells me Mr. Sunderlin is trying to get him a commission as Major of this Regt. If that is so of course he is'nt appointing me. Now seems to me if Mr. Ogden should take hold of this matter correctly, he get Mr. Sunderlin to aid me, even though he may prefer Bassett. They must write on some man or they certainly cant do anything with the Gov. When he sees so much strife between applicants from the same county he will think neither of them amounts to much. If Ogden received any encouragement from the Gov. I want him to go to Albany again and if Sunderlin can be fixed all right have him go too. It will certainly be too bad if any such man as Capt. Munson is made Major of this Regt. When that is done, then there is no doubt in my mind but the 126th Regt has seen its best days.

Neither of them^ Baird or Munson^ have character or stamina enough to sustain the reputation of a setting hen As long as Smith [Brown] stays here then I can remain contentedly, but when he goes then I go.

Nothing in this world, next to entering Richmond, would please me as much as to be able to go back to Geneva with this Regt when its three years are up, & it is mustered out of the service. Would'nt that be a proud day? I am confident that I have done my duty, as well as I know how; and now if

Munson is made Major it is more than I am willing to bear. Munson was not with us at all during the Gettysburg campaign. He has been absent sick about one half of the time since the Regt left Centreville. Now if the ones who have been through the thick and thin are going to be set aside for some local benefits, then they want to count me out. Capt. Scott and I are the only two Capts in the Regt who have not spent more or less of their time absent in Genl Hosptl or home on sick leave. I would a great deal rather he would be made Major than Munson although I so thoroughly despise him.

I think mother you have a wrong idea about these colored troops. You know there is no one who more heartily despises a darkey than I do that is a worthless, shiftless, good for nothing nigger.[12]

But then you take a Regt. of them and properly drill and discipline them & if you dont have a good Regt. its your own fault. I have sent in my application for examination, & am posting up hard & if I can get a Major commission I will take it. If I make a good officer I will be promoted. then I think the darkeys are going to retained after this war is over, and then if a fellow has a Major or Lt. Cols. or Col's commission he is all on the square. A salary from eighteen hundred to twenty five hundred is not to be sneezed at. The officers who go into Colored Regts are as far as I have any knowledge the very best officers in the army. You can tell that from the severe examination which they have to pass before that board of which Maj. Genl. [Silas] Casey is president. Then I will come home and get married. Who to? Jennie I want you to Exert yourself, Jennie, to provide for me Eva Harris' address! Send it to me immediately. Try hard! Work fast! Do your duty!

When you write anything about Sam Hammond or anything the kind, always write it on a separate piece of paper for Dr. always reads all of your letters.

Write *often*
Your aff. son Morris.

[On the edge of first page:]

__ book "What will he do with it" by Bulwer to Frank Smith. Send ____ home with Dr. Hammonds overcoat Dont neglect the book! Since the Sutlers left we are having pretty hard fare. Ham & pork with __ little pork and ham now and then, is "our all."

It will take me a good while to recover from my delightful visit home. A person can not tell what the events of this life consist of until he is compelled to live as we have since we came into the army.

Capt. Winfield Scott (*Source:* Interlaken Historical Society)

This is the unexpurgated Morris Brown. He would accept another's promotion—even of C Company Captain Winfield Scott, who he despised—if merited. And, like many of his comrades, Brown was a warrior, not an abolitionist. Apparently his mother had tried to discourage him from applying for command of an African-American regiment. His use of the offensive, but commonplace, term *nigger* underscores his feelings as well. Yet, he had such confidence in his leadership—and indirectly in African-Americans—that he claimed he could make a regiment composed of them as successful as any. And, probably not surprising for a young man in his prime, Morris shows a love interest. But this is the first mention of marriage in extant letters. It is unclear whether this was a genuine desire or simply his fulfilling expectations for nineteenth-century American males. Above all, however, he wants a command commensurate with his experience and leadership for the upcoming campaign.

Morris's sense of impending battle was prescient, though possibly no greater than any officer observing the increased activity in camp. He expected a battle within two weeks. And he correctly predicted the bloody harshness. However, he failed to mention that he was headed to Washington that day and "expects to be Lt. Col. in a negro regiment," according to Captain Richard Bassett, then on provost duty at division headquarters. But Morris simply ended the letter with the soldier's usual lament: not enough letters from home.[13]

Camp of 126th N.Y. Vols.
Sunday afternoon
April 24th 1864

My dear parents

I must write but have nothing to say. I want this vignette of Bill Long to be placed in my album for safe keeping. Now do not let it lay around there on the table a week or two. If you hav'nt yet had my picture framed take it to Geo. Cornwells if he has a frame which will correspond with those you have already but if not take it to Elliss and have it done immediately.

Great preparations are being made for a forward movement. Everything is being sent to the rear—that is to Washington.

To night it looks as though we were going to have a terrible storm. If so, it will probably delay operations for some days. Undoubtedly before another Sunday unless this storm delays us the greatest battle of the war will have been fought.

This army was never in a better condition & we all have the greatest confidence in Grant.

Two weeks at the farthest will in my judgement see the pending battle fought. I dont relish it much I can assure you. I have seen enough of it—not to be anxious as I was when we were at Centreville.

A great many must fall. I wonder who in this Regt.

Baird starts for home to morrow with his wife—sick.

Put in for my commission before he gets to Geneva or the people there will help him to have Munson appointed Major.

Dont leave a stone uncovered but make a thorough trial and then if we are worsted we will try something else. One thing is certain. If I have any honor left—any self respect or any respect—for my friends I will never remain here under Baird & Munson, & that too when my company is down to seven privates for duty. Jennie has'nt sent me Eva Harris address yet. I do not want her to neglect this a single day.

You dont write often enough

Morris

Brown's next letter also shows the building tension. Though wanting to command a regiment, he had "seen the elephant" at Harpers Ferry, Gettysburg, Auburn, and Bristoe. He was all too aware that his chances of surviving diminished with each battle.

Camp near Stevensburg
May 1st 1864

My dearest sister Jennie

I was very glad I assure you to receive your good long letter of April 24th and am led to believe that my last visit home is going to be some some benefit anyway—that I will receive more letters from home than I used to.

You all speak of having such stormy weather up there. I cant see how it can be possible for we have been having such beautiful weather here—I never saw finer in my life. The peach and plum trees have been in full bloom nearly ever since I returned. The grass is green and looks beautifully and everything begins to look and seem as though Spring was here in full force.

I almost wish it would rain here, for every day of fine weather brings us nearer to the terrible battle which must be fought here in Virginia ere many days passed around. You can bet I aint "spiling for a fight" as I used to be when encamped at Centreville a year ago. I have seen enough. The more battles a person gets in, the more he dreads the next. The only wonder to me now is, how anyone escapes unharmed.

This army is being placed in the best possible trim now, and we are receiving heavy re-inforcements constantly. [Maj. Gen. Ambrose] Burnsides whole [IX] Corps numbering forty or fifty thousand men have joined the Army of the Potomac besides a great many Regts which have been on detached service in forts in different portions of the northern states.

I dont believe this army was ever in as good a fighting condition as at present or it will be when we advance.

If Genl Lee has an army large enough to engage us this side of the defenses of Richmond, you can bet we are going to have a terrible battle. I hope and trust we will beat him, and that so badly so that an end to this war will soon come.

If I can only live to see Richmond ours & be able to return to Geneva with this regiment, if there aint more than twenty five of us left, I will be satisfied; and will feel that our effort[s] have not been in vain.

As I said in one of my former letters, one cannot tell what the "beauties" of this life are until he lives in the army a year or two. Everyone who is disatisfied with his condition while living at the north should be compelled to enlist & serve three years in the army. I will warrant that when his time is out—he will return home satisfied, & with a disposition to grumble less than when he left home.

How I would love to pick out a company of one hundred men there in Penn Yan and bring them down here to the front, and compel 'em to march around Virginia, with me, through mud and rain this summer. You can well guess where I would commence.

It will be terrible lonesome here now. Smith has really gone for good. I dont expect I will see him with this Regt again, unless he should meet us at Geneva when our time expires and we go home to be mustered out.[14]

But I am glad he has gone for now he has a magnificent situation as well as a place where his health will undoubtedly improve. I dont believe he could have stood another summers campaign.

Why dont you send me Eva Harris address! Seems to me you ought to put yourself to a little inconvenience to obtain and send it to me.

Now Jennie write me again. Dont let this letter suffice for all summer; but write me once a week. You have nothing else to do & if you could appreciate how much I love to hear from you. I know [as we?] advance then I will have very little time to write & that with no conveniences whatever. Have to write on my knee or a stump. Now dont forget to obtain for me Eva Harris address immediately.

I want you Jennie to take this photograph to Mrs. Judd and tell her I sent it to her, because she always met me so cordially when home last.

Will write to [sister] Lina to morrow.

The next correspondence was a hasty note without salutation and signed simply "Good by!!" The expected, but dreaded, command to move out had been given.

May 3d 1864 4. P.M.

We march to night immediately after dark & will probably be *in front* of the rebel army to morrow or next day.

I am in command of the Regt & have everything to
do. Good by!!

Morris

Now Brown had the chance to lead that he had so ardently sought
earlier. It was a heady moment and heavy responsibility for a twenty-
two-year-old. Also how it came about is a bit of a mystery. With his
brother in Wisconsin and Lt. Colonel Baird absent, Captain Winfield
Scott outranked Brown (time in grade). And, as he wrote, he had
"everything to do" to ready the regiment for the long-awaited spring
campaign. Rations and ammunition had to be distributed, wagons had
to be loaded with provisions for a march of indefinite length, company
commanders had to be apprised of what lay ahead—at least as far as
Brown was aware—supplies had to be accounted for, and thousands of
seemingly minor details had to be attended. The noise and bustle alone
were troubling signs. Teams of horses snorted, their drivers cracked
their whips, and the general confusion contributed to an unease that
accompanied a campaign.[15]

Seven hours after scribbling the brief note, Brown, appointed acting
126th New York commander only three days earlier, was headed toward
Lee's Army of Northern Virginia. During that dark night, sounds were
magnified. The tramp, tramp, tramp of feet and the rattling of canteens
seemed louder, more ominous, than during the day. Then after crossing
the Rapidan River at Ely's Ford about 8:00 a.m. the marchers confronted
crowded roads. Two hours later the head of the column dropped to the
ground near the Chancellor House, which marked a Federal disaster
almost exactly a year earlier.

What General Meade would come to label "Epoch One" of the
Spring Campaign had begun. Grant intended to interpose the Army of
the Potomac between Lee's Army of Northern Virginia and Richmond. It
was a big task—and a gamble. He had to maneuver close to seventy-five
thousand men and four thousand trailing wagon trains through fifteen
miles of scrub forest known as the Wilderness. The V Corps, commanded
by General Warren, and the VI, led by Major General "Uncle" John
Sedgwick, were headed toward Germanna Ford, where they would cross
the Rapidan River before turning west on the Orange and Fredericksburg
Turnpike. To reduce overcrowding on the narrow roads the II Corps,

once more commanded by General Hancock, was sent farther east, after which it was to drop down below the Orange Plank Road and loop west. Then the three corps were to follow parallel roads and confront Lee in open country, where, as Morris Brown had alluded, the Federals had the numerical advantage.

Early on May 5 General Grant was relieved that the three corps had safely crossed the Rapidan, but shortly thereafter his plans went awry. General Richard Ewell's three divisions smacked into Warren's V Corps, forcing the latter hurriedly to engage his men in a battle for which he was unprepared. General Sedgwick was equally startled. Almost simultaneously A. P. Hill's Corps marched east on the parallel Orange Plank Road, bent on trapping the two Union corps between his and Ewell's corps. Meade had to hastily reroute Hancock's men so they could secure the intersection of the Plank and Brock Roads before Hill arrived. To Captain Morris Brown and others in the II Corps, it seemed to be the usual army blundering: march and countermarch.

While Hancock hurried to connect three divisions with Warren's in the heavy underbrush south of the Turnpike, he detached General Barlow's division to occupy high ground where artillery could be positioned. Barlow's Third Brigade, including Brown's 126th New York now commanded by Colonel Paul Frank, was instructed to hold the junction of the Orange Plank and Brock Roads. Meanwhile, the combatants fought almost blindly in that tangled Wilderness. At best, Warren and Sedgwick held on, but Longstreet's Corps, which had not arrived, could well determine the outcome if reinforcements from Burnside's IX Corps were delayed. Behind hastily constructed breastworks, Captain Morris Brown's inactive regiment listened to firing that wailed like a tempest and nervously fingered their weapons. A gloom descended upon them at nightfall.[16]

Later, he recalled for brother Smith how they lay in the breastworks along the Brock Road and awaited the attack, which began May 6, for the Confederate prisoners had said they must have the intersection of the Orange Plank Road and the Brock Road or they were whipped.

Grant hoped that an early morning attack the next day, May 6, would not only extricate the Federals, but would result in victory.

At daylight the most furious musketry commenced that ever I heard. Oh! how it did rattle. About 7 a.m. we were ordered in

& away we went throughout that terrible wilderness—coud'nt see ten rods in front of us.

Initially it appeared Hancock's hopes would be realized. He was elated when his men blunted, then pushed Hill's corps back close to a mile, but his success was short lived.

Well we drove the rebs at least a mile & a half, but they being hurriedly re-inforced [by Longstreet's Corps about 10:00 a.m. which] drove us clear back [on the Plank Road] behind our breast works & charged us again & again—planting their colors on our works.

This fight commenced at daylight & lasted till dark All musketry—not a cannon was fired. The wilderness is so dense that cannon could not be used. This day the 126th lost 71 killed & wounded out of our 180. Such musketry I never heard!!!!¹⁷

[Late that night, the bloody two-day battle ended.]

Though the battle was at best a standoff, Brown, now commanding both the 126th and the 125th New York (in the absence of the latter's commander), attested to the bitter fighting in which they, the only brigade in Barlow's division, were engaged.

Ten miles below Chancellorsville
Thursday 2 P.M. May 6th

My dear parents

Broke camp at Stevensburg Tuesday eve & marched all that night & next day till noon & reached Chancellorsville.

Encamped on those historic grounds for the night—within twenty rods of the Chancellorsville town itself. Yesterday marched nearly all day around our place [?] & another until we finally halted near where we are now about twelve oclock last night.

This morning our Brigade was thrown forward about a mile & a half when we very hotly engaged the rebels until every field officer in the Brigade was either killed or wounded but the Major of the 39th N.Y. Vols, when they charged on us and drove us back the whole distance

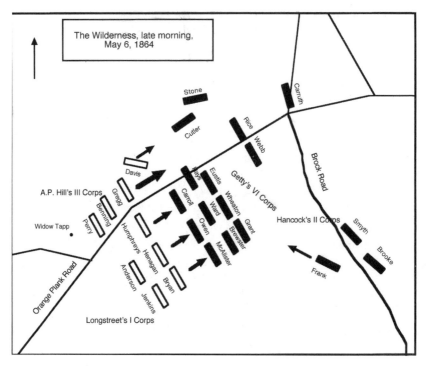

The Wilderness, late morning, May 6, 1864 (*Source:* Wayne Mahood)

I am in command of the Regiment. I have only one Sergt & five Privates left in my Company. The Regt is about in the same proportion.

A terrible battle has been fought to day with no apparent advantage to either side as I can discover. They are fighting *now* very hard to our right [the Orange Plank Road] & the indications are that we will soon be called upon to resist an attack, & one which promises to be very heavy. How this thing is to come out we cant tell yet of course.

If the rebs attack us where we are we can repulse them I think—without doubt.

Our loss has been very heavy. Who next will fall? Good bye—Good bye

Morris

Brown's listing of casualties to the *Yates County Chronicle* the next day attested to the ferocity of the fighting. Indeed, as he would write later, "The battle of May 6th was a terrible one." The Union counted 17,666 casualties; the Confederates, an estimated 7750. Brown's list of casualties in the 126th New York took virtually an entire column in Penn Yan's newspaper. Six men were killed, fifty-five were wounded, and ten were missing. The losses, more than a third of those in the regiment who were engaged, were fairly evenly distributed. Six of the wounds suffered by eight men in his Company A were severe, including that of Sergeant Phineas Tyler, whose right arm was amputated. Yet, Brown claimed "We whipped 'em."[18]

But, in an abrupt break from the past, there was no rest for the two opposing forces. Unlike his predecessors, General Grant did not withdraw his army and allow it to lick its wounds. Instead, he intended "to fight it out on this line if it takes all summer."[19]

CHAPTER 6

"Fight All Day and March All Night"

As Northerners and Southerners alike came to realize, the naturally reticent General Grant was a man of his word. Though he proclaimed his intent privately, he meant to pursue Lee's Army of Northern Virginia relentlessly. And his troops would pay the price. As Captain Morris Brown, the 126th New York's commander, wrote to his parents back home in Penn Yan on May 16, "What a terrible campaign this has been." But, unknown to him, the campaign had just begun. It would be waged with only an occasional letup for another month, when Grant laid siege to Petersburg. Thereafter the Army of the Potomac's battles, however deadly, would be described more accurately as "continuous skirmishes."

In his subsequent letters, beginning on May 16, Brown vividly relates the agony he and his comrades suffered in this spring campaign, including the battle near Spotsylvania Court House on May 12. Though not as deadly for his outfit as the Battle of the Wilderness, it was murderous. Even prior to Spotsylvania, at the Po River, Brown's regiment came close to annihilation.

The campaign's Epoch Two began almost immediately after the Wilderness Battle, with another night march toward Spotsylvania Court House, near the Richmond and Fredericksburg Railroad and the hub of a number of radiating roads. Grant intended to outrace Lee's Army of Northern Virginia and force a fight in the open. Hancock's II Corps began the advance down the Brock Road at approximately 6:00 a.m. on May 8. The corps had scarcely begun when it was confronted by A. P. Hill's Corps at Todd's Tavern, where Barlow's Division, including Colonel Paul Frank's Third Brigade, was briefly engaged on May 9. The

127

next day the Confederates advanced in force on Barlow's Division near the Po River, resulting in another deadly engagement.

On the tenth, General Hancock spotted a Confederate wagon train and redirected his corps to attack, but the Po River proved an obstacle to a successful engagement. So, the corps, minus Barlow's division, was directed to withdraw back across the Po. Now isolated, the division, including Brown's regiment, was ordered to skirmish with Confederate General Henry Heth's division to allow the other divisions to withdraw. Skirmishing was dangerous duty, one that most Union soldiers never performed. Those who did, knew well the perils of skirmishing: "where soldiers were thrown largely on their individual resources . . . where every advantage was taken of the nature of the ground, of fences, trees, stones, and prostrate logs; where manhood rose to its maximum and mechanism sank to its minimum, and where almost anything seemed possible to vigilance, audacity, and cool self-possession." There was barely time to throw up entrenchments to meet Heth's advance, which was emboldened when the brigades of Brigadier Generals Nelson Miles and Thomas Smythe safely recrossed the river.[1]

Captain Brown lamented that "this was the worst place I ever was in yet—for the rebs outnumbered [us] so much that they nearly encircled us before we gave away and then the only way we escaped being taken prisoner was—the woods in our rear were afire and we plunged through this and the smoke being so thick they were afraid to follow us." Though prone to exaggerate, Brown was not guilty here. One Union soldier recalled that at one point "Our men were falling like game before hunters."[2]

Once safely across, Brown and his men uttered a collective sigh of relief. Hancock was unusually complimentary: "Their right and rear enveloped by the burning woods, their front assailed by overwhelming numbers of the enemy, the withdrawal of the troops was attended with extreme difficulty and peril." Their "unyielding courage . . . their . . . steadiness in the presence of dangers so appalling" merited "the highest praise."[3]

However, with barely a moment's rest, the race to Spotsylvania resumed.

General Grant intended to engage the enemy at the first good opportunity. Unfortunately, almost miraculously Lee's Army of Northern Virginia won the race to Spotsylvania Court House and quickly entrenched. Still, Grant believed this was as good a place and time as any to destroy Lee's army and the Confederacy. However, like too many battles, whatever could go wrong for the Federals, did. First, there was inadequate reconnaissance. Second, the heavy, early morning fog on May 12 obscured the target. (The combination led General Barlow, expressing a "forlorn hope" for success, to hand over his personal effects to a friend.) And finally, there was the spirited last-minute Confederate counterattack.[4]

At first, the battle went well for the Union. Grant massed his troops at a single point, the so-called Mule Shoe. Hancock's II Corps was ordered to lead the attack. After a half-hour postponement to gain some visibility, Barlow's men, forming the advance, attacked, hitting the east angle of the Mule Shoe. They tore at the abatis, the pointed wooden sticks aimed at the enemy, and sent the Confederates into a wholesale retreat. The entire Confederate line was threatened, but the massing of Union columns resulted in a debilitating confusion and allowed a Confederate counterattack. What had portended so well for the Union became a furious dogfight, possibly the war's most serious hand-to-hand combat.

Morris Brown's letters tell the story from a combatant's perspective, and though tending to be repetitive, they reveal how much he wanted to tell the story of the ordeal he had been—and was—undergoing. However, the detail he offered depended on the intended correspondent, for he claimed to have had "a peculiar aversion" to describing to his parents what he had experienced.

Near Spotsylvania Court House
May 16th 1864.

My dear parents

Well, this is the first days real rest we have had since we left our camp at Stevensburg. the rebels seem to have evacuated the strong position where we have been fighting them for the last three or four days & to be, moving off—for everything seems to be very down on our part.

*What a *terrible campaign* this has been. You up there will never know what we have passed through. We cant tell it let alone writing it. We fought the enemy more or less every day for ten days & with the exception of the day they drove our division across the river Po we have whipped them *every* time that is as far as I know.[5]

I suppose the newspapers will be full of accounts of the great charge made by the 2d Corps on the 12th of May. It was grand but terrible. There were twenty thousand men all massed which moved against the enemys strongest position. We captured twenty two guns & six thousand prisoners. It will be one of the greatest charges in the history of the world.

I was hit in this charge just as I was on top of the enemys rifle pits. My knee is getting along*

Well Lovin' I have requested a few leisure moments of your time in correspondence with me and you have kindly acquiesced—now what can I write to most interest you. There are so many different subjects to choose from now-a-days that one, in the *beginning*, hardly knows how or when to commence. If I should follow the dictations of my concience or rather if I should write about those things which at present interest me most I am afraid my letters would be filled with to much of the horrible & terrifying to suit the tastes of those less accustomed to these awful scenes, than we who are hourly *compelled* to witness them. While I can hardly divert my thoughts from the terrible scenes I have passed through during the last thirty five days together with a realizing sense of what may be expected in the future you in your peaceful house with its many pleasant associations can think & will of those reminiscences of your bygone days which so often & memory so distinctly recalls, even amid the excitement & confusion of battle.

It seems to be almost an impossibility for me to think or write of anything excepting in relation to the terrible scenes I have been hourly compelled to witness for the last thirty five days & still I have a *peculiar* aversion describing them—for what reason I hardly know

You may think it very singular that I should express the above sentiments so freely but it is not. If you could realize a one millionth part of the difference between our conditions here & when at home I know you would not think it strange that I would be willing to write the above a *certain duty*, which

I think every young man owes to his country at this time, alone *compells* me to remain here and I am not ashamed to say that this kind of life has but few pleasures for me. I believe I should feel ashamed to remain at home during these perilous times. But I'm afraid I am writing to much "on the melancholy" & unless I can write of something else I will certainly have to tell a story. You will at once observe in my epistle that I always write *first what* I think perhaps too much so sometimes but it is not "my style" to dive down into the depths of the rolling billows, or get lost in the shady groves, or roam about over the waving meadows &c &c to find something to write about, but to talk English according to Blair & ask for charity. Just think! I hav'nt spoken a word to a single female since I left home *that* Monday morning & I must add that I deem the loss of society our greatest privation, for here we have none whatever not even gentlemen & one can never realize this position until there.

How I would love to be in P.Y. during the pleasant summer months when boat rides, picnics &c predominate. Well we propose to take Richmond this summer if Grant *only* merits our expectations; and then next summer we can all be home & then—whew! what a time we will have Wont we make up for lost time eh?

By that time we will fully learn what real pleasure is and act accordingly.

Am glad you liked Cudjos Cave. I did not read it. only saw it very highly mentioned. did'nt really know its character. Should judge from what you say that it is similar to Uncle Toms Cabin. If so seems to me I should not like it much. Am glad Aunty Franklin is flourishing so finely. Wonder if she has entirely recovered from her trip to Elmira. Guess not.[6]

*For the last week have been having a pretty nice time here in the army—that is we have been acting purely on the defensive & therefore no fighting of any consequence has taken place. yet there has been constant skirmishing between the two lines & this keeps us close to *mother earth*, for we are so near the "Johnnys" if a person desires to gratify his curiosity by a sly peep at the "____" he first wants to make peace with his Maker for the moment a man lifts his head, away goes that man into eternity. *We are literally living, as it were, in our own graves* [emphasis added], for every man has excavated for himself a hole in the ground about two feet deep to escape the fire of the enemy which would be instant destruction were he to remain on the surface. We have to get in these pits before daylight in the morning & remain there till after night without moving hardly.

Is'nt it pleasant. how I wish you could witness some of our "doings" down here, when the life of a man is not as much valued as that of a good mule. But "the end is not yet" A few weeks more will undoubtedly determine whether this war is to end this summer or continue indefinitely. Our Regt. is now reduced to some forty odd privates "present for duty" with eleven officers. You can see at once that our several commands are very limited & not in accordance with our rank. This sometimes leads me to wish that I might honorably resign & go into some other branch of the service, or rather into some other regiment where one would feel that he was repaying the government for its bountiful pay & emoluments.

I sometimes feel that I was not doing my duty even in remaining here for I only have five men left in my company present. ~~I had eighteen when we crossed the Rapidan. the rest have been killed & wounded.~~

Send me all the daily papers from May 4th to the end of the fight.

Here Morris was unusually reflective, sharply contrasting with his past, more aggressive, positive letters. He had just fought one of the war's bloodiest battles, Spotsylvania. The war was taking a toll.

Whatever "aversion" Morris had to describing events vanished when he wrote brother Smith, as the next letter reveals.

May 19th 1864 6 a.m.

My dear brother

Last night we received a few letters for the first time since we broke camp & among them three of yours of the 7th inst.

Capt. [Robert] Seabury was killed in the wilderness, so I took back your horse—paying Genl [Joshua T.] Owen the $25 he had advanced & sold him to Q.M. [John K.] Loring on the same terms. Is it right?[7]

I would have kept him but we have been cut down to three & five pds of oats per day & I was unwilling to run the risk of loss.

Talk about campaigns. Gettysburg was not a circumstance to this so far. With the last two days exceptions we have had no rest at all.

If this rain storm had not come up I dont know what we would have done for we were just about exhausted.

We have lost 116 out of the number we had when at Stevensburg = 2/3 Gen Owen was not wounded. [General Alexander]Hays was killed. Four of his staff were killed & three wounded. [Capt. James] Sullivan was the only one who escaped unhurt.[8]

[Brown was not exaggerating. The II Corps had lost 11,553 men since May 5.]

I left Stevensburg with 15 in my company & 10 of them are gone. Sergt [Phineas] Tyler lost his right arm. [Pvt. Francis] Pool his right hand & part of his left. [Sgt. Smith] Fuller probably will die. He was wounded & lay inside the rebel lines for two days [.] [W]hen we were driving them away we came across him. [Lt. Col. William] Baird has returned. he was here in time for the big fight yesterday & did very well too.[9] We are now temporarily consolidated with the 125th. Col. Meyers [the 125th New York's Lt. Col. Aaron Myers] was killed. Every field officer who started with us (in our brigade) has been wounded or killed. Our Regt has been in five terrible battles besides all the little skirmishing which you know is not foolishness.

Capt. [Henry] Owen was killed. Capt. [Ira] Munson was mortally wounded. Lt. [George A.] Sherman wounded & taken prisoner or dead on the field. I was hit on the right knee—in the great charge made by our corps on the 12th inst. just as I mounted their first line of breastworks. It kept me back a couple of days & is quite painful at times since.[10]

I believe Grant will have to pull back & give this job up as a bad one. I dont believe we have advanced a foot in a week. Yesterday morning our Division charged a place where the charge [?] could'nt get over if there was'nt a man behind it & of course was repulsed after a trial of at least two hours. [Brig. Gen. Francis] Barlow says we disgraced ourselves.

Your aff. brother

Morris

For Brown and others in Barlow's division, indeed, the entire II Corps, the battle on the 18th at Spotsyvania Court House was worse than the primary one fought on the twelfth. It was a disaster from the outset, when they struck out through the dense early morning fog. Confederate General Richard Ewell's Second Corps Artillery, safely entrenched, waited until the Federals were virtually upon them and then let loose with a barrage. One survivor remembered "Heads, arms and legs were blown off like leaves in a storm."[11]

Shortly before 9:00 a.m. on May 18, five hours after launching the attack, Army of the Potomac commander George G. Meade recognized the attack's failure and called it off. By then the carnage shocked even weary veterans.

In his letter home Morris offered his family a small taste of what he had experienced, but ended with the soldiers' lament: the lack of letters from home.

May 19th

My dear parents

Am all right yet. We made another charge yesterday but were repulsed. Barlow says our Brigade did not do well.

Our thinned ranks show this to be false.

Our Regt started with about 150 from Stevensburg & now 116 of them are gone.

Capt. [Winfield] Scott was wounded yesterday by a solid shot—dont know how badly. Seems to me my turn will come before long. So far I have been exceedingly fortunate.[12]

Received your letter, Lina [Emeline], & pa's last night.

It's the first mail we have received since we left Stevensburg—& this only a small one.

Everyone of you should write me. Heard from Smith last night He seems to be very much pleased, & well he may be. I am glad he is out of this anyway.

Remember me to all my friends. Good bye.

Affectionately
Morris

May 20th/64 2 P.M. [Po River]

[Likely, this was written before the other letter to Smith this date.]

This time I wont address my letter to anyone, but say, my dear all, for since I last wrote I have received letters from pa, ma, Jennie, Lina & Smith—although with one exception they were all written in April or the first week in May.

Am sorry those contrabands turned out so poorly, but that is what I expected. They are a miserable set of beings anyway.[13]

Well I am alive so far; but oh! what terrible scenes I have passed through. We have lost 121 out of our Regt. Only had 150 when we left Stevensburg. Capt. [Henry] Owen was killed instantly. Capt. [Ira] Munson was mortally wounded & has since died. Lt. [George A.] Sherman was wounded badly & is either dead or a prisoner. Lt. [John H.] Hurlburt was also badly wounded.

Capt Scott was severely wounded—rather bruised by a solid shot in the fight day before yesterday. I expected not to get through alive from a dozen places I have been in, in the past two or three weeks, but I feel as though the prayers of the loved ones at home have been answered. Certainly it is a miracle that I have thus far escaped. What is the reason? A merciful Providence must be guarding me.

I dont believe any troops on this continent & perhaps none in the world ever experienced a severer campaign than this has been—fight all day & march all night.

Have not changed my underclothes or any clothes in three weeks, so you can well imagine what my condition is after lying around in the dust, mud & rain for three weeks.

Last night is the second time I have been under a shelter tent since we left Stevensburg.

Cant you get me a commission as Major now Munson is gone? It would be a great satisfaction to me even if I could not get mustered.

I sent _____ _____ to Louise Laphants [Lapham?], Jennie Was it that one you were reading & if so how did you know she had it? Did she tell you or Em Franklin?

I saw it very highly spoken of in the Washington papers. Have not read it.

Have not heard anything from my darkey examination so I guess I did not pass. Dont care much anyway.[14]

Smith seems to be very much pleased with his new position & well he may be. I am so thankful he has escaped this terrible campaign.[15]

Write often
Morris

The following letter, written the same day, offers the most details about the campaign, from the Battle of the Wilderness through Spotsylvania, though his chronology is off somewhat. The soldiers' suffering, especially those in his regiment, is all too evident.

On the bank of river Mattapony [Mattaponi]
May 20th 1864

[To Smith Brown]

Recd your short note my dear brother yesterday requesting particulars of our movements so far &c., &c. but as I am not in a very good condition for writing to day I can only give a very brief schedule of our progress so far.

We broke camp & left Stevensburg about eleven P.M. May 3d—crossed the Rapidan at Elys Ford at daylight & marched to Chancellorsville where we remained until the next morning when we started for Spotsylvania C. H.

When we had reached Todds Tavern our advance was stoped by the Rebs & after some little skirmishing we beat em out. Here we remained till dark when we fell in & marched up the [Brock] road leading from Germanna Ford to Spot. C.H. about six or eight miles when we came upon the rest of the army & they had been fighting all the afternoon.[16]

Gen. Hays was killed the 5th

Well we built breastworks along this road & awaited the attack which must begin at daybreak [May 6] for the rebel prisoners said they must have this road [the Orange Plank Road] or they were whipped.

At daylight the most furious musketry commenced that ever I heard. Oh! how it did rattle. About 7 a.m. we were ordered in & away we went throughout that terrible wilderness—coud'nt see ten rods in front of us.

Well we drove the rebs at least a mile & a half but they being hurriedly[?] re-inforced [by Longstreet's Corps] drove us clear back [on the Plank Road] behind our breast works & charged us again & again—planting their colors on our works.

This fight commenced at daylight [May 6] & lasted till dark All musketry—not a cannon was fired. The wilderness is so dense that cannon could not be used. This day the 126th lost 71 killed & wounded out of our 180. Such musketry I never heard!!! Here we remained during the next day without much fighting & that night (6th) the rebs left & we marched for Spot. C. H. where the 2d Corps had their big fight the next day (7th). The 8th had another terrible fight our Brigade covering the retreat of the 1st Div back across the river.[17]

This was the worst place [Po River engagement] I ever was in yet for the rebs outnumbered so much that they nearly encircled us before we gave away & then the only way we escaped being taken prisoners was—the woods in our rear were afire & we plunged through this & the smoke being so thick they were afraid to follow us. They were so close on to us that they were yelling surrender & halt for ten rods before we entered the fire. Here Capt [Henry] Owen was killed & Capt [Ira] Munson mortally wounded—has since died.[18]

Brown may have understated the danger in which he and others in Colonel Paul Frank's 3rd Brigade, Barlow's 1st Division, found themselves on May 10 at the Po River. Ordered to withdraw his II Corps across the river to support the Union attack west of Spotsylvania Court House, General Hancock pulled his 2nd and 3rd divisions, leaving Colonel John Brooke's and Frank's brigades stranded. Hancock poignantly described the predicament: "Their right and rear enveloped by the burning woods, their front assailed by overwhelming numbers of the enemy, the withdrawal of the troops [across the Po River] was attended with extreme difficulty and peril." In fact, their survival was a minor miracle. Given the urgency (withdrawing across the river before the bridge was destroyed, ducking a Confederate bombardment, and blindly running through woods ignited by the Confederate shelling), formations were lost and "men were falling like game before hunters." Worse, there seemed to be no relief in sight. Hancock claimed their "coolness and steadiness in the presence of dangers so appalling" merited "the highest praise." While Morris Brown fails to mention it in his letter, the successful withdrawal around 5:00 p.m. was not the end of the day's fighting. Rather, once back north of the Po, they were ordered to join in another attack, which was blunted by Ewell's Corps.[19]

After the skirmishes near the Po River General Grant once more meant to draw General Lee's Army of Northern Virginia out of its entrenchments. On May 11, the Union II Corps caught up with the V Corps, which had already made two bloody—and unsuccessful—assaults at Spotsylvania Court House approximately twenty-five miles southeast of the Wilderness and just beyond the Po River. Though more open than the Wilderness, the woods and shrubs near Spotsylvania made orchestrating movements difficult. The corps of Lieutenant Generals James Longstreet and A. P. Hill formed the two Confederate "faces" on the right and left respectively, while Ewell's Corps (Lieutenant General Jubal Early commanding) formed an acorn, the "salient" about two and a quarter miles across, with two "angles."

By 6:00 a.m. Barlow's division had overrun Major General Edward Johnson's four brigades at the angle and had advanced nearly a half mile before running into Brigadier General John B. Gordon's Division. Morris Brown's version here gives a bit of the flavor of what happened next.

Well we did'nt fight much more (that is our Brig.) except some skirmishing until the 12th. On the 11th our Corps was on the extreme right of the line Just after dark of the 11th we fell in & marched to the extreme left when arriving Just before daylight the divisions of the corps were massed in "double column at half distance" preparatory to a great charge. As soon as we could see[,] the word forward was given & away we went, up quite a hill for the enemys works Their fire never stopped us a moment but over their works we went capturing Johnsons entire Division together with cannon & colors.[20]

We here got all mixed & could not take their second line of works which were about a quarter of a mile in the rear of the first with an abattis such that we could not have climbed over even though there were no rebels behind to oppose us. This was probably the greatest & most successful charge of the war.

I was quite severely bruised on the knee just as I had mounted their breast works. Could'nt walk for two days but am all right now

I have written incorrectly We captured two lines of work but could not get the 3d Here they fought all day Lt. [George A.] Sherman was severely wounded & is either dead or a prisoner. Lt. [John H] Hurlburt (a new Lt. Co. K) was wounded during 1st days fight & [1st Lt. Meletiah] Lawrence too in foot—toe amputated.[21]

Well having fought all day we were relieved by the 6th Corps & kept as skirmishers until the 17th when our (1st) Division at daylight again charged the works we failed to take the 12th (massed as before) & this time were repulsed. Our Brigade got up to the works & our colors (126) were planted on their works but we were forced to fall back, which we did & lay down not over thirty rods from their guns.

The other Brigades did not move up as close as we so that while we kept their guns silenced in our front they finally succeeded in training a battery on us from their (enemys) right & the grape & canister coming upon us we were compelled to fall back.

If the other Brigs had kept their guns silenced as well as we did we could have held our own

We think we did the best we could certainly better than the other Brigs. but [Generals] Barlow & Hancock gave us fits. They say they will give us one more chance to redeem ourselves & if we dont do better the Brig. will be broken up.

This is too bad for we certainly do not deserve it Our thinned ranks show what hard fighting we have done I think our Brig. has lost half of the men we had when at Stevensburg. Our Regt has lost 121 out of 180. Does that show cowardice? Its too bad.

If we make another charge I will go into the enemys works, if I can get five men to follow me even if I go to Richmond

[Col. Clinton] McDougall is in command of the Brig. I forgot to say Capt Scott was very severely bruised on the hip by a solid shot in this last charge.

Capt. [Benjamin F.] Lee has resigned. Good enough [Sanford] Platt & I are the only Capts left.

Have not changed my shirt for three weeks.

This has been a terrible campaign—ten times as bad as last summer

I'll bet Grant wishes he was back to Chattanooga but he swears that when he falls back our boat will carry the troops to Washington from Fredericksburg. Baird has your commission as Lt. Col.

Well I guess this is enough. We are in reserve now for the first time.

Write often Morris

[Written on the edges of the paper:]

Capt. Munson lived till he got to Washington. [Adjut Gen. Robert] Seabury lived three or four days Gen Owens was not hurt Every field officer in our Brig. was either killed or wounded

Baird just returned & also McDougall.

You want to add $10 to my a/c against you. Bill spent that ten dollars which we __ _____ postage & it was not reckoned with [N]ow no grumbling—be generous. Now its $120 & some cents Your commutation ought to support you.

Sold the horse (black) to Loring—pays next pay day

[Dr. Charles] Hoyt has been commissioned & mustered as Surgeon of 39th N.Y.V.

However descriptive, Brown fails to note the excitement Barlow's division generated in its charge on the Confederate brigades of Colonel William Witcher and Brigadier General George H. Steuart at Spotsylvania Court House. The II Corps historian characterized the attackers as "crazed with excitement." Nor does Brown adequately describe how successful the II Corps was initially at Spotsylvania. They tore away at the first abatis, sprang over the Confederate entrenchments, and bayoneted and clubbed their opponents. After being momentarily stopped by Confederate artillery spewing grape and canister, they regained their momentum, charged again and captured close to four thousand prisoners—including Generals Edward Johnson and George H. Steuart—and eighteen cannon. It was not until near midnight—roughly twenty hours after the attack began—when both sides, "gorged with slaughter," finally stopped the useless killing. Though exhausted, Brown was aroused sufficiently to defend his regiment's honor in his letter home.[22]

And Brown vowed: "If we make another charge I will go into the enemys works, if I can get five men to follow me even if I go to Richmond."

He correctly prophesied that there would be more charges by his regiment, beginning with a thirteen-hour march on May 20. Figuring Lee was entrenching, Grant planned a flanking movement and ordered

Hancock's corps to march toward Milford Station on the Mattaponi River, the "third consecutive night" with the expectation they would "vigorously" attack at dawn on the next day.[23]

Sunday May 22d

Here I am my dear parents across the river Mattapony opposite Milford Station—five miles below Bowling Green on the Fredericksburg & Richmond railroad.

We left our old position up near Spotsylvania C. H. about eleven oclock Friday evening [May 19] & marched all night & until one P.M. the next day all over Virginia until we finally landed here & commenced throwing up breastworks. Worked nearly all last night & all the forenoon on em & now our Corps have the best works I ever saw our army build As a general thing the rebs construct far better works than we

Our Corps is here all alone. At least we had no communication with the rest of the army this morning.

I suppose it is a flank movement to force Lee to abandon the very, very strong works he held near Spotsylvania C.H.

There is a rumor that we are to move again towards Richmond to night. If this is so Lee must be in full retreat for Richmond with our army in his rear & flank. Probably we will have a big fight tomorrow. Good by again Morris

[On the top edge of the first page:]

Our march yesterday & night before was the hardest one I have been in yet—by far.

[On the side edge of the first page:]

[Forty-two-year-old Private] Warren Allen cooks for me now

[On the side edge of the second page:]

I heard to day that [Samuel] Wilson was very tough now—drinking & swears horribly.[24]

Epoch Three began with the Army of Potomac's crossing of North Anna River and probing to find a weak spot in the Confederate defenses, which initially resulted only in some minor activity for Brown's tired, embattled troops.

On May 23, the Federals charged on the Confederates, bringing on a heavy skirmish with Longstreet's Corps at the North Anna River, causing Hancock to order a fierce artillery barrage, which drove the remaining Confederates back across the river. While it was a minor engagement, members of Brown's regiment recalled the furor that became as hot as the temperature. Heavy fighting temporarily gave way on the twenty-fourth, allowing the weary soldiers to wade across, soaked to the chest in the chilly river, and scale the steep, wooded banks. Then, despite their fatigue, they began an assault.

They were headed toward a trap Lee had sprung by aligning his troops in an inverted V. This would split Grant's army when it attacked, allowing Anderson's and Ewell's Divisions to hammer Hancock's isolated corps. However, word of the Confederates' seemingly impregnable entrenchments ahead led General Meade to call off the attack. The next day the tired soldiers protected themselves from a soaking rain, and some, like Morris Brown, wrote home.

Across the North Anna river
May 25th 1864

Received your letters my dearest mother & Jennie just now. My knee is nearly well. Was in the hospital only two days. Got sick of it. Would rather be with the Regt.

We crossed the river yesterday without much opposition excepting heavy artillery firing & skirmishing. We are about a half a mile across & the rebels are in force about three quarters of a mile farther on. If they give us battle here it will be a terrible one—worse than the wilderness. Grants idea I guess is to flank em for we have been lying still all day & seems to me he would have attacked them before they had time to complete their fortifications had he intended to have driven them out by force.

What awful scenes I have passed through since we left Stevensburg. I believe I am getting nervous at seeing so many men knocked in so many inconceivable shapes. This is a beautiful country down here—the first I have seen worth fighting for.

Did you receive those photographs I sent home [S]ome Generals &c. Frank _____

I wish you would send me all sorts of papers Frank Leslies[,] Harpers Weekly particularly.

Good bye Morris

Across the Pamunky
about two miles south of Hanover Town Va.
Sunday 29th

My dear parents

Well here we are again. We recrossed the North Anna Thursday night & Friday about noon started for this point where we arrived about 4 P.M. yesterday and immediately commenced throwing up breastworks which we completed about ten oclock last night.

We expected the rebels would attack us this morning but they did not. I guess they are getting afraid of us.

Grant can whip em in a fair fight every time

I think our hardest fighting is to come.

With the exception of the fighting in the wilderness & Spotsylvania Court House we have not fought any. Grant has just outflanked Lee every time he attempted it & compelled him to fall back.

Our line of battle is now nearly north and south & if Lee dont look out he will be flanked again & compelled to fall *clear* within the fortifications of Richmond without getting a chance to fight us only behind our own works & with those works we could whip five times our number. I wonder what another week will bring forth. *We will know soon enough.*[25]

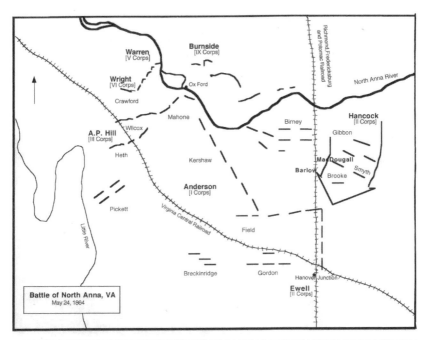

Battle of North Anna, VA, May 24, 1864 (*Source:* Wayne Mahood)

Indeed, he would, for the Federal strategy—to bring on a culminating battle—appeared to be succeeding. Captain Morris Brown rightly presumed that the "hardest fighting is to come." It began with the issuance of six-days rations, the familiar sign of a long march. Night-long marching, crossing the Pamunkey River and tearing up portions of the Virginia Central and Richmond Railroad followed. Shortly they were barely seventeen miles northeast of Richmond, where Brown was ordered to command an expedition to determine how well the ground ahead was defended. The result:

4 1/2 A.M. May 31st 1864

My dear parents

Am all right yet. Had a pretty severe skirmish yesterday. Col. [Clinton] McDougall comdg our Brig was ordered to take some heights about half a mile beyond our skirmish line.

The first thing I heard was ["] Capt. Brown take forty men deploy them as skirmishers & take that ridge.["]

Well I did then feel a little skittish. Only forty men!! I saw at once he only wanted to find out how many rebs were there.

Well I deployed my men & with a yell such as only our soldiers can give we started down the ridge we were on. Oh! Oh!!! how the bullets did whistle. And I with only forty men.

But we pressed forward & crossed the plain driving the Johnnys before us & to my utter astonishment we drove them away from our front on the right & remained there till nearly sundown when Col. Mc fearing we would be taken prisoners if we remained till dark ordered us to fall back across a little creek about half way across the plain. It was a desperate thing & I thought my days were numbered when I first saw what I was to do.

[On the side of the first page:]

I had one of those nice new stockings half shot off mother but the ball did not touch my leg. I would like to have that reb by the neck for spoiling my stockings.

[On the side edge of the first page:]

Recd pa's letter last night. There will be a big fight here in a day or two.

We lost only six men yesterday.[26]

Seemingly indifferent to the staggering losses, General Grant pushed his forces southward. But Lee checked Grant in front of Old Cold Harbor, northeast of Richmond, near where the fateful Seven Days Battle began in 1862. A flank movement now was out of the question, "Richmond was dead in front." So, June 3, the Federals assaulted the Confederates. It was Gettysburg in reverse. Now the Union army had to advance under the withering musketry and cannon fire.[27]

Like other divisions, which seemed to be fighting alone, Barlow's Division, including the Third Brigade, pushed ahead. Initially the

Federals were successful, overrunning the salient and capturing three guns and two hundred to three hundred prisoners, but the stubborn Confederate defense forced a retreat. Other Union commands reported similar results, more losses without compensating gains. The Battle of Cold Harbor may have been Grant's worst generalship—the bloodiest eight minutes of the war—and would result in the epithet, "Butcher Grant." In those few minutes close to 7,000 Federals fell, compared to less than 1,500 Confederates. "The Second Corps here received a mortal blow," the corps's chief of staff Morgan wrote, "and never again was the same body of men." Lt. Col. William Baird's subsequent request for the return of the hundred men on provost duty revealed how depleted the 126th New York was. He had only ninety-seven on his roster: himself, one adjutant, one assistant quartermaster, three captains, three lieutenants, and sixty-seven enlisted men—barely three quarters of a regulation company. (Ten days later, Baird himself was dead.)[28]

The Battle of Cold Harbor was a brutal lesson for Grant and a devastating one for his troops.[29]

Now, Morris Brown and others huddled down prairie dog style in rain-filled trenches to avoid enemy sniper and mortar fire, suffered from lack of sleep and water and hungered for anything other than the tasteless diet of salt pork and hard crackers. More importantly, they reflected on their mortality.

June 5th/64

My dear mother & Jennie

I wont attempt to designate any particular place as Hd. Qrs. for we are all over Virginia every day. We now lie between Cold Harbor & the Chickahominy—perhaps a mile from the river.

Recd your letters, mother & Jennie, this Sunday morning of May 25th. I have only recd three letters from you mother since I left camp near Stevensburg. I have also recd three or four from you Jennie for which I am exceedingly thankful & which I would answer separately were I a little differently situated. I am now sitting flat down in the dirt (*for we cannot stand up for fear of the rebel sharpshooters*) writing, all crouched up in a heap. There is no invisible place I can inform you.

Recd five letters from Smith to day. We dont get a mail only once in a while & cant write only as often.

I wish I could be home when Aunt _____ & _____ are there. How you all seem to be enjoying yourselves.

Could you but know our situation & then compare it with those at home! But I am glad you cannot. I believe I am getting nervous.

Oh! such scenes as I have passed through during the last four weeks.

I now think that if I get out of this place alive—even though I may lose an arm or a leg I will be a fortunate man.

We all begin to think our chances are slight and few. Anyone who comes out of this campaign alive is a very fortunate being surely.

For the last thirty days I have either been in one fight or a skirmish nearly every day or have witnessed other regiments get all cut to pieces which is about as bad.

They are getting so they dont care or notice a fight down here when only lose four or five hundred in killed & wounded. Our lines in some places are not over thirty rods from the enemys & you can bet we have to keep down.

Last night saw the 148th & oh! what a homesick lot of mortals. I fairly pity em![30]

Could write a volume but I want to write Smith & the mail goes out soon.

Good bye again
Morris

He seemed more upbeat four days later. Surgeon Hammond had succored him, and Morris was grateful. Simple pleasures, once taken for granted, were now luxuries. But he remained convinced that, as horrible as the bloodletting had been, it would get worse.

9 miles from Richmond
June 9th 1864

The mail carrier goes in five minutes & I will just say I am all right yet.

Not much fighting during the last three or four days. There must be some tall figuring going on somewhere.

The skirmishers are constantly popping at each other with some casualties each day.

Live better than I did; Went down to the hospital day before yesterday for the first time since I was wounded & told Dr. H[ammond] that I was getting hungry for something else to eat besides pork & hardtack that I wanted something sour &c., &c. Well he went & got me about twenty lemons, a couple bottles of apple jelly, a couple peppers, farina, a bottle of nice brandy & a bag full of ice.

It is pretty tedious to be compelled to live on hardtack & pork alone as we have ever since we left Stevensburg & you cant imagine how hungry one will get for just those things the Dr. gave me.

There is going to be an awful awful!! awful!!! fight here one of these days,

Good by again
Morris

Whatever lay in store for Morris Brown, the next move would be Grant's, and Brown's fate rested with that move.

CHAPTER 7

"Anyone Who Comes Out of This Campaign Alive is a Very Fortunate Being. . . ."

Following the brutal bloodbath at Cold Harbor, barely ten miles northeast of Richmond, both armies paused and took stock. Captain Brown and other Union soldiers crouched in their trenches hastily dug with jackknives and scooped out with broken canteens, spoons, or hands. Then, shortly, still hugging the ground, they inched forward to dig more trenches. Their victuals were no better: pork and hard crackers. It was, as Brown would write, like living in their own graves. In fact, he was sure that he and his fellows were regarded as nothing but cannon fodder.

Sparing his parents the horrors of war (which the same day he reminded his brother to do), Morris Brown is virtually silent about the fighting at Cold Harbor and the casualties in his letter to them immediately afterward.

Near Coal [Cold] Harbor
Sunday June 12th/64

Received your letters my dear father, mother & Lina all right yesterday & was very glad I assure you to hear you were all so well with the exception of Linas cold.

How is that cold? Now keep me posted. Will see Dr. Hammond and ask him about it as soon as I can. Hav'nt seen him but once (or twice) since the 14th of May & then I went after something to eat & got it too. Very little fighting for the last week. We are now diging them out. Slow work We are now living as it were in our own graves, for each man or two has a hole dug just large enough to admit his body & there he remains from daylight to dark—ready to protect the working parties in case of an attack. All work is done under the ground.[1]

We have tunnels & trenches dug from our place to another so we can move about without being "picked off" by the enemys sharpshooters.

I tell you its no fun to be cooped up as we are, for any man who raises his head above the level of the ground wants to first make peace with his Maker, for its a miracle if he dont get half a dozen balls through it. I have seen dozens shot just because they were to curious & wanted to look at the Johnnys when they did'nt want 'em too [sic].

Seems to me we are not progressing very fast now but then we cant tell much about it. They are now constructing some very formidable works about half a mile in our rear which I presume we will occupy with a smaller force than we keep here now while the larger force attacks the enemys right. If this move could be successful it would be a bad fix for the rebs. Time only will develop Grants plans.

Seems to me he "is not waiting here for nothing." Something is up.

Am glad Lina you continue to like Mr. Schofield so much. Pitch in—study hard & you will never regret it.

I learned father that Col. Baird has recommended Capt [Charles] Richardson for the Majority of this Regt. Now Baird promised Dr. H[ammond] before we left Stevensburg that I should be the next one recommended for this place, but as he had sent on Munsons name he did not wish to take it back &c. &c. I dont know as it is so, but will let you know as soon as I learn exactly. But if it is so, the first hard work I propose to do is to get out of this Regt. If I cannot get somewhere on detached service I will offer my resignation even though I run the chances of a dismissal.

Could you not get me some kind of a situation of Hallett on that Pacific R.R. Seems to me that would be a good opening for a young man—particularly at its eastern terminus. Try it! That would be a good place to invest in real estate. Will see Dr. H. as soon as possible & write again.[2]

Your letter Pa was exceedingly interesting & I hope you will write oftener. The mail comes about every day now but we cant tell how long this state of things will last.

Good by *again*
Morris

He was less reticent in a letter to his brother, Smith Brown, in Madison, Wisconsin, where he was serving as Inspector of the State of Wisconsin in the Provost Marshal General's Office. Clearly, Morris continues to anticipate the "terrible battle" that lay ahead. Yet true to form, he was angling for promotion—or the best way out of the army.[3]

Near Coal [Cold] Harbor
Sunday June 12/64

My dear brother.

Have not heard from you since I last wrote. Loring sold the horse to an officer from Maine. I was talking with him yesterday & he told me he would gladly have kept the horse for you had he known of it but added that in his opinion we did well in getting rid of him as we did particularly if he had to remain here in the army. He said that his fore feet were getting very sore & tender & would be very troublesome in a few weeks without *different* care than he could possibly receive here in our present condition.

My feelings in regard to the matter are these. The horse was sold to cheaply at first by you. You could then "have got" more & should have left him with me to be sold—as long as you came to the conclusion not to take him with you west. I think I did just right in selling him as I did as we for the most part have received only from three to five lbs. of oats per day since we left Stevensburg.

Dr. H, Loring & all with whom I have talked think I did the best thing *under the circumstances*. Nevertheless had I received your letters a few days before I actually did I would have kept him here hit or miss.

Had a letter from father mother & Lina last night You must not keep writing to them your fears of my getting hurt &c., &c for it only keeps them in a continual stew.

You know too well the danger I am constantly in, but while I hope I may come out all right I feel that my chances are slight. *If I get off with the loss of a leg or an arm I shall be satisfied.* [emphasis added]

We have actually been under fire every day since the 5th of May—although a good many of these days we lay in rifle pits & were secure.

But I think there have been but very few days of that time that we (our brigade) have not lost more or less in killed or wounded. The lines are now in one front not over four rods apart—that is the rifle pits & not the skirmish lines.

We are living as it were in our own graves. Every one has his own hole dug so as to escape the fire of the Johnnys *mortars* for both sides are using them now. We are having a regular old siege now, & consequently dont do much else but skirmish & dig.[4]

We have underground roads dug to the front—so we can pass around from one pit to the other. Great times these!

They are now constructing some very formidable works about a half a mile to the rear which I presume we are to occupy so as to straighten the line & make it weaker so as to use the extra forces somewhere else. Now we are all mixed.

I think Grant will mass a heavy force & pitch into the Johnnys right flank. At present we are at a halt. We don't seem to be doing anything. There "has got" to be a terrible battle fought here ere many days pass.

We are getting plenty to eat nowadays although it has been pretty rough some of the time.

Just recd your letter of June 5th. Whew! what a small!! Is this your style since arriving at Madison? Whew!!! I must say that this last letter of yours is exceedingly interesting giving so much news & that in a small space. Dont feel flattered.

I heard yesterday that Baird had recommended Capt. Richardson to be Major. Now Baird promised Dr. H. before we left Stevensburg that I should be the next one recommended for this position. I may be mistaken & will write you as soon as I find just how the matter stands.

If Baird has recommended Richardson the first hard work I propose to do is to get out of this Regt even though I have to take the chances of dismissal by forwarding my resignation. I am going to try to get on detached service somewhere first, but if it comes to the worst I shall certainly resign.

Lee (Capt.) has resigned & [Joseph] Hooper mustered in his place. H[enry]. M. Lee has been mentioned as 2d Lt., Co. F & [James] Griggs as 2d Lt. of my Co. [A]

A commission as 1st Lt. came for Randolf [John F. Randolph] but as it will undoubtedly be months before he returns I concluded to have Griggs mustered.

I dont enjoy myself here any more simply because there are no officers left with whom I am willing to associate except Capt. Richardson. [1st Lt. Spencer] Lincoln is a *shirk*. Charley Lisk is about my only companion now—messes [i.e., eats] & tents with me. What a change from last summer![5]

What would you do were you in my place? Write me plainly just what you think.

Does Col. Green have any such retinue of officers about him as Maj. ___ at Elmira?

If so seems to me you ought to get me some place there or in some other portion of the state. Try it. Tell Col. Green that there are only seventy enlisted men left in the Regt, present for duty comprising 47 privates, 14 Corporals & 9 Sergts—& eleven commissioned officers^ and get him to apply to the Sec. of War for me.^ [John B.] Geddis has been mustered Capt. "H" Co—in Owens place He has been in command of all the musicians of the Division during the campaign & keeps back at the hospital.

Hav'nt seen Dr. H. but three or four times since we left Stevensburg. Hoyt is Surgeon of 39th N.Y.V. Loring has been commissioned Capt. C[ommissary].S[ergeant]. but not yet assigned to any particular Brigade.

If I should resign now I could reach home with about four hundred and fifty dollars in my pocket besides what I have at Starks & what you owe me—which would amount to about $650

Why would'nt it be a good idea to go to the eastern terminus of the Pacific R. R. & invest in real estate providing one could get some situation where he could pay expenses. What do you allow? I am bound to get out of this regiment in some shape & now let us all be working for some good place for me to go & "set up shop" The next time you write tell me what your duties are there. I guess not much.

[Captain Richard] Bassett or the Provost Guard have not been under fire yet during this campaign. Your Com[mission] as Lt. Col. is with the train. Will send it to you the first chance I have although you cant get mustered.

A Majors Com[mission] would do me no good; but then I think I deserve it, & it would afford me some gratification as well as my friends at home even though I was never mustered.

Randolph was shot through the shoulder in the night while asleep. Pretty bad wound. Could not find the ball. Heard he was drunk? but cant believe it yet. [Capt. Winfield] Scott was struck with a solid shot on the hip—a very bad bruise. The flesh will probably all slough off & he will have a hard time of it. [1st Sgt. Smith] Fuller is dead. Sergt [Phineas] Tyler of my Co. had his right arm amputated & Sgt [James] Henderson his right leg & F[rancis]. E. Pool three fingers of his right hand.[6]

Twelve of those men I had at Stevensburg when you left have been either killed or wounded. Have six left & three of those returned the other day having been exchanged & sent to the front. Many were taken at Bristoe. Seamans brother lost his left arm. He had'nt been here a week. Have not seen

[Samuel] Wilson. Q. M. [John C.] Stainton saw him. He had a canteen of whisky & was about half tight. Stainton says the first thing he said was "Jesus Christ Stainton how are you." Too bad. Too bad.[7]

[The next part, though it appears to have been part of the June 12, 1864 letter, may have been from Morris's June 18, 1864 letter.]

General Francis Barlow has taken back what he said in regard to our Brig. He now says that those Dutch conscripts in the 52d [New York] caused all the trouble. Your conundrum about ____ & faith is "bully."

Bill is with provost guard [Forty-two-year-old Private Warren] Allen cooks for me.

Did not see Seabury before he died. Huntoon was killed last week—shot by a sharpshooter. They embalmed him & sent him home. [Col. Levin] Crandell is with his Regt. [125th N.Y.V.] Have not written to Eva Harris & guess I wont for I have neither ink or paper—only this. What do you say?[8]

Your row with Mattie is just what I have been expecting. Reason bade me look for it. I am not disappointed. If you are going to be married you want to be about it. You had better make up with Lizzie for you cannot do better. I would love very much to correspond with Eva Harris but hardly know to work it. Lets have some suggestions from you. Send me a copy of that letter you first wrote Mattie? She is worth trying hard for & if I was placed in a little different circumstances would hold my cards pretty close. She is wealthy & finely well educated.

I must own that I am in a fix, as to the better way of starting the thing.

Dont hear anything from Thede. When does his marriage come off? Would send them a nice present, did I but know where or when to send it![9]

What is he doing & what are his prospects for making money? You must not spend more than your commutation under any circumstances.[10]

Try & save something for the future. You will want it yet. Write often Your Aff.

brother Morris

In sharp contrast to the generally light tone of Morris's letter, the Army of the Potomac moved out that night. General Grant was taking another tack, not unlike his successful investment of Vicksburg a year earlier. Actually it was better. In the words of Confederate artillerist, E. Porter Alexander, it was not only brilliantly conceived, but "the most brilliant piece of logistics of the war." Grant intended to sneak clear around Lee's army and Richmond, capture Petersburg, the Confederate rail and supply center some fifty miles away and defended by only six thousand, force the evacuation of Richmond, and cut off any retreat. The keys would be secrecy, speedy marches, corduroyed roads approaching the Chickahominy, ferry boats on call at the James River, and a coordinated attack on Petersburg. It was no easy matter to cross the treacherous Chickahominy and the larger James with five army corps, a cavalry corps, an artillery, and supply train and headquarters detachments, amounting to over one hundred thousand men.[11]

Captain Morris Brown was as surprised as any by the unexpected departure from the rain-filled trenches they had occupied since the blood-letting at Cold Harbor. Shortly before he left Cold Harbor, he scratched out a short note to his father urging renewed efforts to get his promotion.

Father

Col. Baird told Dr. Hammond this afternoon he was sorry he had recommended Capt. Munson for the Majority and said he wished I could get the commission through the influence I could bring to bear on Gov. Seymour from Yates County.

He also said he would revoke Munsons recommendation; but was unwilling to stultify himself to Gov. Seymour.

Morris

The movement began in the evening of June 12, with martial airs, as if it portended another attack on Cold Harbor. General Gouverneur

K. Warren's V Corps, taking the shortest, westernmost route, led off. Hancock's II Corps, stretching five miles, looped east then headed straight south, making twenty miles the first day. The crossing of the James was completed with almost textbook success, but the II Corps was delayed on the fifteenth when rations failed to arrive on time and it got lost. The success of a coordinated attack on Petersburg with Major General William F. Smith's XVIII Corps was seriously jeopardized.[12]

Smith's corps struck around 7:00 p.m. on June 15, even before Hancock arrived at Petersburg, Virginia, the vital Confederate railroad junction. But, mistakenly fearing the entrenchments that encircled the city were too formidable to launch an attack, he opened up with massed artillery. Then near midnight, after Hancock's Corps finally arrived and occupied positions captured by Smith's corps, Smith rested his men. Compounding matters, General Hancock's orders, which followed, were uncharacteristically vague. The surprise was lost, and more Confederate reinforcements arrived, bolstering Lieutenant General Pierre Gustave T. Beauregard's hodgepodge of old men, boys, and recuperating veterans. Grant's brilliantly conceived strategy had failed, as with so many others of the war. Instead of capturing Petersburg, Grant would have to settle for a siege, while doing everything he could to disrupt the Confederate rails and occupy the attention of Lee's army. But that still lay ahead.[13]

Late afternoon, June 16, Army of the Potomac Commander Meade arrived, and, relying on the II Corps' divisions of Generals David Birney and Francis Barlow, directed a grand assault. Captain Morris Brown and others, weary from marching and countermarching for close to twelve hours, were ordered to charge through woods, down a deep ravine, up a hill, and down a deeper ravine while ducking cannon and musketry fire. The final charge took them straight toward the Confederate entrenchments. Dreadful casualties resulted, and Brown overcame his "aversion" to describing the gruesome details to his parents.[14]

Near Petersburg Va.
June 18th 1864

My dear parents

Well I am all right yet, but oh! what terrible fighting we have had for the last two or three days. Night before last we (our brigade) charged the enemys works, took three but with some loss.

Col. Baird was killed also Lt. McDonald. Capt. Richardson was very severely wounded in upper jaw—probably will not live. Adjt. Lincoln has his left arm off & Lt. Dibble badly wounded in leg.[15]

Three enlisted men killed & seventeen wounded.

We only have seventy muskets [men] so you can see our loss is very severe particularly in officers. Lt. [Martin] Stanton was mortally wounded about an hour ago.

Capt. [Sanford] Platt & I are the only two officers left who were with the Regt. when we left Stevensburg. We have two 2d Lts beside but they were just promoted about a week ago.

There are but two of us left *to be chosen from*, in the next fight.

Such fighting I never saw before, & such narrow escapes I never had. A merciful Providence & a God who hear the prayers of the dear ones at home is certainly protecting me.

I am confident of it. My faith is stronger than ever. I feel it more & more every day. I feel different than ever before. I picked up a testament during the battle of the Wilderness on the 7th day of May & since then it has been my constant companion.

I go into a fight now with a different feeling than ever before. I have no fear of death as I used to.

But my dear parents I feel as though I was going through with this campaign safely—still death has none of the terrors it formerly did.

Col. McDougall Comdg. our brigade just told us we probably would charge the city of Petersburg to night. We are only about three fourths of a mile from the city; but I presume their works are very strong & we will lose very heavily. But I think we can take them for we have driven them a good ways to day. We will try it hard anyway.

*Get me a commission as Lt. Col. & Smith a Com[mission] as Col. Col. McDougall told me last night he would gladly recommend me to Gov. Seymour—for good conduct &c. &c.[16]

Will send the letter as soon as I can get some ink to write it with.

Good bye *again*
Your aff. Son
Morris

If his parents needed any reassurance about Morris's survival from the latest combat, Surgeon Hammond, a family friend, provided it:

Petersburgh June 17th

Mr. Brown

We had a hard fight yesterday & a successful one. But at great cost though not so fatal to Officers. Col. Baird was killed.

Capt. Morris Brown, Jr. (*Source:* Yates County Genealogical and Historical Society)

Capt Richardson severely wounded. Morris is all right and in command of the Reg. Go or send to Albany at once. Get a commission Col. for Smith & Major or Lt Col for Morris. Act at once and secure the commissions.

Tell my wife that I am *well, perfectly well* Will write to her as soon as I can.

F[letcher] M. Hammond

Of course, Morris had to tell Smith the results of the latest bloodletting. The constant pounding by Grant's troops to try to break the Confederate will tested the Union soldiers' resolve, as well. Only the combatants truly knew just how awful war could be, but slowly the gruesome details were filtering back home. While lamenting the losses, Morris seemed assured that he would survive and wanted the rank appropriate to his responsibilities as acting regimental commander.

Near Petersburg Va
June 19th 1864

My dear brother

Well you see I am all right yet although since I last wrote you we have seen some pretty rough times.

On the 16th our brigade made another charge on a rifle pit across quite a ravine.

We got within about ten rods of the works where we stopped & then we fought all the afternoon. After dark we outreached ourselves & the next morning (17th) charged the work again capturing five pieces of artillery with horses, caissons &c. complete. also quite a number of prisoners. Col. Baird was killed. also Lt. McDonald. Capt. Richardson was very severely wounded through upper jaw & cant talk now. Adjt Lincoln has his left arm amputated and Lt. Dibble Co. H quite severely wounded in leg.

Yesterday (18) Mart[in] Stanton was mortally wounded. was actg aide on [Brig. Gen. Paul] Frank's staff (who by the way has been returned to duty as the entire court that was trying him have been either killed or wounded) and was shot by a sharpshooter while to[o] far to the front following Frank around he [Frank] being drunk again. Capt. Platt & I are the only two officers left who started with the Regt from Stevensburg. Lts. [James] Griggs, [Henry] Lee & [Milo] Hooper are here. Lee has done very well since mustered. He knows he will catch fits if he dont stand up to the work now I am in command.[17]

Such fighting never was heard of before I dont believe. They not only fight all day but all night.

The night of the 16th we fought all night more or less. The night of the 17th the 2d Div. with a portion of the 9th Corps fought the greater part of the night.

Who can tell what our loss have been tremendous!! I never saw so many dead men before.

Col. [Clinton] McDougall told me he would gladly recommend me to Gov. [Horatio] Seymour but I cant get any paper for him to write it on. Will to day. Richardson will undoubtedly be commissioned Major & I must be as Lt. Col. & you Col.

If you were here now you could be mustered as Lt. Col. but I would rather be where you are with a Majors commission than here as a Brig. Genl. I wish I could get out of it but if I cant I might as well try to be promoted.

We must outfigure Capt Richardson & Scott. Have not recd any letters from you in a good while. not since I last wrote you. Recd a good many papers.

Your affectionate
Morris

Next is an undated, partial letter apparently written to Smith Brown some time after June 16, 1864, possibly as an addendum to one of his June 20 letters.

[no date, likely June 20, 1864]

This piece of poetry in the paper mother sent me is so grand. I want it carefully preserved for me.

There are but two officers in our Regt, who hold their original positions.

Wrote you to day. I forgot to tell you in my letter to day that a man was shot for cowardice in Genl. Owens Brigade this morning.

He was shot about ten rods from our Regt.

It looked hard to see a man shot by our own men, but I have seen so many men blown, torn and mangled in so many different ways during the last two weeks that this dont amount to much.

Day before yesterday I passed over the ground where we made that great charge on the 12th & I saw about a hundred dead rebs all bloated & covered with maggots & worms—worse than they would leave a hog up there in N.Y. Oh such sights! Would that this terrible war was over.

Your Commission as Lt. Col. was in Col Bairds valise & was taken off by his brother in law Isaac Chase who lives at Wilseyville Tioga Co. N.Y. Col Bairds wife lives at Moravia Cayuga Co. & his brother David at Geneva.

When the valise will be taken I dont know but you can get it someplace[?] of one of the above named persons by writing

Place this picture in my album

Whether Morris's apparent callousness toward death, including executions, is for effect or real cannot be determined. It could never have been easy to watch an execution, which typically demanded that the entire brigade, if not division, form into a square to observe the condemned march in, sit upon his coffin blindfolded, and face a firing squad. It was especially painful for the doomed soldier, if not the observers, when the initial firing failed its mission, not all that uncommon. Then an officer was forced to fire his pistol to finish the job. But Brown seems to pass off the latest execution as just one more of what seemed endless deaths.

His next letter offered an ominous warning to his brother. The fighting was too fierce. One Brown family member risking his life was enough.

June 20th 1864

My dear brother

Col. McDougall Comdg. Brig. will recommend me to Gov.
Seymour to day to be commissioned as Field Officer &c.

I think there is some chance yet unless they outfigure
me somewhere at home.

If you can get mustered as Lt. Col. do you think it would
be policy? Would you not have to return to the Regt? If you
run the risk of being ordered back for heavens sake dont be
mustered. Keep out of this. Resign rather than return here.
You have done your duty.

Now mind what I say do not get mustered if you have
to come back here. I would rather remain a Capt then have
you return. Stay where you are. If I get a Majors Commission
I will keep it.

You should put in now for a Cols Commission & I for
a Majors & Lt. Cols.

Dr. H. says Richardson wont accept a Commission [as
lieutenant colonel]

I dont think you could be mustered as Lt. Col. even if
you were here our numbers are so small. Saw Wilson yesterday.
Insulted by his breath the first thing. Rough!

Your brother Morris

And he followed up with an even more portentous letter. The young
officer, who could have been safely graduated from Hamilton College, was
feeling the effects of the fighting and now acknowledged his mortality.
His faith in the Army of the Potomac remained strong, but he worried
about the losses already experienced and likely to result from more attacks
on defended fortifications. This campaign so far had simply been one
brutal battle after another without any compensating success.

Also Morris feared for his brother Smith's health. Apparently
Smith's appointment as Wisconsin inspector general was based in part
on his physical health. To return to the 126th New York, given the

prevailing conditions, would threaten not only his already weakened health, but, more likely, would lead to his becoming a combat fatality. Morris's postscript warning could not have been clearer.

June 20th

My dear brother

Sent a bully good letter from McDougall to Gov. Seymour to father to day & hope it may do some good, but cant tell. An order has just been recd stating that our corps would be relieved to night by the 6th & 9th & we would go back in reserve.

I have heard that we were going back to reorganize—that is the Corps. Certainly it is necessary for you never will believe how badly we have been cut up. The loss of this many will never be known only by a few. 75,000 I believe wont cover it.

Grant cant take Richmond. He may in some way compell them to evacuate the city but as for capturing it with Lee's army there is all nonsense.

We can & have whipped the rebs in every *open* fight but when they get behind their breastworks then we must keep away.

Good bye
Morris

Do not get mustered yet *& resign* if you have to come here.

Yet, despite his warning to Smith and with the fighting intensifying and casualties mounting, Morris tried to assure his parents of his safety and well being. And he remained determined to gain promotion.

June 20th 1864

My dear father

Enclosed you will find a letter from Col. McDougall to Gov. Seymour.[18]

Do what you can for me & spare no efforts or money.

First get me a commission as Major vice [in the place of] Smith promoted then get Smith a commission as Col. & me one as Lt. Col.

If necessary have Ogden & Sunderlin go to Albany. Anyway what you do[,] do immediately.

Dont lose a minute

Morris

Be sure & preserve a copy of this letter [MacDougall's] its different from most every other letter a person obtains.

No fighting by us since the 17th.

Am feeling very well.

Recd mothers[,] Jennie's & Linas letter last night.

Your aff. Son
Morris

[On the top edge of the page:]

Preserve a copy of this letter [MacDougall's] so I can have it published in case of promotion

[On the bottom of the page in different handwriting were the words "Morris's last letter. He very much wanted MacDougall's letter as a memento, but also as news for the local paper. Colonel, later General, MacDougall had written:]

Head Quarters 3d Brig 1st Div 2d Corps
In the field June 17, 1861[1864]

To His Excellency
Horatio Seymour
Gov of New York
Sir.

I most respectfully call your attention to the case of Capt Morris Brown Jr 126th New York Vol. During the fearful charge of last night after his Colonel was killed he assumed command of the Reg and behaved with great gallantry. After reaching the enemies works and driving them out, Capt Brown performed several acts of personal daring which called forth my highest praise at the time. Going at my request from the right to the left and in person ascertaining the position of the enemy upon our flanks, being all the time under a heavy fire.

His conduct upon this occasion was such as in my judgment entitled him to promotion and I most respectfully recommend that your excellency promote him to the position of field officer in his Regt. Capt Brown is an officer of high order & intelligence and entirely capable of filling any office to which he may be promoted.

His own conduct as well as that of his Reg and his lamented Colonel Baird (who was killed) were splendid. The Brigade losing in the charge about 1/2 of their number of enlisted men, and nearly 2/3 the number of commissioned officers present.

Trusting Capt Brown's case may meet with your early attention I have the

Honor to remain
Your obedient servant
C D Mac Dougall
Col 111th N.Y. Vols.
Comdg 3d Brig 1st Div 2d Corps

This was not only welcome praise, it was one of the strongest endorsements for promotion Brown could hope for, from an acting brigade commander and a fellow New Yorker.

However, the "awful" battle that Brown prophesied finally was fought, and Surgeon Hammond reveals the results in a letter to Morris Brown, Sr.

Petersburgh June 22 [1864][19]

Mr. Brown

I have to announce to you the painful news of the death of Morris. He was killed yesterday while leading the Regiment in a charge by a ball in the head. His death was instantaneous. I have not as yet been able to get his body. The Brigade fell back and he was left between the lines. I am making every effort possible to get his body and hope to succeed. I have his property & papers. His watch I presume is lost.

You may rest assured that I will do all in my power aided by Col. McDougall to secure him decent burial where his remains can be had when a proper time comes for their removal. Morris was a noble man and fell on the field without a blemish or a blott [sic] upon his character. I need not say how much I shall miss him as he was the only link that bound me to the Regiment. The rest are all gone. I shall take Warren Allen [Morris's cook] into my service and treat him with favor for his attachment and faithfulness to Morris. Give my sympathy to your wife & mine and believe me when I say that I feel the loss of Morris deeply and pray that this affliction may be softened to you and his mother by knowing that he was respected, trusted and honored by all who knew him.

I will write again soon.

F. M. Hammond

Another, more vivid and troubling description must have been given to Brown's parents by a friend. It could not have offered the Browns any relief:

Camp on the Jones Farm
near Petersburgh June 26 (64)

Dear Cousin & Aunt

I recd your letter last night & hasten to answer it We have had some terrible fighting here in front of Petersburgh &

have lost heavily Our Col. was killed on the 16th & then my Captain was put in command of the Regiment He was from Penn Yan & his name was Brown. He was killed in a charge by our boys the 22d I was up to the front yesterday & our boys were out trying to get him off the field, but the Rebs sharp shooters kept up such a fire that they could not get to him but they saw him He had been stripped of all his clothing & boots & our regiment lost their colors & we have only 19 privates left.

George A. Byington[20]

The next letter referring to Morris's death came from Private Sidney Rice, a Penn Yan native who may have known the Browns, at least Morris Brown, Sr. Writing on corps headquarters stationery July 1, 1864, Rice recalled that initially some members of the 126th New York questioned Morris's promotion to captain, but came to respect him for his courage and leadership. He thoughtfully recalled Captain Brown sharing drinks of water from his canteen before taking a sip himself on the march to Gettysburg.

In this campaign [to capture Petersburg] the men in his company and Regiment fell all around him but he pressed on with what was left and gained the enemys Breastworks.

When our Corp (the 2d Corps) was ordered around on the left of our line we had pretty near reached our destination when a withering fire of musketry was poured on the head of the column. but we drove the enemy and the next day while the troops were forming the line of battle so they could build breastworks and rifle pits. the enemy flanked our Division and there he was killed. note he was shot down by the enemy while trying to rally his men.

Wm Hainer the next day went out and tryed to recover his body but there were some of the enemy watching it and another body so they had to give up all hopes of getting it.[21]

CASUALTY SHEET.

Name: *Morris Brown (First Div.)*

Rank: *Capt.* Company: *-* Regiment: *126*

Arm: *Infty.* State: *New York*

Nature of Casualty: *Killed*

CAUSE OF CASUALTY—(NAME OF DISEASE, &c.)	BY WHOM DISCHARGED.

FROM WHAT SOURCE THIS INFORMATION WAS OBTAINED.

DEGREE OF DISABILITY.

Nominal List of Officers Killed & Wounded during the month of June 1864, in the 2" A.C. Not dated - Sg'd by # Page, 1 - Filed with unindexed Battle Records in D & D. Div. # Army Register shows, Capt. Morris Brown, Jr. Killed in action before Petersburg Va., June 22, 1864. Wd.B.4-19-86.

BY WHOM CERTIFIED.

 # Winf'd S. Hancock Maj. Gen'l. Vols. Com'dg.

DATE OF DISCHARGE, DEATH, &c.

June 22, 1864

PLACE OF DISCHARGE, DEATH, &c.

W. S. Burton
                Clerk.
          (170.)
April 19/86,

Ex'd. B&W.

Morris Brown's Casualty Sheet (*Source:* National Archives)

He was a good friend to me and I shall always cherish his memory and his loss is felt in the Company and Regiment. and he was a brave officer.

I remain very Respectfully
Sid. D Rice[22]

No efforts were spared to retrieve Morris Brown's body, given Colonel Clinton MacDougall's thoughtful and more detailed letter to Surgeon Fletcher Hammond, to whom the Browns must have appealed for more information about their son's death:

Morris Brown's Muster Record (*Source:* National Archives)

Head Qrs Near Petersburg, July 11/64

Dear Dr. [Hammond]

I am in receipt of your letter of July 5 & July 10 and in reply would say I should have answered you first sooner had it not been that I have been sick abed for a few days past.

The only answers I can give to the questions asked by the father of the lamented Capt Brown are these. I saw him fall myself. The bullet entered just back of and along the right ear coming out near the forehead. He died instantly as we were in full retreat being entirely engaged and under a very heavy fire. I had no time to stop to attend him. I had the Brigade in my hands and you may well imagine I had all I could attend to. Genl Barlow himself went into the woods with us and put us in position. The stories written home about his body being stripped by the rebels I think are all false. Upon enquiry I find the men referred to are both at Corps Head Quarters on Provost Guard and of course have no means of knowing anything about it except from hearsay. I have been out twice myself and so has Capt Platt with a detail of men to try and get the body. I find our pickets are not as far out into half a mile as where he fell.

And none of our men could have seen him after we fell back out of the woods that day. The enemies picket lines run along about where he fell, and I am confident they have buried him. Should our lines advance so that his grave can be marked if I am spared I will see to it and so will Capt Platt. The Capt was a very brave and none did their duty better. I recd the article you sent me for which you have my thanks. they were very accept__ ____ Mr. Browns letters. I have been down with fever a few days & have been ___. I would be obliged to give up _____

Very Truly Yours
C. D. MacDougall
Capt Brown was killed
on the 22d when Wilcox Division
of Hills Corps overpowered Barlows[23]

The next day, Dr. Hammond, serving as division surgeon, wrote the grieving parents what he had learned from his inquiries. Hammond's concern for Morris and his parents is obvious:

Citty Point July 12th 64

Mr Brown

Sir

I have received your letters and should have answered them before only that I wanted to get reliable facts to satisfy you as to the manner of Morris death and also about his body. I enclose you a letter from Col. McDougall that you will see contradicts Baker[24] & Byington. I assure you I done all I could to get his body. I offered $200 for it a sum I would gladly have paid. Col McDougall and Capt. Platt as he says were out in search of him [Morris]. Bill Hayner [Hainer] & Pat Manley[25] went out on my solicitation and the promised reward near to where he fell than any others. They did not see the body, were fired on and had to return. Baker and Byington have not been at any time before or since he fell within four miles of the spot. [Private Warren] Allen brought me his sword without scabbard or belt He always carried his sword naked [?] & never wore a belt when in battle or on a march in fact did not own either. Capt. Platt gave the sword to Allen. I do not think he had any amount of money on his person. His papers & clothes I have. His watch is lost. I will send his valise containing his private papers as soon as I can find some reliable person going to Washington. Papers connected with the Regiment & Company have been delivered to the proper persons. His accounts up to the first of April are all settled as you will see from a receipt from the Ordinance Office. There will be no difficulty in settling his accounts with the Government as his papers are all in order. I have the mare in my possession. Will take good care of her until an opportunity offers of sending her home. She is a valuable animal and in fine condition. I shall send Allen tomorrow to Petersburgh to see [Quartermaster] Capt. Loring. Will send you a check for $170[,] Twenty Dollars of it I am sure belonged to Morris. The Capt. [Loring] told me he gave it to him to keep.

I should have written you before but knowing that my letters to my wife were common property in our families and as I had written her all about the death of Morris. Supposed you would know all. I assure you I feel his loss very much. I admired him for his many good qualities. He was brave, generous and noble. A true man in every sense of the word. I have lost all interest in the Regiment since his death and care not if I never join it again. What are left of them are true brave soldiers but Morris is not there or Smith. You speak of a Will. One may be among his papers. I heard him say last winter that he intended to make one for the benefit of his mother. On the 18th of May he showed Allen a paper and said to him "if any thing happens to me I want you to see that my father gets this paper." Allen put it in his coat pocket. A few days afterward he called for his coat and took out some papers and Allen does not know whether he destroyed that one or not. He supposed however that it was with others that were in his pocket. It may be the paper is in with others. I have not looked them over.

I am here in charge of the 1st Division of the 2d Corps Hospital. A place that suits me and for which I think I am fitted. There are 342 patients in my department. I have all the work I want. Am very well. Never better. We all feel hopeful and confident of success. The campaign has been a hard one but the men have stood it well and are ready to meet the enemy at any & all time.

I want you to tell my wife that I will write her tomorrow if I can get time. The Paymaster has not been along yet. As soon as he does come I will pay her debts.

I am going to write to your wife as soon as I can. I sincerely sympathize with you and her in this great affliction and humbly pray the God "who tempers the wind to the shorn lamb" may give you comfort and support to endure whatever trouble and sorrow may be sent. Remember me to your wife, Jennie & Liny and to my family.

Yours Truly
F. M. Hammond
My address
F.M. Hammond
Surgeon 126th NYV
in Charge 1st Division
2d Corps Hospital Citty Point Va

Shortly thereafter the Browns received a letter from Captain Sanford Platt, the only other regimental captain who began the Petersburg campaign—indeed, began the war—with Morris. He offers more details, generally corroborating what MacDougall and Hammond wrote.

Camp 126th N.Y.V.
Near Petersburg Va
July 16th 1864

Mr. M Brown

Dear Sir

Your letter of July 5th was received by me in due time but under the circumstances being on the move ever since I have had no opportunity what ever, till now to answer. Your Son was killed on the 22nd day of June was shot through the forehead and died almost instantly did not live five minutes after being shot. Col. Mac Dougall Comdg Brigade and Corporal Harris[26] of our Regt. saw him after he was shot. The Orderly Sergt of Co "K" 39th N.Y.V. saw him after he was dead and brought in his sword and delivered the same to Dr. Hammond. he layed on his chest and right side. our forces at the time was on the retreat and the men generally were all mixed together. at this time he had on his person all the clothing that he had on when he fell which consisted of a Flannel Blouse[,] Vest & Blue pair of Trowsers. Our forces have not had possession of the ground since. Every thing has been done by myself & (have been out at two different times with a squad of men) the Brigade trying to recover his body without avail. Moreover I think and almost know that his body has not been seen since our retreat and what Baker[,] Byington and others have written home has been premature. I think that his body must have been buried by the Rebels ere this. but think that his Grave must be unmarked and it will be impossible ever to recover his remains or know^ exactly^ where he now lies buried. If there is any more particulars which you wish to know write me again and will willingly give you all information which is in my power

I am
Very Respectfully
S H Platt
Capt Comdg 126th N.Y.V.

Apparently letters from Morris Brown, Sr. and from Dr. Hammond crossed in the mails, for the latter again tried both to console Brown and to allay the elder Brown's concerns. Given his responsibilities at the division hospital—and, apparently, his tardiness in writing his own wife—his thoughtfulness was extraordinary.

City Point July 18th

Mr Brown

I have just received your letters and answer immediately. I wrote one to you some time ago giving you all the information I could in reference to Morris's death and his affairs. I did not write immediately on receipt of your former letter because I knew that Col. McDougall could and would let me know fully on the subject. I enclosed you his letter. I hope you have received it. I sent you yesterday Capt. Lorings Check for $170. I give you my word that the mare shall not go out of my possession without your order. It may be that you will have to wait until I come home before you can get her. I may be ordered to Washington on duty. if so I can take her along. I do not think she can be sent as the property of the Capt. Perhaps Smith might order her to be sent. Warren Allen is with me and will for Morris's sake take proper care of her. Every effort has been made that could be to get his body as you will see by Col. McDs letter. I offered half of all the money due me for it. The offer was not necessary for his men were willing to risk and did risk their lives to obtain it. The story that any had been near enough to see the body is all false. Baker and Byington have not been nearer then four miles of the spot where he fell. Wm Hayner [Hainer] and one other whose name I do not remember Pat Manley [Manly] have been out nearer than any one else and if they had been near enough to recognize him they would have brought him in. Col McDougall was near him when he fell. You will see from his letter what he says about his death. A "flag of Truce" could not be. The rebels would not permit it nor would our side ask it. He fell too near their works for them to allow any of our people to reach the spot. Allen gave me his sword[,] says Capt. Platt gave it to him. I have the sword and will keep it for you. He owned neither scabbard or belt. always carried it in his hand. His valise I will send you as soon as I possibly can. I have preserved every thing belonging to him that I could possess myself of, as I know you would value them highly. I would write you in this letter more of the circumstances but I feel sure you have received Col McD's and my letters ere you will this

The Regiment has not been consolidated and will not be. No officers have been mustered out or will be. That story is all bosh. In marching the 126th, 125th & 57th NYV are for convenience sake under one command. Smith is Lt. Col. of the 126th can be Col if he chooses. The 126th is a Regiment as much as ever though without a field officer present. I feel with Col. McDougall quite sure that Morris's body is buried. It cannot be that the rebels are so inhuman as to permit it to be otherwise when they have had peaceable possession of the ground from the first. I offered any amount of money I could raise but can only regret without avail. I feel his loss deeply. My interest in the Regiment is gone though what is left of it is of the best. It may be I shall not go back to the field again. I have charge of the 1st Division of the 2d C Hospital, a place that suits me and for which I am qualified. You will get some idea of the Hospital from a letter I wrote several. It is called Depot Field Hospital and all the indications are that it will be kept up for some time. I wish you and others would try and get an Asst Surgeon for the Regiment.

The weather is extremely dry and hot. no rain has fallen in the past month. My health is perfect and spirits good. faith strong as ever. Give my respects to your wife and the girls.

Yours &c
F. M. Hammond

Apparently Maria Brown, the grieving mother, wrote Colonel MacDougall directly, rather than going through Dr. Hammond. MacDougall was on furlough at his Finger Lakes home, possibly recovering from the sickness that had hospitalized him near Petersburg. However tired of answering questions about Morris's death he might have been, he wrote a thoughtful letter:

Auburn July 27, 1864[27]

Mrs M. C. Brown

Dear Madam,

Your letter of July 14th reached me at Petersburg while I was sick in Hospital or I should have replied to it sooner. I presume Dr Hammond has either sent or written you the Contents of a letter I wrote him upon the subject. I recd Mr. Browns letters to him, and gave all the information I then could concerning the death of your son. But learning the Doctor may not have sent you the particulars, I will repeat all I know of the circumstances of his death. You are of course aware of the reversal our whole Corps met with on the 22d of June

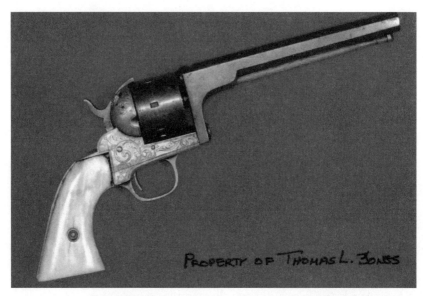

Morris Brown's pistol (*Source:* Thomas L. Jones)

Our Division had advanced about a mile and a half in advance of our old entrenched line through a dense woods, where about in the middle of the woods we were attacked with great fury by AP Hills Corps of the rebel army, and being largely outnumbered besides being outflanked we were obliged to fall back. Immediately commenced the retreat with my Brigade, fighting as I fell back to keep the enemy from closing in upon us and capturing our whole force. It was during this retreat that your son was killed. He was in the act of trying to rally some of his men in the face of the enemy when the fatal bullet hit him. He was shot just back of and quite a distance up behind the right ear and when I saw him he was lying on his face. I should judge he died instantly as the character of the wound was such as in my opinion must produce instant death. He was out front when he was killed. Whether he spoke or not is a question that I am unable to answer. When I saw him a man was pouring water upon his wound. The story that he was stripped by the enemy I think is entirely untrue, as no one has since that day advanced to the spot where he lay. I would gladly have done all in my power to get his body off at the time. But as we were in full retreat at the time, and a Brigade on my hands I of course had not a moment to spare. I went three times to the picket lines myself to see if his body cannot be recovered. But found it impossible to get out where he fell. Capt Platt has also made the effort quite as often. I think you need have no concern about his lying unburied. The enemy occupy that line and there is no danger of their leaving a body unburied. The commanding General has authority to send out flags of truce and it would be fruitless to apply to him to send one out for one body and would not consent to it. I have promised to do all I can toward finding where your son is buried. And when I go back if it be possible I will find his grave and have it so marked that the body can be removed when cool weather comes. We will undoubtedly again occupy that ground in time but it when it will be is hard to tell.

You have my sincere sympathy
in your sad affliction
With much respect
I am Dear Madam
Very Truly Yours
C D MacDougall
Commandg Brig

I omitted to mention that your son fell in a ___ road leading out of the woods, not quite a mile from the open field & from our old line of works_____

However reassuring MacDougall tried to be, he would prove to be wrong on one score. Browns' body was never recovered. Moreover, only recently was anything done to mark his death. In the 1990s, almost a hundred and thirty years after Morris's death, a stone bearing a bronze plaque was placed near his brother Smith's grave in Penn Yan's Lakeview Cemetery. In later wars at least a gold star in the Browns' front window would have marked the family which had lost a member in war. Not so when Morris was killed. In fact, for the next five years, the Browns had only their youngest son's letters, a photograph of him in uniform, and possibly his sword to comfort them.

CHAPTER 8

"Oh, My Poor Poor Brother"

It was obviously painful for Morris's brother Theodore, back in St. Louis and anticipating his August wedding to Lillie Weber, to write his parents:

St. Louis July 2d 1864[1]

My dear Father

Your wholly and entirely unexpected letter announcing the death of Morris has just been received. I cant see to write. I never thought that tears would come to my eyes again but I cant help it. He was such a noble fellow. We were never as intimate as Smith and I have been but I never knew how much I loved him til now. Oh my God that he should have been called to offer up his lifes blood to further the ends of those god forsaken traitors. I have no patience to write in a spirit of faith—religion or tolerance concerning them.

His last letter will be a great consolation to you all as we can feel convinced that he had not changed his condition [and is?] freed from earthly trouble [that?] awaits us where sin and sorrow enter not in [and?] when death and painful feelings are _____. I cant write more. Oh my poor poor brother.

Let me know all facts about and send me all papers concerning his death.

Your affect. son
Theodore

Smith Brown, out in Wisconsin, was slower to write. Likely, it was more painful for him to express himself to his parents. Though seven years apart, Smith, the oldest, and Morris, the youngest, were kindred spirits. Both helped support Theodore's more scholarly pursuits, shared a felt need to join the army, and both were adventurous, even occasionally boastful. They had tented together as fellow officers in the 126th New York, and Morris sought Smith's advice almost as often as their father's. Smith's agony was compounded by his disillusionment with the war and with those whom he accused of profiting thereby.

Actg. Asst. Provost Marshal General's Office Madison Wis., July 8th 1864

My Dear Parents

I have several times essayed to write you but could not. I had no heart to speak of our unutterable sorrow. I could not

John Smith Brown, 126th New York Volunteers (*Source:* Roger D. Hunt)

console when I myself could find no relief. I came back from LaCrosse late Tuesday morning in high spirits having had a very pleasant visit with Mary Baker and Mattie. All the Cameron's are very kind and I intended to write you a long letter. Some young ladies came down the Mississippi with me. Stopped at Madison and Wednesday morning we were at the table at breakfast all laughing and talking when Darling, the orderly, brought me all my letters home from you, Theodore and Aunt Lina. I opened Father's first enclosing Mr. Ogden's and wondered at the concluding sentence where he spoke of desolation. I pondered over it a long time and a sudden fear grew on me. I opened another letter and then it was all told.

I was stunned. I could not realize it. Can not now. It does not seem possible that I shall never see my brother again. I wrote him a long letter Friday. Was a week writing it. He wanted me to give him some advice about writing to Miss Eva Harris, to whom the poor boy had taken quite a fancy. His letters lie before me now. So lately he was well and happy. Now, so soon gone. And not even to him will death come in victory. His life lost by a foolish criminal blunder, a blunder that cost fifteen hundred men killed alone. If he must die it was well he was killed instantly. You can never imagine nor conceive the misery of severe wounds on those fields of battle. The slow lingering torturing death struggle prolonged some times for days and weeks often lying alone in some thicket uncared for till kind death relieves. The whole miserable campaign is a failure. Grant can not take Richmond and even if he could I would not have given Morris for the whole Southern Confederacy. My patriotism was exhausted long ago when I beheld how the men in power prostituted the blood and money so freely given by their countrymen to advance their private fortunes and purposes.

I can not think that I never shall see him again. During the dangers of battle and the weariness of long campaigns we were drawn closer together than perhaps we might ever have been at home. We lay under the same blanket at night and looking at the quiet skies overhead and speculated on the future and hoped, so fondly hoped we might both live to see this war at an end and all once more at home. We laid so many plans commencing "When Thede and you and I all get home together." But now Thede and he and I never will be home together again. It is *so comforting* to remember that we never had a quarrel. Of course we used to dispute and argue. but never was an unkind feeling harbored for a moment and whatever money or anything one had the other could freely share. Of business and such things I will write again. I can hardly collect my faculties now calmly enough to discuss such things. Dr. H borrowed money of Morris in November last and never paid it at least when I left it was not paid. The amount then was $30.00. Whether he borrowed more since or not I do not know.

I would like to have the sorrel mare brought home. She was *our* best friend I can not tell exactly how but it can generally be done. Wm. Baker *loves* the mare and would give all his worth to see her in Penn Yan. But I would not like to see the old mare worked. Let her rest. She has carried the food for herself, Morris and me many a hundred mile on many a weary march and often has Bill and the mare been our only friends. Dr. H. might perhaps help some way. I do not know exactly how though. The Dr. might get a furlough and might not. Uncertain.

If you conclude to wear mourning part of Morris' money should pay for it. I do not know of any way his body can be recovered say by writing Col McDougall to use *every* effort possible. McDougall liked Morris very much—and would do everything he could. Quarter Master Loring should send Stark $175.00 for my black horse. Capt Wilson should send Stark $31.00 he owes me. I guess Loring lent Morris $25.00 on my acct.—maybe more. Aside from Morris' and Loring's matters I owed Morris $104.00 at our settlement.

I recd Jennie's letter of July 3d this a.m. That private Sheppard was always a good honest fellow and always would do anything Morris wanted him to.[2] Show him any kindness he needs. I will write Jennie this evening and will send her the money. Mattie and I are very anxious to have Jennie come as soon as possible so as to visit Mattie and me both. We had many bright plans made last Sunday. I can if necessary meet Jennie in Chicago. If you can only send her as far as Chicago it would be all right. I want Jennie to stay west at least six or eight months unless I am ordered back to my regiment and even then she could remain with Theodore.

If I am ordered back and ever have the chance I have had at the rebels God help them for I never will.

I have no time to write more now. Good bye for a short time.

Your Aff. Son
Smith

On July 7, 1864, barely a week after the *Yates County Chronicle* announced his death, Morris's obituary appeared. Characteristically, it was laudatory, as were the tributes that came in from family and friends. After the usual flowery obituary style of the time the unidentified author, who indicates he knew Morris at Hamilton College, recalled that on vacation after his second year, Morris's "patriotism became enkindled" and he enrolled as a private in Company A, 126th New York.[3]

Then the writer hyperbolically asserted that, "In their first engagement at Harper's Ferry, in the absence of his superiors in rank, as Orderly Sergeant, Brown led the Company into action, and it was his conduct at that trying time which gave promise of his future success as one of the best officers in the Regiment." More factually, he cites Morris's capture of three times the number of prisoners as he had men at Gettysburg and grabbing a Confederate flag, which was "among the trophies of war in the State Capitol Albany."

Following a brief recitation of succeeding battles, leading up to his death on June 22, the long, two-column obituary employs extensive excerpts from Morris's letters to his parents to describe his feelings during the spring campaign. The writer concludes with a sad reminder that Brown's body was not recovered: "Although he now sleeps 'where the foe and the stranger will tread o'er his head,' still we trust the sacred dust of the hero may yet be laid among the familiar scenes of home. . . ."

And the obligatory closing poem:

His few surviving comrades saw
His smile when rang the proud hurrah,
As the red field was won;
Then saw in death his eyelids close
Calmly as to a night's repose,
Like flowers at set of sun.

After the Confederate surrender in April 1865 and the Grand Reviews in Washington a month later, most of the veterans returned home and tried to adapt to civilian life. For the most part Morris Brown, Jr. was forgotten until March 6, 1869, when a Medal of Honor, bestowed on those whose bravery or self sacrifice was above and beyond the call of duty, was awarded him posthumously. He was cited for his capture of a Confederate flag at Gettysburg. Normally recommendations had to be made within two years of the cited act and the medal awarded within three years, but posthumous awards could be made within five years from the act justifying the honor. While initially only enlisted men were eligible for the honor, by the time of Morris's flag capture in 1863, officers were also eligible. Importantly, Morris's name was not stricken after a board of five retired general officers met in 1916 to determine whether any Medals of Honor should not have been issued and the names of 911 Civil War soldiers were removed as undeserving. Largely these medals were granted to entice individuals to remain in service after expiration of their terms.[4]

By then Morris's mother and brother Smith were dead. Maria had passed away almost exactly a month earlier and Smith almost three years previous (on April 27, 1866), less than a year after he was mustered out of the 126th New York. Morris Brown, Jr. then faded into obscurity. An exception was a Morris Brown Camp, Sons of the Union Veterans, which existed at least for a short time in the 1900s. Another exception was a brief reference in Penn Yan's *Chronicle Express*, February 13, 1936, noting the passing of Theodore Morris Brown, who went by his middle name and who died December 24, 1935. However, C. T. Burrill, the author of this reminiscence and nephew of the officer who recruited Morris Brown, Jr. for the 126th New York, inaccurately recalled this Morris as the son of Morris Brown, Jr., not of Theodore.[5]

Because Morris's body was never recovered, there was no funeral. Thus, there was nothing to recall Morris until the mid 1990s when a

Penn Yan veterans' group placed a stone with a bronze plaque identifying Morris as a Medal of Honor recipient near Smith Brown's gravestone in Penn Yan's Lakeview Cemetery.

Epilogue

So, how is the young hero to be remembered; that is, who was Morris Brown, Jr.? We might best rely on Morris's letters, for they are the most candid revelations.

First, we learn that he embraced the Union cause as tightly as anyone could. He did so as a War Democrat, not a Republican. He opposed secession, not slavery. By his own admission he despised the "darkeys" with whom he was familiar. Yet, he believed African-Americans could be good soldiers, given his leadership. However, he offered nothing to suggest their postwar future.

Morris was brave. It takes courage to face death daily when one has seen it with all its horrors first hand. The bravado that he demonstrated at Centreville in 1863—before Gettysburg, Auburn, Bristoe, and the

Morris Brown's gravestone (*Source:* Wayne Mahood)

Wilderness—was long gone by his untimely death just over a year later. He was even willing to sacrifice an arm or leg, if allowed to muster out at home leading his depleted regiment.

He was a leader, as he amply showed when he commanded little more than a squad against the Confederates at Gettysburg, capturing greater than double the number of prisoners and a battle flag, which proved to be an especial prize. Morris had proved he and his regiment were not the cowards they were portrayed after the embarrassing rout at Harpers Ferry, barely a month after the regiment mustered at Geneva. Clearly, his inspired leadership induced Colonel, later General, Clinton MacDougall to encourage New York's governor to promote him.

Still, Morris could be boastful, as his letters almost routinely revealed. He was convinced he had few, if any, equals in his regiment. Yet, he gave credit to those who had demonstrated courage, even if he detested them, as in the case of his peer, Captain Winfield Scott. If a man stood up under the trials to which he was subjected, Morris would serve under him.

Morris Brown, Jr. was mature beyond his years. He wanted promotion not only for the recognition and opportunity to lead, but for the money. He was already planning his postwar future. His attention to money, including investing in property, strongly suggested his aims. He never indicates any intention to return to Hamilton College to complete his education, though there is nothing to suggest later he might not read law, as his father did, whereby he could foster his goals.

And he was ambitious as Lucifer, as his letters amply revealed. He pulled out all stops to obtain a desired promotion, using whatever influence his father or others could bring to bear. Yet, he was willing to put his neck on the line to prove his worth.

Morris Brown, Jr.'s story is not unique, but it is a poignant reminder of a dark period in American history and the sacrifices many families made.

Fortunately, Morris Brown, Jr.'s memory was kept alive either by his sister, Jennie, or a like-named niece who maintained a scrapbook containing the bulk of Morris's letters to his family. Eventually the scrapbook found its way into the hands of Christopher Cedzich of Nashville, Tennessee, who had obtained it from his father, an antique dealer. And propitiously, it is now being preserved at Hamilton College, Morris Brown's alma mater, a testament to a young man not yet in his prime who made the ultimate sacrifice for his patriotism.[6]

Notes

Chapter 1

1. *Yates County Chronicle*, May 2, 1861, November 15, 1860. Walter Wolcott, *The Military History of Yates County, NY* 1 (Penn Yan, New York: Express Book & Job Co., 1895), 23, claimed that five thousand attended the meeting, but this seems unrealistic.

2. W. W. Clayton, *History of Steuben County* (Philadelphia, PA: Lewis, Peck & Co., 1879), 61, 63, 411; Undated Assessment Roll, Village of Penn Yan, Yates County, linkny.com/~history/PY1856.html and linkny.com/~history/PY1856.+html; Grantee Deeds, Book 33: 538, Yates County Historian's Office; Frances Dumas, Yates County Historian; Twila O'Dell, Steuben County Historian; Minutes of the Urbana Town Board, courtesy of Terry Bretherton, Hammondsport Village Historian; Richard Leisenring, Jr., Curator, Curtiss Museum, Hammondsport, New York; 1860 Census. Young Brown alludes to this in a letter to his father December 1863, see chapter 4. The Brown house at 322 Main Street was torn down in 1965 when the Penn Yan School District purchased the property.

3. Grantee Deeds, Book 33: 538; 1860 Census, Frances Dumas, Yates County Historian; Twila O'Dell, Steuben County Historian. By this time, Brown's real estate was valued at $20,000 and his personal estate at $5000. Unusual for the time, Maria's personal estate was valued at $4000. Her father, John Smith, would leave "the rest and residue" of his estate for the "comfort and support of Hannah Grant, a colored women who has served us faithfully during her natural life," Will of John Smith, Yates County Probate Court.

4. "Breaking Apart: The Road to 1861," Yates County Web page www.yatescounty.org/upload/12/historian/prewar.htm; *Yates County Chronicle*, November 11, 1862. The issues were clearly revealed in the 1862 Gubernatorial election, wherein the village of Penn Yan registered 149 voters for the Union candidate, James S. Wadsworth, and 106 for Democrat Horatio Seymour, the winner, in what was described as an "unparalleled vote."

5. J. H. French, *Gazetteer of the State of New York* (Syracuse, NY, 1860), 717, 718, 150, 104.

6. *Yates County Chronicle*, May 2, 1861; May 23, 1861; Brown Genealogy, Yates County Historical Society, Penn Yan, New York. The "Keuka Rifles" became a company in the 33rd New York Volunteers. Inconsistently, Smith Brown was listed as Ira Smith Brown in Frederick Phisterer, comp., *New York in the War of the Rebellion*, 5 vols. (Albany, NY: J. B. Lyon Company, 1912); hereafter, *War of the Rebellion*, 4316; cf. Form B, New York Bureau of Military Statistics, courtesy of Roger D. Hunt. Phisterer, *War of the Rebellion*, 4316, states John Smith Brown enlisted at Washington, no date, which differs from what Brown wrote on Form B on August 27, 1864.

7. *Yates County Chronicle*, May 23, 1861, May 30, 1861, September 21, 1861, October 3, 1861.

8. *Yates County Chronicle*, August 29, 1861, November 7, 1861; Charles A. Stevens, *Berdan's United States Sharpshooters in the Army of the Potomac, 1861–1865* (Dayton, OH: Morningside Reprint, 1984), 5, 3.

9. Robert H. Graham, comp., *Yates County's "Boys in Blue" 1861–1865: Who They Were and What They Did* (Penn Yan, NY: Private Printing, 1926); *Yates County Chronicle*, June 19, 1861, June 26, 1861, July 31, 1861, September 4, 1861.

10. *Yates County Chronicle*, July 24, 1862, August 7, 1862. Other county committeemen were Yates County Judge William S. Briggs, Dr. Charles S. Hoyt, Meletiah H. Lawrence, Hon. Darius A. Ogden, and General Alexander F. Whitaker, Wayne Mahood, *"Written in Blood": A History of the 126th New York Infantry in the Civil War* (Hightstown, NJ: Longstreet House, 1997), 8; hereafter *Written in Blood*. The Town of Milo (Penn Yan) supplied the most, 48, of that original 220 quota, *Yates County Chronicle*, August 28, 1862; Stafford C. Cleveland, *History and Directory of Yates County* (Penn Yan, NY: S. C. Cleveland, 1873), vol. 1, 762.

11. *Yates County Chronicle*, August 28, 1862; Phisterer, *War of the Rebellion*, 3502. On September 2, 1862, Smith Brown obtained his discharge from the USSS, though he would not join the 126th New York Vols., until November 17, Phisterer, *War of the Rebellion*, 3498, 4316. The information about Theodore is found in *The American Chess Journal* II, no. 4 (September 1877): 53–55.

12. Maurice Isserman, *On the Hill: A Bicentennial History of Hamilton College 1812–2012* (Clinton, NY: Trustees of Hamilton College, 2011), 99–101.

13. Mahood, *"Written in Blood,"* 12, 13; notation by Professor of Latin and Greek Edward North and *Delta Upsilon Decennial Catalogue*, 1902, Hamilton College Archives. Myron Adams would be honored later by having a Grand Army of the Republic post named after him and by the success of his muckraker-novelist son, Samuel Hopkins Adams. Another member of Morris Brown's Hamilton class of 1864 was Elihu Root, whose distinguished career

included a Nobel Peace Prize and service as U.S. Secretary of War and State and a term as U.S. senator from New York.

14. Mahood, *"Written in Blood,"* 13, 14. Hammond was married to Maria Brown's sister Sarah.

15. Ibid., 16, 17.

16. Phisterer, *War of the Rebellion,* 3502; Morris Brown, Jr. Military Service Record, Record Group 94, AGO, National Archives; Mahood, *Written in Blood,* 18, 19. Brown's appointment, signed by Colonel Sherrill on August 11, lists him as First Sergeant.

17. Mahood, *Written in Blood,* 19, 20.

18. Morris Brown, Jr. Letters, Brown Scrapbook, Hamilton College Archives, Clinton, New York, used with permission of the College Library. This and the bulk of the letters were in a scrapbook maintained by "Jennie," Brown's younger sister or niece, which the college purchased in 1991. Details of the serendipitous discovery of and purchase of the letters are in the sidebar to my article, " 'Morris is a Hero' A Saga of the Civil War," *Hamilton Alumni Review,* (Fall-Winter, 1991–1992), 10–14.

The punctuation and spelling in Brown's letters are changed only where necessary for clarity. Asterisks (*) for emphasis are in the original and the carets (^) are added to indicate where Brown inserted comments.

19. This reference, apparently to Colonel Jesse Segoine, commander of the 111th New York, is unclear. Segoine had not yet been mustered when Confederates occupied or skirmished near Harpers Ferry from May 1861 to February 1862, when Federals reoccupied it, nor during Jackson's Valley Campaign in early 1862.

20. *Yates County Chronicle,* August 28, 1862; Smith Brown's statement, Form B, New York Bureau of Military Statistics; Phisterer, *War of the Rebellion,* 3498, 4316.

21. Myron Adams Letters (September 3, 1862), Hamilton College Archives; Dennis Frye, "Stonewall Attacks: The Siege of Harpers Ferry," *Blue & Gray* 5, no. 1 (August-September 1987), 10–11.

22. Regimental Order No. 4, September 4, 1862, Record Group 94, National Archives; Frederick A. Dyer, *A Compendium of the War of the Rebellion* (Dayton, OH: Morningside Reprint, 1978), 1524, 1652; hereafter *Compendium of the War.*

23. *The War of the Rebellion: A Compilation of the Official Records of the Union and Confederate Armies* (Washington: 1880–1881), Series 1, Volume 19, Part 1: 600, 792. Hereafter *OR* and Series I, unless otherwise noted.

24. Shelby Foote, *The Civil War, a Narrative,* 3 vols. (New York: Random House, 1963), vol. 1, 667; James Longstreet, *From Manassas to Appomattox* (New York: Mallard Press, 1991 reprint), 286.

25. For extended treatments see Frye, "Stonewall Attacks: The Siege of Harpers Ferry," 9–27, 47–54; Wayne Mahood, " 'Some Very Hard Stories Were

Told': The 126th New York Infantry at Harpers Ferry," *Civil War Regiments* 2, no. 4: 7–41.

26. *Yates County Chronicle*, October 16, 1862.

27. Paul R. Teetor, *A Matter of Hours, Treason at Harper's Ferry* (Rutherford, New Jersey: Fairleigh Dickinson Press, 1981); *Ontario County Republican Times* (Canandaigua, New York), October 15, 1862.

28. OR, Ser. II, 4: 266–67.

29. Richard Bassett Letter, September 22, 1862, Civil War Papers, 1861–1870, Account #2001.116, Ontario County Historical Society; hereafter *Bassett Letters*.

30. Brigadier General Daniel Tyler's report, OR, Ser. II, 4: 596, 595, 596; Michael Stout Letters, Interlaken Historical Society, September 28, 1862; Newman Eldred, "Newman Eldred's Account of Service in the Civil War," *Yesteryears* (Summer 1979), 82; hereafter "Eldred's Account."

31. General Tyler's report, OR, Ser. II, 4: 595. The parolees were the First Brigade, commanded by Colonel Frederick D'Utassy (his own 39th New York, the 111th and 115th New York, the 65th Illinois, and a battery of the 15th Indiana Artillery); the Second, commanded by Colonel William F. Trimble (his 60th Ohio, 9th Vermont, 126th New York, and the 1st Independent Indiana Battery); the Third, commanded by Colonel Thomas H. Ford (his 32nd Ohio, a battalion of the 1st Maryland Home Brigade, Company F of the 5th New York Heavy Artillery, and "Corliss's squadron" of the 7th Rhode Island Cavalry); Colonel William G. Ward's Fourth Brigade (the 12th New York Militia, Company A of the 5th New York Heavy Artillery, Captain Silas Rigby's Indiana Battery and the 8th Ohio). Independent commands were the 1st Maryland Potomac Home Brigade, Colonel Arno Voss's 12th Illinois Cavalry, 1st Maryland Cavalry (detachment), 3rd Maryland Home Brigade and those of Colonel Grimes Davis's 8th New York Cavalry who had not escaped prior to the surrender.

32. Newman Eldred, "Eldred's Account," (Summer 1979), 8; OR, Ser. II, 4: 106.

33. General Tyler's report, OR, Ser. II, 4; 644, 645; Arabella M. Willson, *Disaster, Struggle and Triumph: 1000 "Boys in Blue"* (Albany, NY: Argus Company, Printers, 1870), 117; hereafter Willson, *Disaster Struggle*, Triumph; Eldred, "Eldred's Account," (Fall 1979), 9; "Co. D," *Ontario County Repository & Messenger*, October 29, 1862; Sergeant Harrison Ferguson Letter, October 20, 1862; hereafter Ferguson Letters, courtesy of descendants, Mrs. Eleanor Ferguson and Mr. Donald Wheat.

34. Letter of Company A's Peter Paris, October 2, 1862, courtesy of descendant Terry Murphy; Letter of First Lieutenant Richard Bassett, October 21, 1862, Bassett Letters.

35. OR, Ser. I I, 4: 720, 750.

Chapter 2

1. Bassett Letters, December 1, 1862; Special Orders No. 393, War Department, issued December 13, 1862, charging Barras with living in Washington without authorization and in violation of General Orders No. 414.

2. Brown Scrapbook; Walter Pilkington, *Hamilton College* (Clinton, New York: Hamilton College, 1962), 164, 215.

3. Sid Rice Letter to Brown's parents, July 1, 1864, Brown Scrapbook.

4. Ferguson Letters, March 29, 1863; Letter of Orin J. Herendeen, C.W. Coll. 77, Box 1, Geneva (N.Y) Historical Society, hereafter Herendeen Letters. Just over a year later Carpenter enlisted in the 179th New York as a private, and December 23, 1864 was promoted captain, Phisterer, *War of the Rebellion*, 4033.

5. Smith Brown Letter, December 27, 1862, *Yates County Chronicle*, January 15, 1863.

6. George F. Waring, *"The Garibaldi Guard" in the First Book of the Author's Club. Libor Scriptorum* (New York: The Author's Club, DeVinne Press, 1893), 570–71; Ferguson Letters, December 21, 1862; Letter of George Yost, courtesy of his descendant Michael Yost, January 9, 1863, hereafter Yost Letters; Bassett Letters, January 12, 1863.

7. Bassett Letters, January 15, 1863.

8. George T. Fleming, ed., *The Life and Letters of Alexander Hays* (Pittsburgh, PA: Gilbert A. Hays, 1919), 370, 357, hereafter *The Life and Letters*.

9. Winfield Scott, "Pickett's Charge," California Commandery of the Military Order of the Loyal Legion of the United States (MOLLUS), February 8, 1888, 6; Ezra D. Simons, *A Regimental History: The One Hundred & Twenty-fifth New York* (New York: Judson Printing Co., 1888), 191.

10. Morris Brown, Jr., Military Service Record, Record Group 94, AGO, National Archives.

11. Darius Ogden, Rev. Frederick Starr, likely, and Congressman Daniel Morris, who were New York 26th Senatorial District military committeemen from Yates County.

12. General Hays's letter, January 27, 1863, Fleming, *Life and Letters*, 304.

13. The Stark to whom he refers is Oliver Stark, who exchanged sight drafts on New York City banks and served as a fire and life insurance broker. Stark's ads appeared regularly in the *Yates County Chronicle*. Smith, of whom Morris is so critical, is Franklin Smith, a Penn Yan clothing store owner and Town of Milo supervisor. Biographical information about Smith was found in Lewis Cass Aldrich, *History of Yates County* (Syracuse, NY: D. Mason, 1892), 520. The references to Jones and "Lieut. Smith" are unclear.

14. The Battle of Chancellorsville, May 1–4, 1863, initiated by Army of the Potomac Commander General Joseph Hooker, largely was fought just

west of Fredericksburg, Virginia. Well-planned to force General Robert Lee to do battle, the much-heralded flank movement by General Jackson on May 2 badly scattered the Union XI Corps and may well have caused Hooker to abandon the engagement and retreat back across the Rappahannock River early on May 4.

15. Yost Letters, April 25, 1863; Herendeen Letters, April 7, 1863.

16. Morris Brown, Jr., Military Service Record, Record Group 94, AGO, National Archives; Phisterer, *War of the Rebellion*, 3502.

17. Apparently he refers to Company C Captain Bennett Munger of the historic "Ellsworth Avengers," named for Colonel Elmer Ellsworth, the Union's first martyr, Phisterer, *War of the Rebellion*, 2289, 2302. By this time the 44th New York had fought in the Battles of the Seven Days (June 25–July 1, 1862), Second Bull Run (August, 1862), Antietam (September 17, 1862), Fredericksburg (December 13, 1862), and Chancellorsville.

18. Brown jumped the gun here. Vicksburg didn't fall until July 4, 1863 after a prolonged siege.

19. Herendeen Letters, June 20, 1863.

20. Diary of Benjamin Swartout, June 19, 1863, Swartout Collection, Waterloo Library and Historical Society; hereafter Swartout Diary; Herendeen Letters, June 20, 1863.

21. William LeMunyon, "War Record of W. F. LeMunyon," U.S. Army Military History Institute, Carlisle Barracks, Pennsylvania, hereafter "War Record," 13; Newman Eldred, "Eldred's Account," 14; Herendeen Letters, July 1, 1863; Francis A. Walker, *History of the Second Army Corps in the Army of the Potomac* (Gaithersburg, MD: Olde Soldier Books, Inc., 1988, reprint of Charles Scribner's Sons, 1887), 259–60; hereafter Walker, *History of the Second Corps*. Walker says Hays's men joined the II Corps at Gum Springs.

22. Myron Failing, "Gen. Alex Hays at Gettysburg," *National Tribune*, October 15, 1885, 5: 3.

23. Ferguson Letters, June 28, 1863; Josiah Favill, *Diary of a Young Officer* (Chicago: R. R. Donnelly & Sons, 1909), 241, hereafter Favill, *Diary of a Young Officer*, 241; General Hancock's report, OR 27, pt. 1: 367; Ferguson Letters, June 28, 1863.

Chapter 3

1. Stephen Sears, *Gettysburg* (Boston: Houghton Mifflin, 2003), 144, 145.

2. Yost Letters, July 6, 1863; Sidney D. Rice Letter to Brown's parents, July 1, 1864, Brown Scrapbook.

3. "Eldred's Account," 38; Smith Brown's account, Arabella M. Willson, *Disaster, Struggle, Triumph*, 177.

4. Willson, *Disaster, Struggle, Triumph*, 177.

5. Eric Campbell, " 'Remember Harper's Ferry': The Degradation, Humiliation, and Redemption of Col. George Willard's Brigade," *Gettysburg Magazine* (July 1992), pt. 1: 64, 75; General Hays's report, *OR*, vol. 27, pt. 1: 453.

6. Bassett Letter, July 11, 1863, Ontario County (New York) Historical Society; Charles A. Richardson reunion speech, Willson, *Disaster, Struggle, Triumph*, 178. Canister, effective at three hundred yards, was a tin can filled with small lead balls which scattered after leaving the muzzle and created a particularly deadly effect on charging troops. Grape shot, three layers of lead balls linked by two iron plates and rings with an iron plate through the plates and rings (effective at seven hundred yards), released on discharge, had an equally devastating effect.

7. Benjamin W. Thompson, "This Hell of Destruction: The Benjamin W. Thompson Memoir," *Civil War Times Illustrated*, vol. 12, no. 6 (1973), 18, claims that Willard was struck even before the brigade advanced across the swale. Other accounts, including by the 126th New York's Lt. Col. James Bull, Adjutant Smith Brown and Lt. Richard Bassett, assert Willard was hit after the successful attack when attempting to withdraw the brigade. Ezra D. Simons, *A Regimental History, the One Hundred and Twenty-Fifth New York State Volunteers* (New York: Simons, 1888), 112, is in accord. Simons also suggests that Willard had been ordered to withdraw the brigade. Thompson claimed that Colonel Sherrill "seeing that we were not needed" after the Union line was reformed by the III and V corps, ordered the withdrawal, Thompson, "This Hell of Destruction," 19; Brown's note to General Hays's aide, Captain George Corts, July 3, 1863, Brown Scrapbook.

8. Clinton MacDougall's Letter to Major Charles Richardson, June 20, 1886, 126th Regiment New York Volunteers, Assorted Papers, Box 1, Folder 2, Ontario County Historical Society.

9. Willson, *Disaster, Struggle and Triumph*, 11; Thompson, "The Hell of Destruction," 20; *Annual Report of the Adjutant-General of the State of New York*, vol. 36 (Albany, NY: Oliver A. Quayle, 1904); hereafter *Adjutant-General' Report*.

10. Thomas F. Galwey, "An Episode of the Battle of Gettysburg," *The Bachelder Papers*, 3 vols., edited by David L. Ladd and Audrey J. Ladd (Dayton, OH: Morningside House, 1995), vol. 2, 871; Elwood W. Christ, *"Over a Wide, Hot Crimson Plain:" The Struggle for the Bliss Barn at Gettysburg* (Baltimore: Butternut & Blue, 1993); "Letter of Lt. Charles Hitchcock," in *The Bachelder Papers*, vol. 2, 1183, 1188, 1184; "Letter of Brig. Gen. Alexander Hays," ibid., 1179–80.

11. "Letter of Capt. Charles A. Richardson, in *The Bachelder Papers*, vol. 1, 316; Campbell, "Remember Harper's Ferry!," *Gettsburg Magazine*, part 2, January 1993, 102.

12. "Letter of Lt. John L. Brady," in *The Bachelder Papers*, vol. 3, 1396; "Letter of Capt. David Shields," in *The Bachelder Papers*, vol. 2: 1068; Frank

L. Byrne and Andrew T. Weaver, eds., *Haskell of Gettysburg: His Life and Civil War Papers* (Kent, OH: The Kent State University Press, 1989), 142; Sears, *Gettysburg*, 394.

13 "Eldred's Account" 41, 42; Gary W. Gallagher, ed., *Fighting for the Confederacy: Personal Recollections of Edward Porter Alexander* (Chapel Hill, NC: University of North Carolina Press, 1989), 257; Henry J. Hunt, "The Third Day at Gettysburg," in *Battles and Leaders of the Civil War*, ed. Robert Underwood Johnson and Clarence Clough Buel (New York: Century Company, 1884, 1887, 1888), vol. 3, 372.

14. George R. Stewart, *Pickett's Charge* (Boston: Houghton Mifflin Co., 1959), 142, 143; George H. Washburn, *A Complete History of the 108th Regiment, New York, Volunteers, From 1862 to 1894* (Rochester, NY: E. R. Andrews Press, 1894), 52, hereafter *History of the 108th New York*; Eric Campbell, " 'Remember Harper's Ferry': The Degradation, Humiliation, and Redemption of Col. George L. Willard's Brigade," *Gettysburg Magazine*, July 1992, pt. 2, 103, 104.

15. Winfield Scott, "Pickett's Charge," California Commandery of the Military Order of the Loyal Legion, Robert. L. Brake Collection, Carlisle Barracks: U.S. Army Military History Institute, 9.

16. Washburn, *History of the 108th New York*; Stewart, *Pickett's Charge*, 166.

17. Scott, "Pickett's Charge," 10, 11.

18. Washburn, *History of the 108th New York*, 52; Michael W. Taylor, "North Carolina in the Pickett-Pettigrew-Trimble Charge at Gettysburg," *Gettysburg Magazine*, January 1, 1993, No. 8: 67–83; David G. Martin, *Gettysburg July 1* (Conshohocken, PA: Combined Books, 1995), 401–404, 500–501. Davis's brigade, the 11th, 42nd, and 2nd Mississippi and the 55th North Carolina, had suffered heavily on the first day's battle west of Gettysburg. Brockenbrough's brigade consisted of the 22nd Bn, 40th, 47th, and 55th Virginia. Scales's brigade was made up of the 16th, 22nd, 34th, 13th and 38th North Carolina, while Lane's were also Carolinians: the 7th, 37th, 28th, 18th and 33rd North. Scales's men had suffered heavy casualties, including the wounding of Scales, two days earlier along Seminary Ridge, west of town. For the most part Lane's brigade, like Pickett's Division, had been spared on the First. The quote is from Rod Cragg, *Covered With Glory* (New York: Harper Collins, 2000), 157.

19. "Letter of Lt. John L. Brady," in *The Bachelder Papers*, vol. 3, 1397.

20. Taylor, "North Carolina in the Pickett-Pettigrew-Trimble Charge at Gettysburg," *Gettysburg Magazine*, 74; David Schultz and Richard Rollins, "A Combined and Concentrated Fire," *North & South* 2, no. 3 (March 1999), 40, 54, 56; Cragg, *Covered With Glory*, 204.

21. General Winfield S. Hancock, "Testimony of Major General W. S. Hancock, Report on the Conduct of the War," 2nd Sess., 38th Cong. (Washington: GPO, 1865), 1: 408, hereafter CCW; Stewart, *Pickett's Charge*, 208; T. M. R.

Talcott, "The Third Day at Gettysburg," *Southern Historical Society Papers*, 41: 46.

22. Smith Brown Letter, July 4, 1863, Brown Scrapbook.

23. Brown letter, July 16, 1863, Brown Scrapbook. Brown's recall of the number of men with him on that flank attack reflects the fact that his company, once 100 men, had been reduced to 53 prior to the battle. The ranks of the retreating Confederate regiments were also quite reduced.

24. Receipt for the captured flag, dated July 17, 1863, James M. Bull, 126th New York Infantry Regiment, Book 40–48, Lewis Leigh Collection, in which Leigh corrected the record as to the North Carolina regiment; Adjutant General's Office, May 21, 1888, to Charles Richardson, 126th New York Infantry, Assorted Papers, Box 1, Ontario County Historical Society.

25. "Invoice of Flags Captured at Gettysburg, PA, July 3rd, 1863, By Third Division, Second Army Corps, Commanded by Brigadier General Alexander Hays," Fleming, *The Life and Letters*, 467–69; Statement of Lieutenant Colonel James M. Bull, 126th New York, July 17, 1863 and of Maj. Gen. George G. Meade, October 17, 1864, Adjutant General's Office, May 21, 1888, 2126 A.G.O. 1888; OR 27, pt. 1: 473; Military Service Records of Capt. Brown, Sgt. Dore and Pvt. Wall, National Archives; "Report of Lt. Col. Charles H. Morgan," in *The Bachelder Papers*, vol. 3, 1364.

26. Numbers differ with the source. Compare General Hays's report, OR 27, pt. 1: 453; John Busey and David G. Martin, *Regimental Strengths and Losses at Gettysburg* (Hightstown, NJ: Longstreet House, 1986), 270, 271, 261, 262; General Meade's report, OR 27, pt. 1: 177; General Hays reported 1285 casualties for his division, ibid., 455; *Annual Report of the Adjutant-General of the State of New York*, vol. 36 (Albany, NY: Oliver A. Quayle, 1904).

27. Smith Brown letter, July 4, 1863, Brown Scrapbook. Herendeen and Sherrill were mortally wounded, and, as noted, the flag proved to be the 28th North Carolina's, not the 14th.

28. Letters Sent, Adjutant General's Office, Record Group 94, National Archives; Special Order No. 180, August 15, 1863, Continental Commands, Record Group 383, National Archives.

29. *Yates County Chronicle*, August 6, 1863.

30. General Halleck's dispatches to General Meade, July 8, 1863, OR 27, pt. 1: 84, 82; General Meade's reply to Halleck, ibid., 85.

31. John Ryno Diary, July 8, 1863 (Interlaken Historical Society); hereafter Ryno Diary; *The Frederick, Maryland Examiner*, July 8, 1863.

32. Yost Letters, July 28, 1863.

33. Ibid.; Coleman letter to Surgeon Hoyt, November 27, 1866, Bassett Collection; Bassett Letters, August 8, 1863. Baird's reinstatement is reported in the *Yates County Chronicle*, August 13, 1863, but he was not mustered until November 5, 1863, Phisterer, *War of the Rebellion*, 3498, 3501.

34. Walker, *History of the Second Corps*, 310–12. Official returns list 9,032 present for duty, OR 27, Pt. 1: 152; Willson, *Disaster, Struggle and Triumph*, 210

35. He was promoted lieutenant colonel on May 2, 1864, and mustered, but not commissioned, colonel on July 27, 1864, Phisterer, *War of the Rebellion*, 3498, 3502; John Smith Brown military record, Brown Scrapbook.

36. Walker, *History of the Second Corps*, 316, 317; Willson, *Disaster, Struggle and Triumph*, 209.

37. Fleming, *The Life and Letters of Alexander Hays*, August 10, 1863, 476.

Chapter 4

1. General Hays's letter to his wife, September 14, 1863, Fleming, *The Life and Letters*, 483; General Longstreet to General Lee, September 2, 1863, and General Lee's telegrams to President Davis, September 6, 1863, OR 29, pt. 2: 693, 694, 700, 701; G. K. Warren Papers, Box 22, Coll. No. SC10668, vol. 5, New York State Library, Albany, New York, hereafter Warren Papers; William Swinton, *Campaigns of the Army of the Potomac: A Critical History of the Operations in Virginia, Maryland, and Pennsylvania, from the Commencement to the Close of the War, 1861–1864* (New York: Charles B. Richardson, 1866), 374, 375.

2. General Hays's letter to Annie Hays, Fleming, *The Life and Letters*, 484; Ferguson letters, September 17, 1863. There is some confusion about the date, with Ferguson offering one date, Hays another.

3. Walker, *History of the Second Corps*, 310, 311; Warren Papers; Letters Sent, October 17 and September 24, 1863, Adjutant General's Office, Record Group 94, National Archives. Conscripts were draftees; bounty jumpers signed up for the monetary inducement with no intention of serving.

4. Brown was referring to the Battle of Chickamauga (Tennessee), where Maj. Gen. George Thomas earned the sobriquet "Rock of Chickamauga" for withstanding Longstreet's attack, which threatened the Union's hold on Tennessee and had sent Maj. Gen. William S. Rosecrans and subordinates back to Chattanooga.

5. Francis A. Lord, *They Fought For the Union* (New York: Bonanza Books, 1960), 123. Why Brown was paid at the end of September is unknown, because army regulations called for paying the soldiers on the last day of even numbered months. However, issuance of pay was often irregular, even depending on when an advance of the army was anticipated.

6. Frank J. Welcher, *The Union Army: Organization and Operations*, 3 vol. (Bloomington, IN: Indiana University Press, 1989), vol. 1, 463, 472; Swinton, *Campaigns of the Army of the Potomac*, 376, 377; Brig. Gen. Joshua T. Owen's report, OR 29, pt. 2: 242; General Hays's letter to his wife, October 3, 1863,

Fleming, *The Life and Letters*, 492; William D. Henderson, *The Road to Bristoe Station: Campaigning With Lee and Meade, August 1–October 20, 1863* (Lynchburg, VA: H. E. Howard, Inc., 1987), 74, hereafter, *The Road to Bristoe Station*.

7. Henderson, *The Road to Bristoe Station*, 70, 71; Circular, Warren Papers, Box 22, 5, October 10, 1863; General Warren's report, OR 29, pt. 1: 235.

8. Circulars, Warren Papers, October 12, 13, 1863; Warren's report, OR 29, pt. 1: 236, 237; Organization of the Army of the Potomac, OR 29, pt. 1: 217–223.

9. General Warren's report, OR 29, pt. 1: 238.

10. Henderson, *The Road to Bristoe Station*, 156; General Warren's report, OR 29, pt. 1: 238, 239; Telegram from Maj. Gen. Humphreys to Maj. Gen. Warren, October 14, 1863, Warren Papers.

11. Henderson, *The Road to Bristoe Station*, 157; General Hays's letter to his wife, October 17, 1863, Fleming, *The Life and Letters*, 498; Ferguson Letters, October 18, 1863; General Hays's letter to his wife, October 17, 1863, Fleming, *The Life and Letters*, 498.

12. Henderson, *The Road to Bristoe Station*, 158.

13. Winfield Scott, "Letter from Winfield Scott," December 15, 1890, unidentified publication, courtesy the late Maurice Patterson, President, Interlaken (New York) Historical Society, hereafter Scott Letters; General Hays's letter to John B. McFadden, October 17, 1863, Fleming, *The Life and Letters*, 498; General Hays's report, OR 29, pt. 1: 289.

14. Scott, "Letter from Winfield Scott," December 15, 1890, Scott Letters.

15. Telegrams from Maj. Gen. Humphreys to Maj. Gen. Warren, October 14, 1863, Warren Papers; General Warren's report, OR 29, pt. 1: 241.

16. James I. Robertson, *General A. P. Hill: The Story of a Confederate Warrior* (New York: Random House, 1987), 234, 235, hereafter *General A. P. Hill*; General Hill's report, OR 29, pt. 1: 427.

17. General Warren's report OR 29, pt. 1: 242; Charles W. Cowtan, *Service of the Tenth New York Volunteer (National Zouaves) in the War of the Rebellion* (New York: Charles H. Ludwig, 1882), 222.

18. Walker, *The Second Corps*, 352; Brown Letters, October 15, 1863, Brown Scrapbook.

19. Cowtan, *Service of the Tenth New York*, 222; General Warren's report, OR 29, pt. 1: 242; Captain John G. Hazard's report, ibid., 305; W. J. Martin, "The Eleventh North Carolina Regiment," *Southern Historical Society Papers*, 23: 47, 48; Charles D. Page, *History of the Fourteenth Connecticut Volunteer Infantry* (Meriden, Connecticut: The Horton Printing Company, 1906), 194.

20. General Warren's report, OR 29, pt. 1: 243.

21. General Heth's report, OR 29, pt. 1: 432; William W. Hassler, "The Slaughter Pen at Bristoe Station," *Civil War Times Illustrated*, 1, no. 2 (May

1962): 13; General Warren's report, OR 29, pt. 1: 243, 244; Ferguson Letters, October 18, 1863; Favill, The Diary of a Young Officer, 268; General Hays's letter to his mother-in-law, October 19, 1863, Fleming, The Life and Letters, 500.

22. General Orders No. 96, October 15, 1863, Walker, The Second Corps, 363; General Warren's report OR 29, pt. 1: 245, 249; Hassler, "The Slaughter Pen at Bristoe Station," 13. General Lee reported a total of 1381 casualties, 205 killed and 1176 wounded, OR 29, pt. 1: 414.

23. Strobridge would survive this, but not a wound incurred March 26, 1865, near Petersburg, Virginia.

24. Company A musters, 126th New York Volunteers, Assorted Papers, 1862–1877, M122, Box 3, Folder 29, Ontario County Historical Society. The October muster, printed in the Yates County Chronicle, November 26, 1863, listed 226 officers and men present for duty, including 16 officers (1 "in arrest" and 4 sick) and 210 enlisted men, including 4 "in arrest." Morris's report on the letter from Private Beyea was submitted to the paper by his brother, the regimental adjutant, on November 6, 1863, ibid., November 12, 1863.

25. General Hill's report, OR 29, pt. 1: 427; General Lee's dispatch to Jefferson Davis, ibid., 428. Confederate losses are in General Hill's and General Heth's reports, ibid., 428 and 433.

26. General Hays's letter to his wife, October 18, 1863, Fleming, The Life and Letters, 496.

27. General Meade's telegram to General Halleck and Halleck's reply, OR 29, pt. 2: 409–410, 412; Meade to Halleck, ibid., 424; Circular from Meade to his corps commanders, ibid., 425–427; Meade to Halleck, ibid., 429; General Hays's letter to his wife, November 16, 1863, Fleming, The Life and Letters, 520.

28. Swinton, Campaigns of the Army of the Potomac, 391.

29. General Humphreys to General Newton, November 22, 1863, OR 29, pt. 2: 477 and General Meade's report, December 7, 1863, OR 29, pt. 1: 13; General Warren to General Humphreys, November 22, 1863, OR 29, pt. 2: 477; Circular from General Meade, November 22, 1863, ibid.; General Meade to corps commanders, November 22, 23, 1863, ibid., 477, 478; Circular from General Meade, November 23, 1863, ibid., 480.

30. General Orders No. 72, dated November 25, 1863, 126th New York Volunteers, Assorted Papers, 1862–1877, M122, Box 1, Folder 6, Ontario County Historical Society; Surgeon Fletcher Hammond's letter to Morris Brown, June 22 [23] 1864, Brown Scrapbook.

31. "Extract from a Private Letter from the 126th N.Y.V.," Yates County Chronicle, December 17, 1863, likely from Smith Brown, who apparently had learned to be circumspect after being court-martialed by General Hays the past August. General Warren's report, OR 29, pt. 1: 694, 695; "Extract from a Private Letter from the 126th N.Y.V."; General Hays's letter to his wife, December 3,

1863, Fleming, *The Life and Letters*, 523; General Warren's report, *OR* 29, pt. 1: 696. Smith Brown was promoted major on November 20, 1863, Phisterer, *War of the Rebellion*, 3498.

32. General Warren's report, *OR* 29, pt. 1: 698; General Warren's dispatch to General Meade, November 30, 1863, *OR* 29, pt. 2: 517; Thomas Livermore, *Days and Events, 1860–1866* (Boston: Houghton, Mifflin, 1920), 303, 304; "Extract from a Private Letter from the 126th N.Y.V.," *Yates County Chronicle*, December 17, 1863.

Chapter 5

1. *Yates County Chronicle*, January 14, 1864, February 25, 1864. Morris's military service record lists him as present for January and February, 1864, but inconsistently lists him on detached recruiting service for February and March, National Archives. Theodore's return was reported in the *Yates County Chronicle*, December 3, 1863. A letter from Colonel Bull in Canandaigua, dated March 3, 1864, suggests that Morris Brown was still on recruiting duty March 3 and asking about travel arrangements to return to his regiment, Morris Brown Scrapbook, Hamilton College Archives.

2. Walker, *History of the Second Corps*, 392–93; *Yates County Chronicle*, January 21, 1864, November 11, 1863, December 3, 1863, January 14, 1864.

3. Bruce Catton, *A Stillness at Appomattox* (New York: The Fairfax Press, 1984), 461 (reprint of 1953 edition); Letter to the editor from D. A. O[gden], *Yates County Chronicle*, March 3, 1864.

4. Roy P. Basler, *The Collected Works of Abraham Lincoln*, 10 vols. New Brunswick, NJ: Rutgers University Press, 1953, vol. 8, 339; T. Harry Williams, *Lincoln and His Generals* (New York: Knopf, 1952), 297, 298. The reorganization was in General Orders No. 115, March 23, 1864, *OR* 33: 717, 718, with clarification in General Orders No. 10, March 24, 1864, *OR* 33: 722–23.

5.Ezra J. Warner, *Generals in Blue: Lives of the Union Commanders* (Baton Rouge, LA: Louisiana State University Press, 1986, reprint of 1964 edition), 18, 19.

6. *Yates County Chronicle*, March 24, 1864, May 12, 1864. Privately Coleman admitted that he was not proud of the way he left the regiment, but made it clear that he would not serve under "that fellow [Smith] Brown," whom Coleman labeled "a rascal and a coward who owed his continuance in the service to my forbearance," Letter to the 126th New York's surgeon, Dr. Charles Hoyt, November 27, 1866, Civil War Papers 1861–1870, Acc #2001.116, Ontario County Historical Society. Baird had rejoined the regiment November 5, 1863 after having successfully argued his case for reinstatement all the way to Secretary of War Stanton. He had been wrongly dismissed after the 126th's surrender at

Harpers Ferry. While officially reinstated shortly after Gettysburg, there were no vacancies at his rank until November. Mahood, *Written in Blood*, 195, 196.

7. *Yates County Chronicle*, May 5, 1864, June 1, 1864; Smith Brown's Military Service Record, National Archives; Phisterer, *War of the Rebellion*, 3498. Inconsistently, in less than a month, he was promoted lieutenant colonel of the 126th New York, resulting from the resignation of Colonel Bull on April 18, and Lt. Col. Baird's succession as regimental commander. Later Smith Brown would be promoted colonel, but like Baird, would never be mustered at that rank, ibid., 3502, 3501. The Adams brothers' and Sheldon's post-126th New York service can be traced in ibid., 4158 and 4210.

8. *Yates County Chronicle*, April 7, 1864. It appears that Jones, a wealthy land owner in Penn Yan completed the sale of twenty-five acres for $500 on September 23, 1865, more than a year after Morris's death, Deeds, Book 47, page 36, Yates County Clerk. At the time of the court case against Jones in April 1864, the elder Brown and Prosser also were quite active as counsel in a murder case, for which they obtained an acquittal, and a rape case, in which the jury disagreed over the appropriate charge, *Yates County Chronicle*, April 7, 1864.

9. General Orders No. 129, March 30, 1864, OR 33: 769; General Grant to General Halleck, ibid., 770; General Orders No. 17, April 7, 1864, ibid., 816, 817; Circular, April 8, 1864, ibid., 822; General Grant to General Meade, April 9, 1864, ibid., 827, 828.

10. Probably Company F Lieutenant Ira Munson.

11. OR, 33: 828; General Grant to General Halleck, ibid., 729; Grant to Meade, April 9, 1864, ibid., 828.

12. Apparently, he did not have an African-American servant, as his brother, Lieutenant Bassett, and Captain Charles Richardson did in spring 1863, Bassett Letters, May 28, 1863, Civil War Papers 1861–1870, Acc #2001.116, Folder 5B, Ontario County Historical Society; Yost Letters, March 2, 1863.

13. Bassett Letters, April 26, 1864.

14. Smith Brown had been appointed Inspector General of Wisconsin by the secretary of war on April 20, 1864, and incongruously was promoted lieutenant colonel of the 126th New York on May 2, 1864, with rank from April 18, Smith Brown Military Service Records, National Archives. He would serve in that rank until May 11, 1865.

15. Morris Brown was appointed commander of the 126th New York on April 30, 1864, OR 33: 1037.

16. Walker, *History of the Second Corps*, 421–22; Colonel Thomas Smyth's Report, OR 36, pt 2: 450,

17. Brown's May 20, 1864 letter to his brother Smith.

18. *Yates County Chronicle*, May 19, 1864. Of the Union's 17,666 casualties—2,246 were killed, 12,037 wounded, and 3,383 missing—or 17 percent of

effective troops, OR 36, pt. 1:133; Thomas Livermore, *Numbers and Losses in the Civil War in America, 1861–65* (Dayton, OH: Morningside, 1986), Morningside Reprint, 110, 111. Over half of the casualties in the 126th New York, 12 of 21, were suffered by recruits. Confederate casualties were only four percent less, Walker, *History of the Second Corps*, 440; Gordon C. Rhea, *The Battle of the Wilderness, May 5–6, 1864* (Baton Rouge, LA: Louisiana State University Press, 1994), 440.

    19. General Grant, *OR* 36, pt. 1: 4.

Chapter 6

    1. Walker, *History of the Second Corps*, 451.

    2. Excerpt from Brown Letter, May 12, 1864, Morris Brown Scrapbook, Hamilton College Archives. The original has mysteriously disappeared and this is taken from Mahood, *Written in Blood*, 248. The quote from the Union soldier is in Gordon C. Rhea, *The Battles of Spotsylvania Court House and the Road to Yellow Tavern* (Baton Rouge, LA: Louisiana State University Press, 1997), 137.

    3. General Hancock's report, *OR* 36, pt.1: 332, 333.

    4. Walker, *History of the Second Corps*, 469; Richard F. Welch, "Boy General Francis Channing Barlow," *America's Civil War*, March 1998, 38.

    5. Asterisks before paragraph two and after paragraph four, undoubtedly for emphasis, are in the original.

    6. *Cudjo's Cave* was an 1864 novel by John Townsend Trowbridge, which chronicles the experiences of Unionists in northwest Virginia, near the Kentucky line, focusing on a runaway who hides in a cave.

    7. Seabury was Adjutant General, II Corps, 1st Division, 3rd Brigade; Owen was the 3rd Brigade commander; and Loring, the 126th N.Y.'s quartermaster.

    8. Sullivan was the Assistant Adjutant General to Brigadier General Alexander Hays, formerly the 126th's brigade, later acting division, commander. In time, Sullivan became the late general's son-in-law.

    9. Tyler would survive and be discharged December 23, 1864; Pool would be transferred to the Veteran Reserve Corps, January 10, 1865; while Fuller had died on the 12th, *Adjutant-General's Report*, 1012, 974, 912.

    10. Munson died May 14, 1863, and Sherman was listed as killed in action, May 12, 1864, ibid., 959, 992.

    11. Gordon C. Rhea, *To the North Anna River, Grant and Lee, May 13–25, 1864* (Baton Rouge. LA: Louisiana State University Press, 2000), 144.

    12. Scott's wound, his fourth, would lead to his discharge. His postwar experiences as a missionary and army chaplain resulted in his owning eight hundred acres in what is now Scottsdale, Arizona, Richard E. Lynch, *Winfield*

Scott: A Biography of Scottdale's Founder (Scottsdale, Arizona: The City of Scottsdale), 1978.

13. Freed blacks who came into Union lines; that is contrabands, or spoils of war, which the victors claim. General Benjamin Butler is credited with this usage of the term. It is unclear to whom or to what Brown is referring here.

14. Officers' examination to command a U.S. Colored Regiment.

15. Recall Smith Brown was on detached service as U.S. Inspector General for the State of Wisconsin at the capital.

16. Here he is referring to the Battle of the Wilderness.

17. Again, his chronology is off; the Po River engagement was May 9 and 10.

18. Owen was killed on May 12, at Spotsylvania Court House, and Munson, of whom Brown had been so critical, was wounded at the Po River engagement and died four days later, on May 14, *Adjutant-General's Report*, 966, 959.

19. *OR*, 36, pt 1:332, 333; Rhea, *The Battles for Spotsylvania Court House, May 7–12, 1864*, 137.

20. Major General Edward Johnson's Division belonged to General Ewell's Corps.

21. Sherman was reported killed May 12; Hulbert, who was promoted Second Lieutenant on May 3, 1864, would be discharged November 22 because of injuries; Lawrence would be discharged for disability August 10 and, coincidentally, years later would be buried quite near Smith Brown's grave in Penn Yan's Lakeview Cemetery, *Adjutant-General's Report*, 992, 934, 944.

22. Walker, *History of the Second Corps*, 470, 475; G. Norton Galloway, "Hand-To-Hand Fighting at Spotsylvania," in *Battles and Leaders of the Civil War*, vol. 4, 173.

23. Rhea, *To the North Anna River, Grant and Lee, May 13–25, 1864*, 170.

24. Wilson, formerly a Company A first lieutenant, had been commissioned captain of the 39th U.S. Colored Troops in March, *Adjutant-General's Report*, 1022.

25. Because the letter lacks the usual valediction, it may be that part is missing.

26. Again, the lack of valediction suggests this is a partial letter.

27. Martin T. McMahon, "Cold Harbor," in Underwood and Buel, *Battles and Leaders of the Civil War*, vol. 4, 217.

28. William Baird's June 6, 1864 memo in Assorted Papers, 1862–1877 M122, Box 11, Folder 11, Geneva Historical Society. The regimental morning reports are consistent with Baird's count.

29. Grant "always regretted that the last assault at Cold Harbor was ever made . . . no advantage whatever was gained to compensate for the heavy loss we sustained," Ulysses S. Grant, *Personal Memoirs of U. S. Grant*, 2 vols. (New

York: Charles L. Webster & Company, 1886), vol. 2, 276; Walker, *History of the Second Corps*, 522.

30. The 148th New York, which mustered less than a month after the 126th New York, included men from Penn Yan and the area from which most of the 126th New York was drawn. Their first major battle was at Cold Harbor on June 3. Subsequently five men were awarded Medals of Honor, two posthumously, Anon, *America's Medal of Honor Recipients* (Golden Valley, Minnesota: Highland Publishers, 1980), 727, 835, 922, 928, 934; Phisterer, *War of the Rebellion*, 436, 443, 448, 449.

Chapter 7

1. Dr. Hammond was working at the 1st Division hospital.

2. Brown's referring to the Union Pacific Railroad, which had been authorized by Congress in July 1862 to run from Nebraska to Utah, where in 1869 it would connect with the Central Pacific Railroad.

3. Individual Record of Officers and Enlisted Men, New York State Bureau of Military Statistics, Albany, New York August 24, 1864, prepared by Smith Brown.

4. Mortars, fixed to fire at a high angle, are designed especially to drop on entrenched troops.

5. Regimental Commissary Sergeant Charles Lisk.

6. This is a partial list of those wounded May 12 at Spotsylvania, *Adjutant-General's Report*. Scott's wound, his fourth during the war, would lead to his discharge.

7. Private William Seamans, mustered March 31, 1864, was wounded at the Wilderness, May 6, 1864, and was discharged for disability due to the wounds, February 27, 1865, ibid., 989.

8. 1st Lt. Asbrah Huntoon was mortally wounded on June 5, 1864, at the battle of Cold Harbor and died two days later, ibid, 934.

9. Brother Theodore M. Brown married Lillie Weber of St. Louis on August 30, 1864, Brown Genealogy, Oliver House, Yates County Historical Society.

10. "Commutation" is money allotted for travel away from regular duty.

11. Gallagher, ed., *Fighting for the Confederacy*, 419; Andrew A. Humphreys, *The Virginia Campaign of '64 and '65*. Vol. 12 of *Scribner's Campaigns of the Civil War* (New York: Thomas Yoseloff, 1963, reprint), 198.

12. Charles A. Dana to Secretary of War Stanton, OR 40, pt. 1: 19; General Hancock to General Humphreys, OR 40, Pt. 2: 59.

13. Walker, *History of the Second Corps*, 530.

14. Ibid., 535. From here on, reports are so fragmentary that exact locations of the 126th New York cannot be determined with any certainty. Newly promoted regimental commander Captain John B. Geddis's report of Petersburg takes up less than seven lines in OR 40, pt. 1: 353. The 126th's Morning Reports are equally sparse after May 3. The report of Captain Nelson Penfield of the 125th New York is of little help either, ibid., 352–353.

15. Baird's death on June 16 was particularly poignant, for he had been dismissed November 27, 1862 (effective November 8) based on a Court of Inquiry's finding that he was guilty of "bad conduct" at Maryland Heights mid October 1862. He appealed successfully to Secretary of War Stanton, was reinstated just before the battle of Gettysburg, but with no regimental vacancies, could not return to duty until November 5, 1863. It seemed to those who watched him that he was especially aggressive, as if proving his worth as an officer after his return, *Adjutant-General's Report*, 861. 1st Lt. John A. McDonald is listed as killed on June 16, 1864 "before Petersburg," ibid., 953. Both Capt. Charles Richardson and 2nd Lt. Pratt Dibble survived and were discharged in September, ibid., 982, 900. Adjutant Spencer Lincoln, who had attended Baird before he succumbed, was struck shortly thereafter and died two days later from complications following amputation of his arm, ibid., 946.

16. Asterisk in original, likely for emphasis. MacDougall followed through with his promise. See Morris's June 20, 1864 letter to his father.

17. Charges of drunkenness had been brought against Frank. The fighting Brown describes has been rather vaguely called "Assaults on Petersburg" or even more vaguely, "Before Petersburg."

18. Colonel Clinton MacDougall was now commanding the reorganized 3rd Brigade in Barlow's division (39th, 52nd, 111th, 125th, and 126th New York). The letter was reprinted in the July 7, 1864 *Yates County Chronicle*.

19. This appears to be misdated. Morris was killed June 22.

20. Private George A. Byington, 32, from Starkey, outside Penn Yan, was a member of Morris Brown, Jr.'s Company A, Brown Scrapbook, Hamilton College Archives.

21. Forty-year-old Private William Hainer from Penn Yan was a member of Company A, *Adjutant-General's Report*, 920.

22. Sidney D. Rice, a twenty-year-old, also was from Penn Yan and in Company A, Brown Scrapbook, Hamilton College Archives.

23. Brown Scrapbook, Hamilton College Archives.

24. Likely, Private Eugene C. Baker, Company A, *Adjutant-General's Report*, 861.

25. Twenty-year-old Corporal Patrick Manly, from Penn Yan, another member of Brown's Company A, ibid., 950.

26. Cpl. George V. Harris, from Naples, New York, who had transferred to Company A from Company K, ibid., 922.

27. Brown Scrapbook, Hamilton College Archives.

Chapter 8

1. Brown Scrapbook, Hamilton College Archives.

2. Probably Albion Shepard, a twenty-three-year-old from the Town of Jerusalem, a member of Company A, *Adjutant-General's Report*, 991.

3. It is unlikely we'll ever know who wrote the obituary, the bulk of which appeared in Frank W. Plant, comp., *Statistics of The Class of 1864 of Hamilton College* (Utica, NY: L.C. Childs, Book and Job Printer, 1865), n. p., Hamilton College Archives, courtesy Frank Lorenz. Plant was identified as "Class Secretary." There is also a reference to the Chi Psi fraternity, of which Brown was a member. Whether Plant borrowed from this obituary or the reverse cannot be determined.

4. References to Morris's Medal of Honor and the history of the award are OR 27, Pt 2: 282; Anon, *America's Medal of Honor Recipients* (Golden Valley, MN: Highland Publishers, 1980), 724, 1, 1108; Patricia L. Faust, ed., *Historical Times Illustrated Encyclopedia of the Civil War* (New York: Harper Perennial, 1991), 484. Unfortunately, there is no record of what happened to Morris's medal subsequently.

5. Even today Morris Brown, Jr. is virtually unknown in his home town; at best a small file on him is maintained in the Yates County historian's office. Records about Theodore's son's passing are in conflict. The Obituaries file in the Yates County Historical and Genealogical Society lists him as having died on December 25, 1901. The Morris Brown Camp was mentioned as participating in the 1912 Memorial Day parade, "Yates Past" May 2005, 5, but no record of a Grand Army of the Republic post named for Brown has been found yet.

6. Credit for obtaining the scrapbook bearing Morris Brown's letters is due to Frank Lorenz, former Editor of College Publications and volunteer archivist, Hamilton College. Unfortunately, we'll never know who maintained the scrapbook, Morris's sister alternately known as Mary Jane, Jean, or Jennie (the latter 1860 Census) or, more likely, his brother Smith's daughter, Jennie M. Burrell (also Burrill); how it got into the Nashville, Tennessee antique dealer's hands; or what happened to Brown's sword.

Bibliography

Manuscripts and Primary Sources

Adams, Myron. Myron Adams Letters (September 3, 1862), Hamilton College Archives, Clinton, New York.

Baird, William. June 6, 1864 memo in Assorted Papers, 1862–1877 M122, Box 11, Folder 11, Geneva Historical Society.

Bassett, Richard. Bassett Letters, Civil War Papers, 1861–1870, Account #2001.116, Ontario County Historical Society.

"Breaking Apart: The Road to 1861," Yates County Web page, www.yatescounty.org/upload/12/historian/prewar.htm.

Brown, John Smith. Smith Brown Letters, Brown Scrapbook, Hamilton College Archives, Clinton, New York.

Brown, Morris, Jr., Letters. Brown Scrapbook, Hamilton College Archives, Clinton, New York.

Brown, Morris, Jr., Military Service Record, Record Group 94, AGO, National Archives.

———. Statement, Form B, New York Bureau of Military Statistics.

Bull, James M. Statement of Lieutenant Colonel James M. Bull, 126th New York, July 17, 1863 and of Maj. Gen. George G. Meade, October 17, 1864, Adjutant General's Office, May 21, 1888, 2126 A.G.O. 1888.

Coleman, William. Letter to the 126th New York's surgeon, Dr. Charles Hoyt, November 27, 1866, Civil War Papers 1861–1870, Acc. #2001.116, Ontario County Historical Society.

Company A musters, 126th New York Volunteers, Assorted Papers, 1862–1877, M122, Box 3, Folder 29, Ontario County Historical Society.

Dore, George. Military Service Record, Record Group 94, AGO, National Archives.

Ferguson, Harrison. Letter, October 20, 1862, courtesy of descendants, Mrs. Eleanor Ferguson and Mr. Donald Wheat.

Grantee Deeds, Book 33, Yates County Historian's Office.

Herendeen, Orin J. Letters, C.W. Coll. 77, Box 1, Geneva (N.Y) Historical Society.

Minutes of the Urbana (New York) Town Board.

Paris, Peter. Paris Letters, courtesy of descendant Terry Murphy.

Receipt for flag captured by Morris Brown, Jr., dated July 17, 1863, James M. Bull, 126th New York Infantry Regiment, Book 40–48, Lewis Leigh Collection (Adjutant General's Office, May 21, 1888, to Charles Richardson, 126th New York Infantry, Assorted Papers, Box 1, Ontario County Historical Society).

Regimental Order No. 4, September 4, 1862, Record Group 94, National Archives.

Rice, Sidney. Letter to Morris Brown, Jrs.'s parents, July 1, 1864, Brown Scrapbook, Hamilton College Archives, Clinton, New York.

Special Orders No. 393, War Department, issued December 13, 1862.

Warren, Gouverneur K., Warren Papers, Box 22, Coll. No. SC10668, Vol. 5, New York State Library, Albany, New York.

Undated Assessment Roll, Village of Penn Yan, Yates County Web page: linkny.com/~history/PY1856.html and ibid., 1856+. html

U.S. Census 1860.

Wall, Jerry. Military Service Record. Record Group 94, AGO, National Archives.

Yost, George. Yost Letters, courtesy of Michael Yost, January 9, 1863.

Primary Printed Sources

Basler, Roy P., ed. *The Collected Works of Abraham Lincoln*, 10 vols. New Brunswick, NY: Rutgers University Press, 1953, vol. 8, 339.

"Letter of Lt. John L. Brady." In David L. and Audrey J. Ladd. *The Bachelder Papers: Gettysburg in Their Own Words*, 3 vols. Dayton, OH: Morningside, 1994, vol. 3, 1397.

Cowtan, Charles W. *Service of the Tenth New York Volunteers (National Zouaves) in the War of the Rebellion*. New York: Charles H. Ludwig, 1882.

Delta Upsilon Decennial Catalogue, 1902, Hamilton College Archives, Clinton, New York.

Dyer, Frederick A. *A Compendium of the War of the Rebellion*. Dayton, OH: Morningside Reprint, 1978.

Eldred, Newman. "Newman Eldred's Account of Service in the Civil War," *Yesteryears* 8 (Winter 1979), 41, 42.

Failing, Myron. "Gen. Alex Hays at Gettysburg," *National Tribune*, October 15, 1885, Vol. 5: 3.

Favill, Josiah. *Diary of a Young Officer*. Chicago: R. R. Donnelly & Sons, 1909.

French, J. H. *Gazetteer of the State of New York*. Syracuse, New York, 1860.

Galwey, Thomas F., "An Episode of the Battle of Gettysberg," in *The Bachelder Papers*, 3 vols. David L. Ladd and Audrey J. Ladd, eds. Dayton, OH: Morningside House, 1995), vol. 2, 871.

Gallagher, Gary W., ed. *Fighting for the Confederacy: Personal Recollections of General Edward Porter Alexander*. Chapel Hill: University of North Carolina Press, 1989.

Galloway, G. Norton. "Hand-To-Hand Fighting at Spotsylvania," in Robert U. Johnson and Clarence Clough Buel, eds., *Battles and Leaders of the Civil War*. Four Volumes. New York: The Century Co., 1884, 1887, 1888, 4:173.

Grant, Ulysses S. *Personal Memoirs of U. S. Grant*, 2 vols. New York: Charles L. Webster & Company, 1886.

Hancock, Winfield Scott. "Testimony of Major General W. S. Hancock," *Report of the Committee on the Conduct of the War*, 2nd Sess., 38th Congress. Washington: Government Printing Office, 1865, 1: 408.

Hays, Alexander. "Letter of Brig. Gen. Alexander Hays." In David L. and Audrey J. Ladd, eds. *The Bachelder Papers: Gettysburg in Their Own Words*, 3 vols. Dayton, OH: Morningside, 1994, vol. 2, 1179–80.

Hitchcock, Charles. "Letter of Lt. Charles Hitchcock." In David L. and Audrey J. Ladd, eds. *The Bachelder Papers: Gettysburg in Their Own Words*, 3 vols. Dayton, OH: Morningside, 1994, vol. 2, 1183, 1188, 1184.

Hunt, Henry J. "The Third Day at Gettysburg." In Robert Underwood Johnson and Clarence Clough Buel,. *Battles and Leaders of the Civil War*, 4 vols. New York: Century Company, 1884, 1887, 1888, vol. 3, 372.

Johnson, Robert Underwood and Clarence Clough Buel, eds., *Battles and Leaders of the Civil War*, 4 vols. (New York: The Century Company, 1884, 1887, 1888.

LeMunyon, William. "War Record of W. F. LeMunyon," U.S. Army Military History Institute, Carlisle Barracks, Pennsylvania.

Livermore, Thomas. *Days and Events, 1860–1866*. Boston: Houghton, Mifflin, 1920.

———. *Numbers and Losses in the Civil War in America* (Dayton, OH: Morningside Reprint, 1986).

Longstreet, James. *From Manassas to Appomattox*. New York: Mallard Press, 1991 reprint.

Martin, W. J. "The Eleventh North Carolina Regiment," *Southern Historical Society Papers*, vol. 23: 47, 48.

Morgan, Charles H. "Report of Lt. Col. Charles H. Morgan." In eds. *The Bachelder Papers: Gettysburg in Their Own Words*, 3 vols. David L. and Audrey J. Ladd, eds. Dayton, OH: Morningside, 1994, vol. 3, 1364.

Page, Charles D. *History of the Fourteenth Connecticut Volunteer Infantry*. Meriden, Connecticut: The Horton Printing Company, 1906.

Phisterer, Frederick, comp., *New York in the War of the Rebellion*. 5 vols. Albany, NY: J. B. Lyon Company, 1912.

Plant, Frank W. comp., *Statistics of The Class of 1864 of Hamilton College*. Utica, NY: L.C. Childs, Book and Job Printer, 1865, Hamilton College Archives, Clinton, New York.

Richardson, Charles. "Letter of Capt. Charles A. Richardson." In *The Bachelder Papers, Gettysburg in Their Own Words*, 3 vols. David and Audrey J. Ladd, eds. Dayton, OH: Morningside House, 1994, vol. 1, 316.

Ryno, John. Diary, July 8, 1863 entry, Interlaken Historical Society.

Scott, Winfield. "Pickett's Charge," California Commandery of the Military Order of the Loyal Legion of the United States (MOLLUS), February 8, 1888, 6.

———. "Letter from Winfield Scott," December 15, 1890, unidentified publication, courtesy the late Maurice Patterson, President, Interlaken (New York) Historical Society.

Simons, Ezra D. *A Regimental History: The One Hundred & Twenty-fifth New York*. New York: Judson Printing Co., 1888.

Swinton, William. *Campaigns of the Army of the Potomac: A Critical History of the Operations in Virginia, Maryland, and Pennsylvania, from the Commencement to the Close of the War, 1861–1864*. New York: Charles B. Richardson, 1866.

Talcott, T. M. R. "The Third Day at Gettysburg," *Southern Historical Society Papers*, 41: 46.

Washburn, George H. *A Complete History and Record of the 108th Regiment, New York Volunteers, From 1862 to 1894*. Rochester, New York: E. R. Andrews Press, 1894.

The War of the Rebellion: A Compilation of the Official Records of the Union and Confederate Armies. Washington: Government Printing Office, 1880–1891. 128 vols.

Newspapers

Ontario County Republican Times (Canandaigua, New York), October 15, 1862.
Ontario Repository and Messenger (Canandaigua, New York), October 15, 1862.
The Frederick, Maryland Examiner, July 8, 1863.
Yates County Chronicle

Books

Aldrich, Lewis Cass. *History of Yates County*. Syracuse, NY: D. Mason, 1892.

Anon, *America's Medal of Honor Recipients*. Golden Valley, MN: Highland Publishers, 1980.

Busey, John W. and David G. Martin. *Regimental Strengths and Losses at Gettysburg*. Hightstown, NJ: Longstreet House, 1986.

Catton, Bruce. *A Stillness at Appomattox*. New York: The Fairfax Press, 1984, reprint of 1953 edition.

Clayton, W.W. *History of Steuben County*. Philadelphia: Lewis, Peck & Co., 1879.

Cleveland, Stafford C. *History and Directory of Yates County*, 2 vols. Penn Yan, NY: S. C. Cleveland, 1976, reprint of 1873 book.

Cragg, Rod. *Covered With Glory*. New York: Harper Collins, 2000.

Faust, Patricia L., ed. *Historical Times Illustrated Encyclopedia of the Civil War*. New York: Harper Perennial, 1991.

Fleming, George T., ed., *The Life and Letters of Alexander Hays*. Pittsburgh, PA: Gilbert A. Hays, 1919.

Foote, Shelby. *The Civil War, a Narrative*, 3 vols. New York: Random House, 1963.

Graham, Robert H., comp. *Yates County's "Boys in Blue" 1861–1865: Who They Were and What They Did*. Penn Yan, NY: Private Printing, 1926.

Henderson, William D. *The Road to Bristoe Station: Campaigning With Lee and Meade, August 1–October 20, 1863*. Lynchburg, VA: H. E. Howard, Inc., 1987.

Lord, Francis A. *They Fought For the Union*. New York: Bonanza Books, 1960.

Lynch, Richard E. *Winfield Scott: A Biography of Scottdale's Founder*. Scottsdale, Arizona: The City of Scottsdale, 1978.

Mahood, Wayne. *"Written in Blood": A History of the 126th New York Infantry in the Civil War*. Hightstown, NJ: Longstreet House, 1997.

Martin, David G. *Gettysburg July 1*. Conshohocken, PA: Combined Books, 1995.

Pilkington, Walter. *Hamilton College*. Clinton, NY: Hamilton College, 1962.

Rhea, Gordon C. *The Battle of the Wilderness, May 5–6, 1864*. Baton Rouge, LA: Louisiana State University Press, 1994.

———. *The Battles of Spotsylvania Court House and the Road to Yellow Tavern*. Baton Rouge, LA: Louisiana State University Press, 1997.

———. *To the North Anna River, Grant and Lee, May 13–25, 1864*. Baton Rouge, LA: Louisiana State University Press, 2000.

Robertson, James I. *General A. P. Hill: The Story of a Confederate Warrior*. New York: Random House, 1987.

Sears, Stephen. *Gettysburg*. Boston: Houghton Mifflin, 2003).

Stevens, Charles A. *Berdan's United States Sharpshooters in the Army of the Potomac, 1861–1865*. Dayton, OH: Morningside Reprint, 1984.

Stewart, George R. *Pickett's Charge*. Boston: Houghton Mifflin Co., 1959.

Teetor, Paul A. *A Matter of Hours: Treason at Harper's Ferry*. Rutherford, NJ: Fairleigh Dickinson Press, 1981.

Walker, Francis. A. *History of the Second Army Corps in the Army of the Potomac*. Gaithersburg, MD: Olde Soldier Books, Inc., 1988, reprint of Charles Scribner's Sons, 1887.

Warner, Ezra J. *Generals in Blue: Lives of the Union Commanders*. Baton Rouge, LA: Louisiana University Press, 1986, reprint of 1964 edition.

Welcher, Frank. J. *The Union Army: Organization and Operations*, 3 vols. Bloomington, IN: Indiana University Press, 1989, vol. 1, 463, 472.

Williams, T. Harry. *Lincoln and His Generals*. New York: Knopf, 1952.

Willson, Arabella M. *Disaster, Struggle and Triumph: 1000 "Boys in Blue."* Albany, NY: Argus Company Printers, 1870.

Wolcott, Walter. *The Military History of Yates County, NY*. Penn Yan, NY: Express Book & Job Co., 1895.

Periodicals

Campbell, Eric. "'Remember Harper's Ferry': The Degradation, Humiliation, and Redemption of Col. George Willard's Brigade," *Gettysburg Magazine* (July 1992), pt. 1, 64, 75.

Campbell, Eric. "'Remember Harper's Ferry': The Degradation, Humiliation, and Redemption of Col. George L. Willard's Brigade," *Gettysburg Magazine*, January 1993, pt. 2, 103, 104.

Frye, Dennis. "Stonewall Attacks: The Siege of Harpers Ferry," *Blue & Gray* 5, no. 1 (August-September 1987): 10–11.

Hassler, William W. "The Slaughter Pen at Bristoe Station," *Civil War Times Illustrated* 1, no. 2 (May 1962): 13.

[Mahood, Wayne] " 'Morris is a Hero' A Saga of the Civil War," *Hamilton Alumni Review* (Fall-Winter, 1991–1992), 10–14.

———. "PennYan's Morris Brown, Jr. is a Hero," *Crooked Lake Review*, Issues 134, 135 (Winter 2005, Spring 2005).

Mahood, Wayne. " 'Some Very Hard Stories Were Told': The 126th New York Infantry at Harpers Ferry," *Civil War Regiments* 2, no. 4: 7–41.

Schultz, David and Richard Rollins. "A Combined and Concentrated Fire," *North & South* 2, no. 3 (March 1999), 40, 54, 56.

Taylor, Michael W, "North Carolina in the Pickett-Pettigrew-Trimble Charge at Gettysburg," *Gettysburg Magazine*, January 1, 1993, 67–83.

Thompson, Benjamin W. "This Hell of Destruction: The Benjamin W. Thompson Memoir," *Civil War Times Illustrated*, vol. 12, no. 6 (1973), 18.

Waring, George F. *"The Garibaldi Guard" in the First Book of the Author's Club. Libor Scriptorum.* New York: The Authors' Club, DeVinne Press, 1893, 570–71.

Welch, Richard F. "Boy General Francis Channing Barlow," *America's Civil War*, March 1998, 38.

Index

Baltimore & Ohio Railroad, 13
Baltimore, Maryland, 126th New
York Infantry fed, 12
Banks, Maj. Gen. Nathaniel, 14;
ordered to take Mobile, 110
Barksdale, Brig. Gen. William,
CSA, flanked Union right at
Harpers Ferry, 19; countered by
II Corps brigade at Gettysburg,
59
Barlow, Maj. Gen, Francis, 138, 141,
173; appointed II Corps, Third
Division, commander, 104;
assaulted Petersburg, 159; Cold
Harbor, 146–147; criticized II
Corps, Third Division, 139–140;
fears before Spotsylvania, 129;
ordered division to occupy high
ground, 122; overran Johnson's
Division at Spotsylvania, 139;
Po River engagement, 123, 127,
128; retracted criticism of Third
Brigade, 157
Barras, 2d Lt. Samuel, 126th New
York Infantry, 26, 28, 40;
altercations with Capts. Bassett
and Phillips, 31; dismissed, 31;
praised by Morris Brown, Jr., 14,
22; recruiting, 7
Bassett, Capt. Richard, 126th New
York Infantry, 59, 114, 156;
altercation with Lt. Barras, 31;
arrested "stragglers" from Camp
Douglas, 30; claimed Morris
Brown took exam to command
U.S. Colored regiment, 117;
critical of 39th New York Infantry, 35; described Gen. Hays, 35;
on provost guard, 117; promoted,
114; protested Lt. Col. Baird's
return, 73

Beauregard, Gen. Pierre Gustave
T., commanded hodgepodge at
Petersburg, 159
Beckham, Maj. R. F., CSA, 88
Bellows, Sanitary Commission Head
Henry W., described Camp
Douglas conditions, 29
Beyea, Pvt. Daniel J., 126th New
York Infantry, prisoner of war, 97
Birney, Maj. Gen. David, assaulted
Petersburg, 159
Bliss Barn, skirmishing at, 59;
torched, 61
Bolivar Heights (Harpers Ferry, West
Virginia), 13, 16, 18
Boonsboro, West Virginia, 17, 18
Brady, Lt. John L., recalled odds
against the Union at Gettysburg,
65
Bragg, Lt. Gen. Braxton, CSA, 76,
78, 84; commanded Army of the
Tennessee, 86
Bristoe Station, Virginia, xii, 91, 98;
engagement, 91–98
Brockenbrough, Col. John, CSA, 64,
65
Brough, 2nd Lt. John H., 126th New
York Infantry, described Harpers
Ferry, 13; wounded, 68
Brown, Emeline (Lina), 2, 37, 120,
135, 151, 152, 154, 167, 176
Brown, Jennie (Mary Jane, Jean), 2,
37, 40, 48, 106, 107, 115, 118,
120, 135, 136, 143, 147, 167,
176, 186, 187, 190
Brown, John (abolitionist), 13
Brown, John Smith, 7, 9, 27, 28, 34,
38, 40, 42, 43, 44, 47, 49, 51,
54, 71, 75, 79, 83, 84, 85, 98,
107, 108, 111, 114, 120, 122,
132, 135, 136, 148, 153, 160,

Brown, Morris Jr. (continued)
Chancellorsville, and Maj. Gen.
George Stoneman's raid, 47, 48;
reported departures of I, XII and
part of V Corps, 86; requested
leave to handle "important
business," 102; reported Smith
Brown's promotion to lieutenant
colonel, 164; requested files from
home, 109; reviewed battles of
the Wilderness, Po River, Spotsylvania, May 5–May 19, 1864,
129–130, 132–138; saw 148th
New York Infantry, 98; sent
copy of MacDougall's promotion
recommendation home, 167;
showed love interest, 106, 117,
157; shared canteen with Pvt.
Sidney Rice, 56; spared fatal
charges, July 3, 1863 morning,
59; stated Col. Frank drunk,
163; slightly wounded near Mine
Run, 100; threatened to court
martial Sgt. Charles Forshey, 97;
threatened to resign, 110, 111,
112, 132, 152, 155, 156; toured
Manassas (Bull Run) battlefield
with John Smith Brown, 34;
urged appointment for his father,
38; visited Penn Yan on leave,
103; vowed to take regiment to
Richmond, 104; wanted letters from home, 120; wanted
Theodore to come home, 75,
81; warned Smith Brown not to
return, 166; Wilderness battle
May 6, 122–125; Wilderness and
Spotsylvania losses, 125, 133,
134, 135
Brown, Morris, Sr., 12, 37, 39, 40,
43, 44, 45, 46, 48, 51, 52, 81,
101, 102, 108, 109, 151, 152,
154, 158, 166, 175, 183, 184,
185, 190; appointed district
military committeeman, 17;
background, 2; chaired Vigilance
Committee, 4; presided at war
rally, 1, 2, 3; presided over meeting to form home guard, 5; sued
Ebenezer B. Jones on behalf of
Morris Brown, Jr., 106
Brown, Theodore, 1, 2; went to Germany, 7; letter of condolence to
parents, 183; returned to Penn
Yan, 103; supported by Morris
and John Smith Brown, 48, 78,
81, 82
Brown, Theodore Morris, 188
Buford, Maj. Gen. John, defended
Gettysburg, July 1, 58
Bull Run (Manassas), Virginia, 16,
33, 34, 35
Bull, Col. James, 126th New York
Infantry, 38, 79, 83, 85, 86; act-
ing regimental commander, 32,
appointed lieutenant colonel, 11;
Auburn-Bristoe Station engage-
ment, 89–92; commanded bri-
gade, 68; debt of Morris Brown,
Jr. repaid, 79; praised by Gen.
Hays, 98; replaced Col. Sherrill
as commander of 126th New
York Infantry, 73, 76; replaced
by Lt. Col. Baird, 102
Burnside, Maj. Gen. Ambrose,
expected at Wilderness, 122;
IX Corps to link with Army of
the Potomac, 119; to reinforce
Meade, 110
Burrill, C.T., 188
Burrill, Capt. Truman, 126th New
York Infantry, 45, 47; absence,

Crandell, Col. Levin, 125th New York Infantry, 60; returned, 157

D'Utassy, Col. Frederick G., 39th New York Infantry, 16; described, 34, 35
Davis, President Jefferson, CSA, 47
Davis, Brig. Gen. Joseph R., CSA, 64, 65, 66
"Deathlike silence," July 3 morning, 62
Delaware Volunteers, 1st Delaware Infantry, 61, 64, 65
Delta Upsilon fraternity, 9
Desertions, 28, 30, 49, 70
Dibble, Lt. Pratt, 126th New York Infantry, wounded, 160, 162
Dix, Maj. Gen. John, 16, 25
Dix-Hill Cartel (prisoner exchange procedure), 25
Dore, Sgt. George, 126th New York Infantry, captured flag, 67
Douglas, Sen. Stephen A., 25

Elmira, Jefferson and Canandaigua Railroad, 12
Elmira, New York, military depot, 4, 12, 22, 131, 155
Ely's Ford, 99, 121, 137
"Epoch One," Spring Campaign 1864, 121–125
"Epoch Three," Spring Campaign 1864, 143–147
"Epoch Two," Spring Campaign 1864, 127–142
Ewell, Lt. Gen. Richard, CSA, 58, 88, 99, 100; Bristoe Station, 92; artillery at Spotsylvania, 134; attacked Cemetery Hill, July 3, 1863, 61; formed "salient" at Spotsylvania, 138; march to

Gettysburg, 55; North Anna, 143; to flank Union army near Warrenton, 87; Wilderness attack, May 5, 122
Executions, 74, 77, 164

Farrington, Lt. Dewitt, 125th New York Infantry, 34
Ferguson, Sgt. Harrison, 126th New York Infantry, 32; criticized 125th New York Infantry, 89; described execution, 77; march to Gettysburg, 54; withdrawal from Bristoe Station, 95
Finch, Sgt. Daniel W., 126th New York Infantry, severely wounded, 97
Folger, Sen. Charles J., 11
Foote, Shelby, 16
Forshey (Forshay), Sgt. Charles, accused of running from battle, 97; Brown threatened court-martial, 98; "ran" at Gettysburg, 68
Fort Sumter, South Carolina, 1, 8
Frank, Col. Paul, Brown accuses him of being drunk, 162; Po River engagement, 127, 138; told to hold Wilderness intersection, 122
French, Maj. Gen. William, 87, 91; commanded I, II and III Corps November 1863, 99; replaced by Hays, 58; collided with Johnson's Division near Mine Run, 100
Fry, Col. Birkett D., CSA, 64
Fuller, Sgt. Smith, mortally wounded, 133, 156

Galwey, Lt. Thomas F., 8th Ohio, anxious about defenses, July 3, 1863, 61

Garnett, Brig Gen. Richards, CSA, "Pickett's Charge," 64
Geddis, Captain John, 126th New York Infantry, 155
Geneva, New York, 7, 11, 12, 13, 14, 26, 27, 108, 114, 118, 119, 120, 164, 190
Germanna Ford, 99, 121, 137
Gettysburg, Pennsylvania, xii, 32, 55; battle of, 57–67; casualties, 68; described, 56–57
Gibbon, Brig. Gen. John, 65, 87; at Gettysburg, 58; situation July 3 morning, 62
Gilder [Gelder], Pvt. Barnard F., 126th New York Infantry, killed, 97
Gillett, James M., 2
Goff, 1st Sgt. David, wounded, 61
Gordon, Maj. Gen. John B., CSA, routed Union skirmishers, 89; stopped Barlow's advance at Spotsylvania, 139
Grant, Hannah, 2
Grant, Lt. Gen. Ulysses, 35, 51, 109, 118, 125, 131, 134, 140, 144, 149, 152, 154, 159, 162, 166, 185; difficulty moving large army, 122; flanked Army of Northern Virginia, June 1864, 158–159; labeled "butcher," 147; North Anna, 143; planned spring 1864 offensive, 110, 121; Po River engagement, 138; post Wilderness pursuit, 127–129; promoted Union Army commander, 104; race toward Spotsylvania, 128; Spotsylvania, 129
Gregg, Brig. Gen. Irvin, 87
Green, Col., 155

Griggs, Lt. James, 126th New York Infantry, 113; recommended for promotion, 155

Hainer, Pvt. William, 126th New York Infantry, court-martialed, 100; tried to recover Brown's body, 170, 174, 178
Halleck, Maj. Gen. Henry, criticized Maj. Gen. Meade after Gettysburg, 71; ordered troops to remain at Harpers Ferry, 15
Hamilton College (Clinton, New York), xi, 8, 9, 24, 32, 45, 165, 187, 190
Hamlin, Mrs. Charley, 107
Hamlin and Latimer, 85
Hammond, Dr. Fletcher, 126th New York Infantry surgeon, 22, 90, 96, 111, 114, 116, 158, 172, 173, 176, 177; announced Brown's death, 168–169; appointed surgeon, 12; assured Brown's parents, 161–162; collected Brown's papers, 174; denied claims about seeing Brown's body, 174; efforts to recover Brown's body, 178; family death, 38; fed Brown, 148, 149; offers details about Brown's belongings, 114–115; offered money for recovery of Brown's body, 174; recommended John Smith Brown's return to regiment, 83
Hammond, Sam, 44, 45, 115
Hammondsport, New York, 2, 106
Hancock, Maj. Gen. Winfield, 35, 53, 54; attested to "shock" of Confederate assault at Gettysburg, 65; flanked Army of

that killed Brown, 173, 180;
confronted Union II Corps at
Todd's Tavern, 127; formed
"face" at Spotsylvania, 138;
march to Gettysburg, 55; moved
east on Orange Plank Road,
May 5, 1864, 122; to flank
Union army near Warrenton, 87
Hill, Maj. Gen. Daniel H., CSA,
rear guard on march to South
Mountain, 18
Hobart College (Geneva, New York),
15
Hoffman, Commissary General of
Prisoners William, ordered parolees released from Camp Douglas,
30
Hooker, Maj. Gen. Joseph, 45, 47,
53, 55; resignation accepted, 56
Hooper, Lt. Milo, 126th New York
Infantry, 155
Howard, Maj. Gen. Oliver O., driven
back at Gettysburg, 58
Hoyt, Dr. Charles S., appointed sur-
geon, 39th New York Infantry,
141, 156; reported 126th New
York Infantry's strength, 73
Humphreys, Maj. Gen. Andrew A.,
reported railroad reconstructed,
79; questioned Warren about
delay at Bristoe Station, 91
Hunt, Brig. Gen. Henry, directed artil-
lery fire at Gettysburg, 62, 65
Huntoon, 2d Lt. Ashbrah, 126th
New York Infantry, killed, 157
Hurlburt, Lt. John H., 126th New
York Infantry, badly wounded,
135, 139

Illinois Volunteers,
65th Illinois Infantry, 29

Indiana Volunteers,
1st Ind. Indiana Battery, 16
15th Indiana Infantry, 16

Jackson, Lt. Gen. Thomas ("Stonewall"), CSA, 14, 15, 16; captured Harpers Ferry garrison, 22;
led attack on Harpers Ferry, 17
Johnson, Maj. Gen. Edward, "Old
Allegheny," CSA, 100, advanced
on Warren at Cedar Run. Virginia, 88; overrun, captured at
Spotsylvania, 139, 141

Kemper, Brig. Gen. James L. CSA,
64
Kershaw, Maj. Gen. Joseph, CSA, 19
Keuka Lake (Crooked Lake), 2, 3
"Keuka Rifles" (Co. I, 33rd NY Vol-
unteers), 4
Kilpatrick, Brig. Gen. Judson, attend-
ed II Corps Grand Ball, 104
Kirkland, Col. W. W., CSA, 91, 92

Lane, Brig. Gen. James H., CSA, 65
Lawrence, 2d. Lt. Meletiah, 126th
New York Infantry, attended
II Corps Grand Ball, 104; toe
amputated, 139; wounded at
Gettysburg, 68
Lee, Capt. Benjamin F., 126th New
York Infantry, repaid debt to
Morris Brown, Jr., 79; resigned,
140
Lee, Gen. Robert E. Lee, 15, 56,
85, 110; checked Grant at
Cold Harbor, 146; criticized A.
P. Hill, 98; delayed at Falling
Waters, Maryland, 71; failed to
trap Army of the Potomac at
North Anna River, 147; flanked

Lee, Gen. Robert E. Lee (*continued*)
Union army, fall 1863, 86, 87;
march to Gettysburg, 55; Mary-
land invasion plans, 15; ordered
Hill's Corps's advance to Bristoe
Station, 96; won race to Spotsyl-
vania, 128; Special Orders No.
191 ("lost orders"), 17; withdrew
behind Rapidan, entrenched
near Mine Run, 99
Lee, Lt. Henry, 126th New York
Infantry, praised by Brown, 163
Lincoln, Abraham, call for volun-
teers, 3, 15, 34, 56, 99
Lincoln, Adj. Spencer, 126th New
York Infantry, lost arm, 155,
160, 162
Linkletter, Pvt. Orson R., 126th New
York Infantry, wounded, 97
Lisk, Sgt. Charles, 126th New York
Infantry, 155
Longstreet, Lt. Gen. James, CSA, 15,
19, 35, 64, 122, 137; attacked
Union's III Corps, 59; called
Harpers Ferry a "man trap," 17;
Corps sent west, 176; drove
Union back, May 6, 1864, 123;
formed "face" at Spotsylvania,
138; march to Gettysburg,
Lorenz, Frank K. xiii
Loring, QM John, 126th New York
Infantry, 79, 81, 84, 122, 133,
141, 153, 154, 175, 177, 186;
appointed Commissary Sergeant,
156
"Lost Orders" (Antietam, Sharps-
burg), 17
Loudoun Heights (Harpers Ferry,
West Virginia), 17, 48
Lowrance, Col. W. Lee. J., CSA,
65

MacDougall, Brig. Gen. Clinton, 145,
160, 163, 190; acting brigade
commander, 60; assigned brigade
command, 140; defended Sherrill,
60; recommended Morris Brown's
promotion, 167–168; returned
from leave, 141; searched for
Brown's body, 172; wrote Dr.
Hammond about Brown's death
and efforts to recover body,
172–173; wrote Maria Brown
about Morris's death, 179–180;
wrote Morris Brown, Jr. about
Morris's death, 176–177; wound-
ed at Gettysburg, 68
Mallon, Col. James E., CSA, 92
Manley, Pvt. Patrick, 126th New
York Infantry, tried to recover
Brown's body, 174, 178
Marshall, Col. James K., CSA, 64
Martin, Col. W. J., CSA, 92
Maryland Heights (Harpers Ferry,
West Virginia), 16, 17, 18, 24,
26, 31
Maryland Volunteers,
1st Maryland Cavalry, 22
Mattaponi River, 95
McClellan, Maj. Gen. George B., 30;
conducted Peninsula Campaign,
6; obtained "lost orders," 17
McDonald, 1st Lt. John, 126th New
York Infantry, killed, 105, 106
McLaws, Maj. Gen. Lafayette, CSA,
17, 18
Meade, Maj. Gen. George G., 58,
72, 76, 86, 110; answered Maj.
Gen Halleck's criticism after
Gettysburg, 71; attended II
Corps Grand Ball, 104; can-
celed attack at North Anna
River, 134, 143; countered Lee

near Warrenton, 90; directed
Petersburg assault, 159; forced to
call off Mine Run attack, order
withdrawal, 100; held councils of
war, 61, 71; Mine Run campaign, 99–100; ordered advance
to Bristoe Station, 90; ordered
crossing of Rappahannock, 77;
praised II Corps after Bristoe
Station engagement, 96; succeeded Hooker, 56; ordered to
make Army of Northern Virginia
his target, 99; rerouted Hancock,
May 5, 1864, 122

Medal of Honor, xi, 67, 188, 189

Mexican War, 16, 35

Middleton, Pvt. Arthur W., 126th
New York Infantry, severely
wounded, 97

Miles, Brig. Gen. Nelson, 128

Miles, Col. Dixon S., commanded
Harpers Ferry troops, 16; condemned by Morris Brown, Jr.,
23; killed, 23; ordered surrender
at Harpers Ferry, 21

Milo Center, New York, 2

Milo, Town of, 5, 7, 106

Mine Run campaign, 99

Morgan, Col. Charles H., 147;
Confederate flags captured, 66;
praised II Corps after Bristoe
Station engagement, 96

Mule Shoe (Spotsylvania), 129

Munson, Capt. Ira, 126th New York
Infantry, 152, 158; criticized
by Morris Brown, Jr., 108, 109,
110, 111, 112, 114, 115, 118;
mortally wounded, 133, 135,
136, 138, 141

Myers, Lt. Col. Aaron, 125th New
York Infantry, killed, 133

New Jersey Volunteers,
12th New Jersey Infantry, 61

New York State 26th Senatorial District, 7; military committee, 6, 7,
11, 40, 73, 104, 108, 109

New York Volunteers,
39th Infantry, 16, 33, 35, 59,
64, 104, 123, 141, 156, 176;
described, 34; withdrew from
Bristoe Station, 92

57th New York Infantry, 178

79th New York Infantry, 18, 19

108th New York Infantry, 61, 64,
100

10th New York Infantry battalion,
61, 92

111th New York Infantry, 16, 28,
33, 59, 60, 64, 68, 91, 168; tore
down fences at Camp Douglas,
29; torched Bliss Barn, 61; withdrew from Bristoe Station, 92

125th Infantry, 34, 37, 60, 62;
advance to Gettysburg, 54, 56,
58; attacked McLaws's Division,
59; brigaded with 39th, 111th,
and 125th New York Volunteers,
33; driven back at Bristoe Station, 90; carping among officers,
34; casualties at Gettysburg, 51;
command changes, 73; dodged
shelling at Bristoe Station, 91;
in reserve, July 3 morning, 65;
ordered out as skirmishers, 89;
withdrew from Bristoe Station,
94

126th New York Infantry, xii, 7,
9, 15, 16, 18, 19, 20, 23, 27,
29, 32, 37, 40, 70, 76, 104, 113,
121, 127, 165, 168, 170, 176,
178; advance to Gettysburg,
54–56; arrival at Harpers Ferry,

Strobridge, Cpl. William, 126th New York Infantry, severely wounded, 97

Stuart, Lt. Gen. J. E. B. ("Jeb"), CSA, blocked Warren advance, 88, 89; covered route to Boonsboro, 18

Swift, Brig. Gen. Joseph G., 11

Swinton, William, "Campaign of Maneuvers," 77

Sykes, Maj. Gen. George, 100, led advance toward Cedar Run, Virginia, 87; advance toward Bristoe Station, delayed, 91; advance toward Mine Run, 99; urged Warren to hurry, 95

Taylor, Cpl. David E., 12th New York Infantry, severely wounded, 97

Thompson, Lt. Benjamin, 111th New York Infantry, recalled sounds of wounded, 61

Thompson, Nelson, 2

Tobin, Pvt. Thomas, 126th New York Infantry, killed, 97

Trimble, Maj. Gen. Isaac, CSA, 65

Trimble, Col. William F, commanded 60th Ohio Infantry, 16

Twitchell, Pvt. Thaddeus, 126th New York Infantry, killed, 97

Tyler, Brig. Gen. Daniel, claimed prisoners are mutinous, 29; shocked by desertions, 28

Tyler, Sgt. E. B., 14th Connecticut, Bristoe Station engagement, 92

Tyler, Sgt. Phineas, 126th New York Infantry, arm amputated, 133

Union Army, Casey's Division, 31

Union Army, Defenses of Washington, 31

Union Army, organizational changes 1864, 104

Union Mass Meeting, 1

Union Mills, Virginia, 31, 33, 37, 40

"Union Relief Association," fed 126th New York Infantry, 12

United States Troops, 1st U.S. battery, 62, 64, 65

Hiram Berdan's U.S. Sharpshooters, 4, 6, 7, 15, 69

Upson, Professor Anson J., recommended Brown for promotion, 32

Vermont Volunteers, 9th Vermont Infantry, 16; rioted at Camp Douglas, 29; retained at Camp Douglas, 30

Vigilance Committee, formed, 4

Walker, Brev. Brig. Gen. Francis, 54; predicament at Bristoe Station, 92

Walker, Brig. Gen. John G, CSA, 17, 91

Wall, Pvt. Jerry Wall, 126th New York, Infantry, captured flag, 67

Ward, Samuel, declared Hamilton College's patriotism, 8

Warren, Maj. Gen. Gouverneur, 77, 87, 89, 90, 96, 99; attack at Auburn, Virginia, 88; attended II Corps Grand Ball, 104; march to Wilderness, 121; called off Mine Run attack, 100; ordered Hays's and Webb's divisions to advance on Bristoe Station, 88; praised Gen. Hays after Bristoe Station engagement, 91; replaced Brig. Gen. William Hays, 76; reported perilous situation at